HOW TO BE A REFUGEE

Life lessons learned by one who escaped the Holocaust

By Irene Gabriele Gill (née Zuntz)

The Caseroom Press — Second Printing — Summer 2022
PDW2003, Brayford Pool
Lincoln, LN6 7TS

Typeset in Hawkland
Images & Text © Irene Gabriele Gill
Edited by Tom Gill

ISBN: 978-1-905821-38-9

9 781905 821389

I dedicate this book to my family, and to all refugees, orphans and lost souls, wherever they may find themselves on this little planet of ours.

It was such a pleasant surprise,
meeting you in the covered market.
i hope you enjoy reading this.

Yours

Rene.

Contents

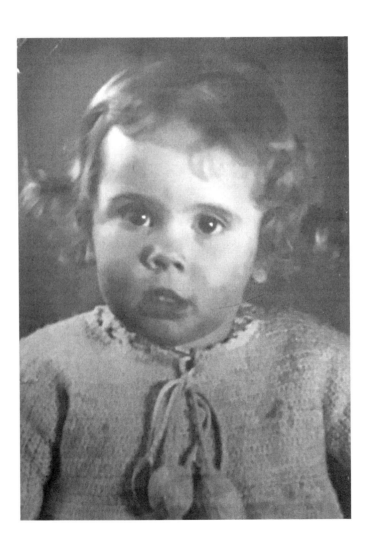

Chapter 1: Early Days

I'm lying on a bed in a shadowy room with light filtering through the blinds of a tall window. There's another bed between me and the window. There's a nun lying on it. Her name is Schwester Permina. She wants me to go to sleep. After a while she turns her head to look at me. I quickly shut my eyes. She gets up and moves silently to the door, her pale grey veil and gown floating behind her, and out of the room. She thinks I'm asleep! I feel triumphant. Fooled her!

That's my earliest memory. We were still in Germany, in Freiburg, in the Black Forest, and I was between two and three years old. At birth I had been named Vera Irene Gabriele Beate Zuntz, but my family called me Gax. Mu, my mother, had left me with the nuns while she went away to arrange for us to go to Denmark. We couldn't stay in Germany, because Mu's mother, my Oma, was Jewish; so was Fe's father, Opa Leo. We were half Jewish, a dreadful thing to be.

My second memory is from Copenhagen in 1936. I am five or six years old.

I wake up in the night and scream: my thumb has swollen and looks like a purple ball. I scream again in terror, and Mu, my mother, comes. She discovers the elastic I had wound round my thumb and forgotten about. She gets it off by snipping it with a small pair of curved scissors and promises me that my thumb will soon be normal again. But because I am still sobbing she lets me come downstairs and sit in the "Mutter-coupé" *- the space behind her in the armchair.*

My favourite place. There are various grown-ups in the room. Mu has explained about my thumb and they have made soothing noises. Now they go on with their conversation: a background murmur which soon has me asleep again.

Another memory from Copenhagen. I am visiting my big brother Peter in hospital: a sharp stone got into his knee when he was playing football, and now he has blood poisoning. He has got enormously fat in the hospital. A nurse comes along with a roll of toilet paper. I am fascinated. Is she going to wipe out the poisoned blood? I want to watch, but Mu hurries me away. Something quite straightforward is to happen - but it's *rude*, I mustn't watch.

And then there's the time I locked myself into the bathroom. I couldn't turn the key to unlock the door again. Mu is on the other side, encouraging me to try again. My big sister Maleen joins her; she tells me I can't be too weak to turn it, since I'd managed to lock the door. My father, Fe, comes home. He tells me to pull the key out and push it out to him under the door. But I can't pull it out. I'm panicking. Mu fetches the concierge. There they all gathered outside, and me a prisoner! There's talk of taking the door off its hinges. Then Peter comes home from school. He pushes his penknife, unopened, under the door. I'm to push it through the ring at the end of the key and then use both hands to turn it. And it works! The door opens and I am free! Tears streaming down my face I collapse into Mu's arms.

That bathroom was the scene of the only physical punishment ever meted out to me. I have no idea what I had done wrong; but Fe, sitting on the lavatory, had me across his lap and looking round I saw his hand, as big as a spade, coming down onto my unprotected bottom and was terrified.

Sometimes we had visitors from Germany - there was one lady who gave us *Katzenzungen* - chocolate "cats' tongues." They were delicious!

Now it's 1938, and we have moved to Birkeröd, a village outside Copenhagen. Oma, my grandmother - Mu's mother - has come to

visit us. Mu was shocked when I said that Oma looked like a capital
B. But at that time Mu was helping me to remember the letters of the
alphabet by pointing out their similarity to other things. Capital A
was like a house; G - rather puzzling, this - a dog kennel with a shelf
for the dog to rest his paws on. So why was it wrong to observe that
my rotund grandmother, with her curving bosom and belly, was
like a B? Mu couldn't explain why, but it was *rude*.

 One sunny day we were sitting on the gravel patch behind the
house for coffee, with the shadows of leaves fluttering over the cups
and jugs on the table, and I was told the story of "The sun will reveal
it": a man robbed and murdered another man in the forest. No-one
else was about, so he thought he was absolutely safe. But the dying
man looked at the sun through the leaves and said - these were his
dying words - "The sun will reveal it". Years later - the murderer
had prospered with the dead man's money - he was sitting just as
we were here, having coffee, and smiled to see the shadows of the
leaves which the sun cast onto the table and shook his head. The
dying man was wrong, no-one had ever found out. He murmured
the fatal words: "The sun has not revealed it." But his wife heard
him - and questioned him - and so the sun had revealed it, after all ...

 While Oma was with us, we had to observe an evening ritual. In
a procession we carried a chair, cushions, a rug, and her writing
things to a gap in the hedge so that she could sit in comfort to watch
the sunset, as she did every evening, wherever she was. There was a
double row of hazels on our side of the fence, and on the other, a field
belonging to a farm where Prepen lived. He was a boy of about the
same age as me, and he liked to make me feel inferior, for instance
because I could not - however hard I tried - emulate the fountain of
urine he unleashed behind a certain great oak tree. I did realise that
our games were *rude* and told no-one about them.

 On one side of our house there was a big gooseberry bed, with
a hedge round it. It was in this hedge that Peter created a stable for
my toy animals. I also had a doll, a wonderful one, called Kirsten,

who shut her blue eyes when she lay down and opened them when I raised her blonde curly head; but mostly I played with my little farm animals

We went for walks with Oma – very slowly, because of her bad knee – along a path beside a green field and up a low hill. She was clad all in black, and had a furled umbrella. Her silver hair was gathered in a bun on top of her head. At one point, she stopped and swung the umbrella round in a circle and sang in a low vibrant voice:

O Täler weit, o Berge	Oh valleys wide, oh hills
Du schöner grüner Wald...	You lovely forest green...

Later in our slow progress she pointed up into the sky, and her grey-blue eyes looked at me over the top of her glasses.

"See the skylark there?" she asked. "Hear it? It's going up and up. If you turn round three times it will be out of sight."

I did so – and she was right: the skylark had vanished into the sky, as she had foretold.

Soon after, Oma had gone to Persia, to live with her older daughter Tante Marianne and her family. It was many years before we saw her again. But we started getting a steady stream of letters from her address in Persia.

Mu often took us out into the country. I would sit in a seat on the handlebars of her bike. Peter and Maleen, being seven and five years older than me respectively, had their own cycles. I remember riding along a curving road towards some woods, a grassy embankment rising on our right. In the shadowy wood, the path split round a massive tree. Maleen and Peter raced each other round either side. Further on we came to a lake called Sjaelsö. Six decades later, in 1998, I went back there with my husband David, and as we cycled along the path with lake Sjaelsö gleaming through the trees on our left, I suddenly recognized the huge tree in the middle of the path, and a little further on, the spot where we used to bathe: Mu swimming out slowly, head up to keep her hair dry; Maleen and Peter having water fights. But I had quite forgotten the round shallow pond just the other side of the path where little streams falling down through the forest had been dammed and diverted into a modest fountain. As soon as I saw it again, I remembered it. I hadn't learned to swim, so I played there while the others bathed. Later, when we were all dry again, we would sit there eating bread and apples and listen to Mu reminiscing about her youth.

My father Günther, whom we all called Fe, was mostly absent: he spent at least half the year in England. When he came, however, I would feel the family was complete, not realising how profound the rift between him and Mu was. I have an indelible memory of him, on one occasion when he had just reappeared, tall and slim and, I suddenly recognized, beautiful, stretching up his right hand to pull a flowering twig down from a tree to sniff at the blossom. There was a large sepia photo portrait of him as a boy indoors; he was looking up with a dreamy expression from a book open on his knees, his shoulder length hair resting on a large lace collar: Little Lord Fauntleroy we called it. Fe was not only beautiful; he was fastidious, whereas Mu was rough and ready. He deplored her slap-dash energetic ways; she despised his fussiness and hypochondria. But that was not the only trouble between them.

I begged to be allowed to go to school, like Peter and Maleen, and so one morning I walked along to the *Komuneskole*, clutching Mu's hand, in a state somewhere between excitement and panic. The brick buildings - huge in my eyes - surrounded an asphalt playground, where drinking water fountains bubbled from the edge of a circular basin. Some of the big boys - so daring! - would sit on one of these fountains and then holler "Ma! Ma! I've wet myself!" They would spit their chewing gum out onto the ground, which was blotched with the flattened pink shapes. I was not above secretly peeling these off to find out what chewing gum was like. When the bell clanged we trooped up the wide stairs to the classroom, where

I sat next to a beautiful fair-haired girl called Inge with fascinating ridged finger-nails. There were tiny white flecks in them; these, she told me, were supposed to appear every time one told a lie. Inge did not deny having told so many lies; she looked at me through her silky lashes and said nothing. Sometimes the wicked boy sitting behind her dipped the end of her pigtail into his inkwell - and she did not tell on him; just gave him a stony stare and wiped off the ink with a blotter. The classroom seemed huge to me; somewhere up in front the teacher sat behind a desk on a platform. Sometimes I was allowed join the Big Girls, and I would sit under the table at which they were sewing, and run my finger nails down the teacher's stockings. She shrieked with laughter because it tickled so, but no-one was ever angry with me. I was a sort of mascot. And presumably I was still picking up the Danish language and didn't understand everything that was said.

Peter would walk home with me. He tried to teach me to whistle. At last I found I could, and hurried to demonstrate it to Mu. But when I got home, I was as always in urgent need of the toilet - so urgent that Mu said I need not go up to the bathroom, but might squat down behind the hazels. By the time I got into the house, the ability to whistle had left me. In fact for a time I could only whistle one note, once a day. I tried to save this one whistle till I got home, but could not resist using it up on the way. It was Peter I most wanted to impress. And Prepen.

When I went back to Denmark with David, Birkeröd had become a suburb of Copenhagen. The place was completely engulfed in nice new houses - small bungalows embedded in lilacs. Finally, after scouting around on hired bicycles, we found the junction of three roads that I remembered; but the shop in the angle of the junction where I used to get *morenkop* - a divine mass of some creamy substance on a stick, coated with chocolate - was now a veterinary surgery, Dahlgaard's Dyreklinik; the short steep road up to our house was now paved and led to a long terrace of town houses.

But going through a gap in the terrace, and across a patch of waste land where some boys were playing football, and past some allotments, some beehives, some ponds - there, suddenly, was our house. Utterly charming. Behind that window was the living room, with the big black wooden settle on which, trying to retrieve my satchel, that had fallen between it and a chair, I hit my head so hard that blood poured out. Mu scooped me up and got me to a doctor somewhere, somehow; I still have the scar. Beyond that room would be the kitchen, where we had our meals, with a window looking out onto the two rows of hazels.

At the local library we found photographs of the Kommuneskole, which had been demolished years ago. But where was the flowering fruit tree by our house? The gooseberry patch? The hedge where Peter made the stable for my toy animals? Prepen's family's farm? All had vanished, except in my memory.

My father was the son of Leo and Edith Zuntz; my mother was the daughter of Hugo and Olga Hempel. Oma Drübbelchen, my mother's mother, told me a good deal about my father's father, Opa Leo, who was at University in Freiburg studying medicine at the same time as her, and they remained friends. After his studies, he wanted to see the world, and worked as a ship's doctor. At the end of his interview before his first voyage to the tropics, the Captain asked him if he had packed everything he was going to need. He said he believed so.

"Have you remembered your butter-brush?"

Leo was alarmed: he had never even heard of this instrument. Then the Captain explained, earnestly, that where they were going it was so hot that butter melted; you could only spread it on your bread with a brush.

It was a JOKE!

Later Leo helped his father, Nathan Zuntz, a famous physiologist, in his Institute, with some of his experiments to examine the effects of high altitudes, using a "pneumatic cabinet" to simulate alpine or aeronautical conditions which became important when aeroplanes came into use. For a time Leo practised in Moabit, a working class area of Berlin, and even when later he ran a fashionable maternity clinic he would never refuse to help a poor person in need.

He married Edith, a shop-keeper's daughter, and not Jewish: a small, refined woman, very different from Olga, who could not stand her affectations. When my father, Günther, was quite a young boy, he came home one day to find his mother unconscious: she had tried to kill herself when she discovered that Leo had been unfaithful to her. Günther was able to summon help in time, and she was restored; but from then on, Leo was abjectly ashamed, and he and their children - there were two girls as well as Günther - treated her with the utmost solicitude.

When Edith was expecting her third child, after two difficult, indeed life-threatening confinements, she asked Leo to deliver the baby, which he did with skill and humanity and none of the terrors and dangers of the first two births. The two families - Zuntz and Hempel - spent several holidays together, little dreaming that Leo's son Günther would one day marry Olga's daughter Lore. Edith was passionately opposed to this marriage, and never forgave my mother for seducing Günther.

Leo died in Berlin in 1937, and Edith came to England; in fact she lived with her daughter not far from us in Oxford, yet I never saw her. Right at the beginning she gave me a ball of blue and silver wool with Smarties hidden in it, which was to encourage me to knit (it did not succeed), but that was the only contact I ever had with her.

1939 came, and we had to go to England, because it seemed likely that the Nazis would overrun Denmark. Mu assured us that she would never let the Nazis catch us alive. She had enough Veronal (a suicide drug) for all of us. So now I became aware of the fact that people in Germany wanted me dead. And yet Germany was that land of woods and lakes and mountains, and true love and courage and constancy, "the land of poets and thinkers" (*das Land der Dichter und Denker*), that was celebrated in the folksongs Mu sang with us, and the stories and ballads she read to us.

Peter didn't want to leave Denmark. He said if the Nazis came, he wanted to help the Danes fight them. But Mu said that he couldn't help them. We would be a danger to our Danish friends if we stayed. It was as if we were infected with a deadly disease. At this, Peter threw himself onto the floor in despair and cried unconsolably.

Mu packed all our things, our furniture and books and clothes and cooking things and everything, and we went to our friends to say goodbye. Then it turned out that we couldn't go to England straight away, because our visas hadn't arrived. For a few days we stayed in a tiny flat with a teacher of Maleen's. Then some kind Danish friends said we could stay on the island of Samsö.

I was given a warm blue winter coat which I wore on one of Mu's farewell visits to a nearby farm. While she and the farmer's wife talked, I played in the yard. My ball rolled out onto a flat brown area. I ran out after it - wondering why the surface was so brittle. It was actually a pool of slurry, but I pursued my ball till I was waist-deep in the stinking liquid. Mu was appalled: the coat was ruined. There was no time to have it cleaned: we were leaving for Samsö next day.

So for a few months we lived on that blessed island, in a tiny house between Tranebjerg and Ballen, surrounded by hollyhocks and with an outside toilet which had a warm, wide wooden seat, and which became my private domain, with a notice on the door: *Gabi Privat*. Behind the house was the farm to which it belonged; along the road to one side we quickly came to the beach, where tall blonde brown-skinned women took a liking to me and bought me ice creams. Mu would help me pile up a hill of sand, patting it firm, adding handfuls of water to make it even firmer. Then we would start tunnelling, she with two fingers from her side, I with my whole hand from the other. Sometimes the hill collapsed before we had reached the middle; sometimes we had misjudged the direction of the tunnels and came out somewhere at the side; but occasionally our hands met in the

By the seaside at Samsö

middle and we laughed with the pleasure of touching each other - warm and smooth and alive - in the gritty depths of the sand-hill.

"When I was your age," Mu said, "my mother - your Oma - played with me just like this in the sand in Ferch, a village on the Lake Schwielowsee, near Berlin. And she told me that she learned to make sand-hills and tunnels like this from her grandfather, when she was a little girl."

"Her grandfather!"

"Yes - my great grandfather, and your great great grandfather!"

"Where did they do it?"

"At Zoppot. If we went on and on towards the sunrise from here we'd get there. Some of this same water has probably been by the beach at Zoppot." Zoppot, also called Sopot, is the city near Danzig (now Gdansk) where Oma lived when she was a girl.

We would roam around Samsö, that green, clean, peaceful island, singly or together, on foot or by bike, always feeling perfectly safe. Everyone was kind and friendly to us; and the weather seems to have been perfect all the time. We wandered along the quiet roads, past huge trees with little houses beneath them, and meadows with cows, and were never far from the sea. There was a windmill and a white, red-roofed church with a stepped façade to the tower. We were happy there, and it is lodged in my memory as an earthly paradise. Ferch played the same role in Mu's consciousness, as the place that encapsulated the innocent time of childhood, the place for which she was helplessly homesick all her life. Zoppot played the same role in Oma's consciousness lifelong.

So the weeks and months we spent in Samsö are like an unforgettable oasis of peace and well-being in my mind. But for Mu, biting her nails as she read the newspapers and knew what was happening elsewhere, and what was threatening, that time of waiting for the documents that would allow us to go to England must have been agony. At last they came, and we set off, first on the ferry to Jutland; then by train. It had to stop twice: first, because there were cows

lying on the line, and then because I had to go to the lavatory. There
was none on the train, and we were the only passengers, so the train
made an unscheduled stop at a small station where there was one.
The family stood outside, begging me to hurry, which I was quite
unable to do. The more I tried, the less I achieved. At long last I was
ready, and the train chugged on, while Peter and Maleen told me just
what they thought of me. When we reached the junction where we
were to board the express to Esbjerg, railway officials came running
towards us, because we were so late, and helped us to get ourselves
and our luggage onto the express, which was waiting for us: the
driver of our local train had telephoned, explaining my embarrassing difficulty. Now another call was made to Esbjerg, and the boat
waited for us, too. As soon as we had run up the gangplank, it set sail.

Years later, Mu told me that when we got to Harwich we were
not at first allowed to disembark; the British authorities wanted no
more refugees, and they scrutinised our papers very carefully. Mu
was afraid they would send us to Hamburg. She explained the situation, the officials listened politely, then went away to telephone
London. We had to wait, and while we waited she took her Veronal
pills out of her bag and ordered tea. If the reply from London was "to
Hamburg" she was going to slip a pill into each cup of tea. She held
those pills in her hand for many hours while we sat there on the
deserted boat in Harwich. But we were allowed in, and she buried
the pills in her bag.

*

When David and I explored Samsö in 1998, the sea was calm despite
a strong cold wind, and some fine yachts, even a schooner, were
sailing in the sunshine all sails set - many places looked familiar
to me: cows and calves and a few horses in the lush meadows with
ponds, little houses like toys with corrugated iron roofs painted red,
or thatched. We took the one and only bus, number 131, through the
rolling green land, through Kolby, Permelille, Ballen, to Tranebjerg,

where we stayed with Asta Rasmussen: a big, warm, welcoming woman, her English - which she was keen to practise - about as hopeless as my Danish. Mrs Rasmussen went in for knick-knacks, hundreds of them, on highly polished surfaces, from tiny china dogs to model bonsai trees.

In the night I had a strange dream: a calf approached its mother to drink milk - no - it sprawled on the ground; she lay beside it; its legs disappeared into her, then its body, then its head; she got up, walked backwards, lowered her head and gently spewed out grass ...And my grey hair turned dark, my six-year-old shape returned, and I was a small child again, on Samsö.

I woke up early and walked along the road toward Ballen, exploring some of farm tracks, looking at the small houses and wishing for some strong sense of recognition, for the present to coincide with my memories; but it was not to be.

Chapter 2: Refugee in Oxford

1939. From Harwich the journey continued by train to London - I have confused memories of the deafening hiss in the black vaults of Paddington as clouds of white steam were let off - and thence to Oxford. It was night time when we got to the house Fe had found for us in Oxford, at 37 Thorncliffe Road, Summertown. While Mu sat wearily on a chair and spoke with Fe, we children rushed around exploring the house excitedly, vying to discover details that the others had missed. But soon I was exhausted and half asleep, which had the curious effect of making everything look a tenth of its actual size. In the pile of luggage and furniture shipped from Germany that was stacked in the hall, Mu found a folding bed, which was opened for me in a small room upstairs. I knew nothing till the next morning, when I sat up and looked out of the window at the yellow brick wall of the next-door house, and beyond, long, narrow gardens separated by brick walls and containing apple trees, their blossom veiled with a soft, gentle rain. I got out of bed and opened the door to a corridor leading to the stairs. A slanting door near the top of the stairs opened into a bathroom with a cast iron bath standing on lion's feet. Two steps up led to more closed doors. But following the noise of the family's voices I descended the stairs and found myself facing the front door, partially glazed with ornamental green glass leaves; and doubling back along the side of the staircase I came to a step down and a door to the kitchen. That was where everyone was.

The chaos was absolute, with things strewn around on every horizontal surface, everyone talking at once, Maleen and Peter arguing, Mu shouting in the scullery beyond and crashing about with saucepans and buckets; and Fe sitting at the head of the table, holding his head in his hands. Pretty soon there was a knock at the front door and visitors started arriving: a woman from the refugee committee with a bag of groceries and a screeching voice – since she spoke English, only Fe could understand some of what she was saying; a German woman called Frau Borcherdt, who wanted to welcome us as fellow refugees. She bowed down to me and smiled archly and said: "Your grandfather brought me into the world." I begged for an explanation, and learned that Fe's father, Opa Leo, had had a clinic in Berlin where women went to have their babies – including the mother of this Frau Borcherdt. Opa Leo was dead now. But Mu told me that he and Oma had continued to be friends, and their two families had gone to Walkemühle on holiday together several times, and later some of the Zuntzes came to the Hempels' summer house in Ferch. And that gave her the opportunity to start telling me about Ferch, where she spent her summers and weekends from 1908 to 1919. Later she wrote about it.

"*I could go on about Ferch for days,*" Mu wrote. (And she did go on about it, throughout her life.) "*The more I think about it, the more I remember. When we were young, in Berlin, we looked forward to the weekend all through the week. On Fridays, Ida, our housekeeper, would be standing at the school gate to give us our rucksacks with our things for the weekend; she would take our school satchels home to the flat. Then we rushed to the underground to get the train to Potsdam, where the garrison church bells rang out the tune of* Üb immer Treu und Redlichkeit *('Always practice faithfulness and honesty') and where we had to change to go to Long Bridge for the Star Steamer which took us to Ferch in two and a half hours. How we landlubbers admired the sailors and the cabin boys when they jumped ashore to tie the ropes and put down the gang-plank!*

*The Captain was the helmsman, and looked very solemn and proud
- And no wonder: our lives were in his hand.*

    *My God, how beautiful the Schwielohsee was, and the River
Havel, with forests everywhere! Past Old Tornow, Hermannswerder,
Caputh - up to that point you were still on the river Havel. But there
our lake opened out, Lake Schwieloh. I can never forget what a joy
it was to see the great lake before us without anything to obscure the
view. It filled you with a kind of pride, you felt like a queen. First we
went across to Baumgarten - you could just about see Ferch from
there - then back to the middle of the lake, and there was Petzow
on the right, an old manor house, where Herr von Rochow lived.
Everyone was afraid of him - there was a rumour that he shot
anyone who entered his park. But I don't know if he really did. Still,
we were always very apprehensive as we passed near Petzow. Yet
we always went to Petzow every autumn - the walk from Ferch took
about one-and-a-half hours - to collect horse chestnuts. On the opposite side of the lake was Flottstelle, a very poor place as I remember
it, very sandy, but with a little café where you could get raspberry
juice, if Mother was feeling very extravagant, which didn't happen
often. And I can still see the rather pathetic blackcurrant bushes
there, all covered in sand. The next stopping place was called Ferch
New Barn, where there was a very popular bathing place - it even
had cabins for changing and a pole in the water with a sign that
said: 'Non-swimmers not allowed beyond this point'. We learned to
swim very early, and it was always glorious. But to get to New Barn
from our house took three-quarters of an hour, along the meadow
path and back up the steep raspberry hill. So we mostly bathed at a
spot nearer home, with no luxuries. We would hide in the rushes to
change, and often got into the water from the rowing boat that was
moored there."*

These stories about her childhood fascinated me, and filled me
with envy.

Thorncliffe Road was the seventeenth and last address in Mu's

My parents

married life; it was to be her home until she died. She moved 16 times in the first 14 years of marriage, and not at all for 54 years thereafter. She came to feel very possessive indeed about the house; it was to be a refuge and a home for the family first and foremost, but for all sorts of needy people in the years to come.

Yet she did not like the house at first. It belonged to a Mrs Monk, who lived in the next street, Beech Croft Road. My parents could have bought it, in 1939, for £400; nowadays it is worth over a million pounds. But my parents didn't have £400, so for decades to come paying Mrs Monk the rent was a priority. It was a late Victorian end-terrace tunnel-back house, of yellow brick, facing the street and the North, so that the front rooms never got any sun. That only shone on the back garden, when the high brick walls surrounding it allowed, and onto the scullery and the bedroom above it. The rear of the house consisted of the kitchen and the scullery; the "tunnel", a narrow sunless passage, ran along the side of it. One corner of the scullery was taken up with a "copper" for boiling laundry; there was a gas cooker beside it, and a sink under the window. There was an outside toilet which backed onto the pantry in the kitchen. Above the kitchen door there was a panel with curious numbered tags which corresponded to bell pushes in all the rooms: the house was designed for servants. Of course we tried all the bells, but none of them worked.

Upstairs there was a large front room which had been claimed by my father for his study; his big black bookcases and his leather-topped writing table were already installed. A fair-sized back-bedroom overlooked the tunnel, as did a small bathroom with the bath on lions' feet, a toilet and a wash basin, a "box room", where my father slept, and a small bedroom overlooking the garden. In the long years that followed, these rooms were allocated and re-allocated, furniture was moved from one to another - which was almost as good as moving house, said Mu, who, for a long time, would have liked to. We reproached Fe, who could have got a much nicer house in Bainton Road with a back garden that ran down to the canal; but he feared that rats might emerge from the canal.

The Brookes family lived on one side. Mr Brookes had a small square car. Mrs Brookes looked like a hen and was soon an enemy. There were two children, Mary and Malcolm. They were all deeply suspicious of "ruddy foreigners", especially us next door. When we were too noisy, she would bang on the adjoining wall, and Mu would retaliate in kind. On the other side was a deaf family, the Harrisons: elderly parents, their middle-aged daughter, all deaf; their booming voices could be heard almost all day. Both the Harrisons and the Brookes's were intensely property conscious. Mr Harrison would laboriously lean his ladder against the garden wall and climb up it to demand to speak to "the Professor" when he had a complaint. None of them ever came to the front door. One complaint was because of an apple core which I had thrown over the wall. He waved it indignantly as he boomed his complaint to the "professor", teetering at the top of his ladder. Another time we spotted him at dawn climbing over the wall into our garden to pick up some apples that had fallen from his trees. Their daughter would hang out of their bathroom window to comb her few grey locks; then she would reappear downstairs with a dustpan and brush to sweep up whatever had dropped from her head onto the concrete paving.

My father's beautiful sister Leonie was living in Oxford, studying Hittite and hoping in vain for a university post; but she did not make any attempt to befriend us. His other sister, Dora, and her English husband, Brian Roberts, a night editor on the Daily Telegraph, once invited Peter to stay with them for a short time in London; thereafter there was no contact with them, either. Their mother, Oma Edith, came and lived with Leonie for a time, but she never called on us, though Fe spent a good deal of time with them in Norham Gardens.

Visitors kept coming in the days and weeks that followed, and Mu would try to get them out of the kitchen and into the front room. We were expected to converse with them, or to join in their homesick singing of songs like *Der Lindenbaum,* from Schubert's *Winterreise.* One of them was Professor Paul Maas, famous as a pioneer of textual criticism. He had taught Fe Greek at University in that other world that I kept hearing about – it came to be called: *Vorm Krieg,* Before the War, or sometimes *Vor Hitler.* Professor Maas would hit a tuning fork against a hard object – his own skull – and give us all our notes; we would sing a Bach Chorale in four parts, with Professor Maas often taking the top line, falsetto, which had us children doubled up with suppressed laughter; or Fe would play the piano and Maleen and I would sing songs and duets by Mendelssohn or Mozart. And we would be expected to take part in the conversation, which was impossible, as they were all talking at the same time, and about things I knew nothing about: *Anschluss* and Czechoslovakia, *Sudetenland,* Fascism, Communism, Anti-semitism, *Lebensraum...* so I would slip out between them and through the steam-filled scullery to the garden, to play with my toy animals. One of my cows was made of metal and looked too old to produce milk, but I half believed that they all came to life in the night, and that then the other, rubber one was milked by elves or dwarves. During the day I patiently fenced in tiny meadows with bits of stick, and found titbits like daisies or apple blossom petals for them to eat, especially my favourite, the foal.

When I slipped back into the house, it was filled up with still more refugees. And so it went on. They would sit and talk endlessly about *Vorm Krieg* and about the latest news, and about people who were still in Germany. Sometimes we had to visit them. There was Frau Kann, who lived in a flat in Woodstock Close and made a lot of fuss about making coffee; there was an elderly couple, the Slutzewskis, who actually lived a little further along our road – at least they were funny to watch, having been actors *Vorm Krieg* and using high-flown quotations from plays all the time: "Emil, my hound of heaven, please pass me your cup," or: "Oh thou my only child that I bore in agony, where have I left my purse?" The Liepmanns had a big house in a nearby street with lodgers. Herr Dr Liepmann had a little goatee which he would thrust out horizontally from time to time. This made him look like a fierce gnome. His thin, puritanical wife, a pastor's daughter, always looked as if she were exercising her Christian forbearance, as indeed she was; her husband was as aggressive as a small dog and would say sharply: "Elizabeth, I would like to draw your attention to the fact that you have just interrupted me for the third time." No doubt she had, as he - a Professor of Economics *Vorm Krieg* - did not speak normally, but lectured, and sometimes she needed to say something. But she was absolutely loyal to him, and had not hesitated to emigrate with him, though she was not Jewish. Later he was one of the small group that founded the global charity, Oxfam.

There was tension between fat Mr Meinhardt and his wife, too. They lived on Woodstock Road, and had a daughter, Marianne, who was my age, and a younger son. Marianne developed a passion for horses, and taught me to ride on Port Meadow: or rather, she taught me to sit on a horse, gallop, and fall off without hurting myself. Another family was the Hammerschmidts: Herr Hammerschmidt had been a pharmacist *Vorm Krieg* and now did almost nothing all day except sit in the house in Museum Road and pontificate. He believed any argument could be settled by a quotation from Goethe, whom he called *Der Altmeister von Weimar* - the Sage of Weimar - and he almost fell off his chair when once, years later, I was not silenced by the quotation, but said, "I disagree with Goethe there". That was blasphemy.

His wife came from a very rich family: she had fur coats and all sorts of expensive tailor-made clothes and hand-sewn shoes in the fashion of the 1930s. They had a housekeeper, Irma, who had a round, Slavonic face and light blue eyes. Their daughter, Gretchen, was mentally disturbed, and their son, Hans, was not like other boys: tall and gangling and cruelly bullied at school. One day he set fire to some paper in the basement, meaning to burn the house down in a misguided bid to persuade his mother to join the peace movement. By chance the housekeeper came home, discovered the smouldering paper, and called the fire brigade. Hans was committed to Broadmoor, the prison for the criminally insane. Later in life he managed to live a relatively normal life, marrying a woman called Olga from the tiny island of Saint Helena and working as a dustman and street cleaner at various times. He had strong political opinions and would expound them while shaking his head from side to side and lisping slightly. He often referred to the human race as "vermin" - like Swift, he liked individual people but could not abide the human race.

Professor Maas worked for Oxford University Press and had a room on the top floor of a house in Beaumont Street. Guided in all things by pure Reason, he kept his water supply in a large battered watering can, as his room was some way from the nearest tap, and he needed water for his tea and coffee and for washing. He rode a large bicycle which he would mount from behind with a dramatic leap after a vigorous run to get up speed - necessary for balance, as he insisted. He was fond of saying: "My principle is to have no principles," and though he was a keen gardener, he drew the line at plants with shallow roots, unless they were to be eaten. Roses were all right, since they have quite deep roots, and he was knowledgeable about pruning them; but once, when I brought him a bunch of flowers, he threw them angrily into his bin: "Do you think I want to be surrounded with these dying things?"

Professor Maas had taught Greek at the University of Königsberg (then part of Germany, now in Russia and named Kaliningrad) until April 1934, when the Nazis purged Jews from all academic posts, the entire civil service, and all the other professions. Clearly it was intolerable to have a Jew lecturing on Greek and Latin prosody, so Paul Maas, then aged 54, was forced to retire. In 1935 the Nuremberg Race Laws made him give up his house to a Nazi family - though he did not go willingly, but fought a fierce legal battle, believing that

Germany was still a *Rechtsstaat* - a country under the rule of law. He still had some money and travelled extensively. He attended the biennial International Congress of Papyrology in Florence in 1935, where a brilliant young British scholar, Enoch Powell, read a paper. Powell was then only 22, and already a fellow of Trinity College Cambridge. He and Paul Maas discovered shared interests in such academic fields as textual criticism and became fast friends. After a lively exchange of letters they met again at the next Papyrology Congress, which was held in Oxford in 1937. Maas stayed at the house of Professor Gilbert Murray on Boars Hill, and also at Enoch Powell's parents' home in Sussex, and with Powell at Trinity College Cambridge. Powell described the relationship between Maas and himself as one of the greatest intellectual romances of his life.

Professor Maas used to visit us quite often to discuss classical topics with my father. Powell, now in his smart Major's uniform, sometimes came too. The three of them were able to converse in classical Greek: there were few other people in the world who could. They were united in their veneration for the civilisation of Athens. When Professor Maas - a penniless refugee - was offered a chance to earn some money teaching the Greek language to a student, he turned it down because the student was African. "They will have to develop through a few more generations before they will be ready to learn Greek," he said. These scholars were racists - as Enoch Powell made very plain some time later with his notorious "Rivers of Blood" speech, which unleashed an ugly upsurge of racism. Yet he had helped to rescue Paul Maas from the Nazis.

When Powell shook hands, he stared into your eyes and gripped your hand so tightly you almost screamed with pain. Maleen was quite flustered by his powerful masculinity. He seemed to be fascinated by my mother, as quite a number of our visitors were, sitting talking round the metal "Anderson Shelter" which served as a table in the kitchen, and under which we were to hide in case of an air raid

- which never came in Oxford. I can remember various men, including Powell, watching Mu at work rather intently. But she would play the part of the traditional German Hausfrau, urging the men to go and talk in the front room while she prepared their coffee and brought it in to them.

Professor Maas had a daughter called Gau, who also became a family friend. She looked like a sweet little troll in a pink beret, and lived in a houseboat near Donnington Bridge that was full of all sorts of junk. On the riverbank alongside it stood the frame and strings of a piano she had rescued from a dump. She called it her "pia-yes-or-no." Small children would bounce up and down on it. She had a colony of mice living on her houseboat, which was a refuge for domestic mice brought to her by children.

When we needed our teeth to be fixed, it was of course to a refugee dentist that we went: Dr Pick, in St John's Street, a small man in a white coat with a lamp on a ring round his bald head. He insisted on speaking "English" - "Gut morrning, pliss tek a sit." His word for "rinse" was a version of the German "spülen": "Spill pliss," he would say. He gave me an injection which made my lips so numb that I could bite through them without feeling anything. I did this a lot, and it led to an inflammation of my mouth; for ages, just at Christmas, I could only eat strained porridge, charmingly called Haferschleim, literally meaning "oat slime."

Old Mrs Rosenberg - Ludwig's mother - lived in St John's Street, too. She had managed to get into England on the scheme which had English people engage refugees as domestic workers. Her employer was a Mrs Gerrard, a professor's widow, a pleasant, easy-going old soul who kept a fine library in her toilet, which had a window overlooking the garden. I know, because years later, when I was transferred to a secondary school, I needed to catch up on a year's French, and Frau Rosenberg undertook to teach me. She was a highly intellectual and intelligent woman, gentle and generous; but she looked like a haggard old witch, with a long purple nose, usually with a drop of mucus hanging from the end of it, so we only ever called her *Hexchen* - Little Witch.

September 1939 came, and Germany invaded Poland. On October 3rd, Britain and France declared war on Germany. We got ration books and we had to put up black-out curtains - sometimes an air raid warden would knock at the door in the evening and warn us that there was a chink of light showing. We were now Enemy Aliens and had to report to a policeman with a walrus moustache from time to time. We were not allowed to travel more than five miles from the house; so when Fe took me for Sunday morning cycle rides into the country, we would hide our bicycles in a hedge at a certain point and walk from there, through the fields and woods round Elsfield and Woodeaton.

We had to start going to school. Peter went to a minor Public School called Saint Edwards, a short walk from Thorncliffe Road. It was not easy for Peter to be a day boy. The boarders looked down on day boys, and moreover he was a bloody foreigner, with a funny name, speaking broken English, a Jew, and a "Jerry" - an enemy. He was bullied and humiliated, and reacted by working incredibly hard to master the language and the curriculum. Soon he was getting top marks. But that did not help: now he was maligned for being a "swot". He burned to be accepted, and realised that sporting prowess was the only thing that impressed these boys; so it was a great relief when, being slight, he was chosen as "cox" of a rowing eight. As he grew and put on weight, his dread of losing his one toehold in the world of sport was so great that for months he deliberately starved himself. Possibly because of this he was often ill with a high temperature - it may have been jaundice. Some years later, in the Sixth Form, he was more or less accepted by a small gang of rather loutish young men who were also day boys, and went out with them in the evenings, getting drunk.

Things were no better for Peter at home, where he was in a state of open conflict with his father. They clashed over everything, even at mealtimes, when they would both stretch out their legs under the table and complain if - as was inevitable - their feet collided.

Maleen and I were sent to Rye St Antony, because we were still nominally Catholic. The Hastings family, devout Catholics, took us under their wing. Mrs Hastings, a short, stout woman with a large nose and blue-tinted glasses, had six children - her husband was usually away, being in the Diplomatic Service - and the youngest, Susan, was my age. We played wonderful games in the bedroom with a big rocking horse at the foot of the bed. Once we played hair-dressers, and Susan cut off my hair, hiding it under the rocking horse, where the maid - they had a maid, who wore a little white apron and cap - found it. In the evening Mrs Hastings drove up in her little square Austin with Susan, who was sobbing and red eyed, to apologise. But Mu, absorbed in the News, had hardly noticed that my hair looked as if it had been ravaged by mice, and was certainly not upset, knowing that it would grow again. In the summer, Susan and I decided to establish an aquarium. For this we needed a large blue bowl, which we would get from Woolworths, which was then a "3d and 6d store". Susan asked her mother for sixpence. "Take a shilling, dear", she replied. When I reported these words at home, the family could hardly believe that we knew such wealthy people.

Rye St Antony school was then in two large houses in Woodstock Road, and on our first day, totally bewildering to me, I found myself sitting at a table in a crowded basement room with a large piece of paper in front of me and a woman circling her hands over the paper. I was fascinated by the rings on her fingers. She was saying something, but of course I could not understand: I only understood Danish and German. Maleen came to the rescue. She had been called in from the bigger girls' classroom and somehow managed to divine the meaning of the English words. In Danish, she told me the teacher wanted me to cover the whole paper with a drawing. So I set to and drew cows and horses and houses and trees. School was fairly pointless for me, since I couldn't understand a word; but I had just learned to stand on my head – a skill I was keen to practise – so my first school report ended with the comment:

Gabi must not stand on her head when the teacher is talking to her.

I was an outsider here in school, enclosed in the language barrier, just as I was regarded as an irrelevant bystander in all the arguments and discussions at home, because I was so young and could not possibly understand.

Mu knew no English either, and what she needed she pieced together from the dictionary and from listening to the news on the radio and studying the paper. She had had less trouble in Denmark, as the two languages are so close, though there had been a famous altercation in a shop when she asked for *Gries* – German for *semolina* – and was presented with a piece of *pork, gris* being the Danish for *pig.* Now she had a heated exchange with a butcher when she asked for some of his *flesh,* the German for *meat* being *Fleisch.* There was a notice in a dark corner between buildings in Oxford with a rather odd notice saying: "Do not commit a nuisance". So when I brought home a girl I had made friends with at school, Mu asked her: "Will you commit a nuisance?" – indicating the toilet door, and pronouncing the word: *nooeesants.*

Almost imperceptibly, we learned the language, and swapped "refugee jokes" – such as:

A: *Spring in the air!*

B: *Why should I? (Springen means jump in German)*

Or the refugee woman on the crowded bus, whose husband has gone to the upper deck, where he could smoke, says to the conductor: *The Lord above us will pay.*

November, and the talk was all about Finland. Finally that dreaded war broke out: Russia, the big bully, attacked plucky little Finland. Mu, always passionately on the side of the underdog, was overwhelmed. Bad enough that the land of Tolstoy and Dostoyevsky, and indeed Lenin and Stalin, whom she had long revered, had entered into a pact with Hitler: this was unbearable for her, and she spent her scant spare time shaking a tin at the corner of Thorncliffe Road in the cold and the rain to collect money to help Finland in this dreadful Winter War. Not until the following March did the Finns surrender, and Mu wept into her saucepans and wash tubs.

Maleen and I were expelled from Rye St Antony, because we did not go to mass every Sunday. Our agnostic parents hadn't realised that this was expected of Catholics. Moreover, when we regaled them with stories of Miss Bailey's harangues – "You're like a lot of sheep: if one of them jumps over a ditch, all of them do", or: "Saint Teresa would be very distressed if she could see some of you girls sliding down the banisters", they could not take it seriously. Indeed, Mu passed the story about Saint Teresa on to Mrs Hastings, expecting her to laugh; but she commented: "But it's a well-known fact that Saint Teresa takes a special interest in girls' schools." So we were transferred – Maleen to Milham Ford, and I to Saint Denys.

Now the talk was all about the possible invasion of Britain, and I started to take an interest in the News. Once again, Mu was assuring us that she would never let the Nazis get hold of us alive. Our dear Denmark was occupied; so was Norway; the Netherlands followed; then the Channel Islands; the little boats crossed the Channel to rescue the troops from Dunkirk; the Battle of Britain and Churchill's speeches had our hearts in our throats; and then came the Blitz, as London and other cities were bombed by the *Luftwaffe*, and the newspapers showed warning pictures of Firebomb Fritz, an angry-looking anthropomorphised German incendiary bomb. Fe joined the ARP (Air Raid Protection) and spent chilly nights standing round in the street ready to spring into action if bombs started falling, and we were all given gas-masks. Mine was in a square cardboard box with a string to go round my shoulders and keep it bobbing up and down on my back as I walked along the Woodstock Road to and from school – except that I very often forgot it. I would notice half way to school, and then be faced with the dilemma: to go back home and fetch it from the hook by the front door – and be scolded for being late – or go without it, and be scolded for forgetting it. To this day, I occasionally experience the old lurch of guilt as my hand goes round to my back and finds no gas-mask there. Forgotten it again!

It was walking along Woodstock Road four times a day that I started pondering about the nature of time. I could not see or feel or touch it, yet nothing happened without it. I would look along to the next lamp-post. Soon, however slowly I walked, I would be there, looking back at this one. What was it that pushed everything into the past like that?

One afternoon, when I got home, Mu came to the front door with the dramatic announcement:

"Your father is in prison."

We refugees were now "enemy aliens". The adults had been questioned by special Tribunals, and assigned to different categories, A, B or C; some women and most men, including Fe, were interned. Now Mu had a new cause. She assumed that, since Fe was in an "internment camp" on the Isle of Man, he must be suffering terrible hardships, and sent him regular parcels of home-made biscuits and any other goodies she could lay her hands on. She included daffodil bulbs in one, to beautify the camp in Spring. But Fe was not grateful: there was something wrong with the onions you sent, he wrote, they tasted awful.

In fact he was very happy in internment. The "camp" consisted mainly of seaside boarding houses. He was among some of the most learned men Germany had produced, and they very quickly organised themselves into a kind of university – a truly "universal" one as professors and experts in the most diverse fields happily lectured to each other on their subjects: E.F. Schumacher (of *Small is Beautiful* fame) lectured on economics, Paul Maas on Greek metre, Egon Wellesz on Byzantine music, and Fe himself on ancient Greek life and literature. The celebrated Rawicz and

Landauer played piano duets, and there was chamber music by the four musicians who later formed the world famous Amadeus Quartet. There were learned debates and physical exercises and chess tournaments - it was as near as my father ever got to the Athens of Socrates and Plato.

Meanwhile Mu filled the house with refugees as her contribution to the War Effort. Enemy Aliens were forced to leave areas near the south coast as part of the preparation for a possible Nazi invasion. Ludwig Rosenbaum had been a teacher at Dartington Hall School in Devon, but was now interned; his wife Anna and their two small children were put in Fe's study. Anna was expecting their third child. She worshipped her son, aged about 5, and one evening at supper time, when he deliberately poured his cocoa over the white table cloth, and Mu asked Anna to tell him to stop, she said dreamily: "No, he must not be stopped. Can't you see how artistic he is? He mustn't be frustrated!"

A home for refugee boys on the coast was closed down and the boys transferred to a home run by an English couple who had lost their only son and cared for these *Kindertransport* orphans to assuage their grief - only to have some orthodox Jewish organisation insist the boys should not be brought up and indoctrinated by Christians. Three of these young boys came to us, though there was no religion of any kind in our family, certainly not Judaism. Their names were Ernst, Stefan, and Kurt. The three of them shared an upstairs bedroom. Kurt had lost his parents and would become my foster brother.

Then there was a Jewish couple, but they did not stay long: when Mu asked them what their profession was, they said, quite coolly: "We are terrorists." Mu thought she had misheard, but no: "We believe Israel must be won for the Jews by terrorism." At that, Mu asked them to leave her house, at once. They were quite surprised at her reaction, but went quietly enough, once they had found somewhere else to stay.

Mu would come home from the weekly market in Oxford loaded with sacks of food and would prepare mountains of vegetables, leaning on her elbows on the kitchen table, reading a newspaper at the same time, which sometimes meant that peels and parings went into the saucepan and some of the cleaned leaves onto the compost heap. Gritty over-done spinach, singed potatoes, leathery fried eggs, greasy meat would appear on our plates as we crowded at the table and woe betide you if you did not eat up - people were starving in China.

And then, miraculously, Hitler broke his pact with Stalin and attacked the Soviet Union. The dreaded invasion of Britain was off.

*

Saint Denys, a primary school for girls, was founded in 1854 by the Anglican nuns of the Holy Trinity Convent in Woodstock Road. On my first day, Mu walked to Winchester Road with me, and I was taken in by a large, bespectacled nun in flowing black veil and habit, with a starched white breastplate: the head mistress, Sister Constance. Her face reminded me of Churchill, and he, in turn, was often depicted as a bulldog on patriotic posters.

There were five classrooms, with a cloakroom where a narrow staircase led up to Sister Constance's tiny office. The toilets were outside in a separate building always referred to as "The Offices". Mrs Silcox was the teacher in Standard One, a thin woman with bulging eyes who impressed me greatly with her artistic skills: for Christmas she produced a frieze of the Holy Land, and helped us to cut out camels and wise men and shepherds and stick them onto the frieze. Sometimes Miss Bamwell was in charge, a large, lumpish woman whose grey hair was twisted into a row of snails on the nape of her neck. Miss Wright was a glamorous young woman who played the piano so brilliantly in our singing lessons that she could make us hear the sound of the sound of the wind on the moor and the galloping horse in the old folk song, Widecombe Fair:

When the wind whistles cold on the moor of a night
All along, down along, out along lee
Tom Pierce's old mare may be seen, ghastly white,
Wi' Bill Brewer, Jan Stewer, Peter Gurney, Peter Davey, Dan'l
Whitten, 'Arry 'Awkes
Old Uncle Tom Cobley and all …

When the American soldiers came to Oxford in large numbers later in the war, Miss Wright was seen one evening kissing one of them in Friar's Entry. Very soon afterwards, she was no longer seen at the school. Perhaps she was replaced by a shy young nun, Sister Catherine, whose teeth protruded.

Behind the school there was an air-raid shelter that had been built "for the duration" (of the war), a dank, dark, windowless brick building in which we spent many hours, either in an "air-raid practice", or because the wailing sirens had gone off - a German bomber had lost its way and had been seen approaching Oxford and no-one had heard the "All Clear". Here we sat on narrow benches, getting very bored, and the teachers would try to keep our spirits up by endlessly singing "Ten Green Bottles," "One Man Went to Mow", or "Neath the Spreading Chestnut Tree".

There never was an air raid on Oxford. Mrs. Brooks next door thought that was because *we* were there - sending radio messages to our compatriots in Germany.

Near the shelter was a patch of gravel where we had PE, jumping and flapping our arms. It was particularly difficult for me as I was wearing heavy knee-high boots - passed down to me from Peter - which I detested. But it was seeing which way everyone twisted, arms akimbo, that taught me "left" and "right". For now I was learning English. There were prayers every morning, and soon I had memorised Sister Constance's favourite bible reading: *Behold ye the lilies of the field …* as well as the Lord's Prayer. We put on plays: in one, I was cast as a banana in a fruit salad (*But nothing's as nice as fruit salad and cream)*; in another, I emerged from Pandora's box wailing: "*We are the TROUBLES!*" In another, my dearest friend, Anne, was King Canute, and I was one of her flattering courtiers. For this I had borrowed a toy sword from Malcolm Brookes, the boy next door, and thrust it through my belt. But while we were flattering the King, culminating in

Even the waves of the sea will obey you!

my belt came undone and my sword started slipping. When Anne said:

We'll see about that! Meet me on the beach tomorrow!

we were supposed to walk off the acting area. I felt I had to maintain the fiction of my sword being in my belt and must not hold it with my hand; so I clutched it unobtrusively between my knees and inched along in such an awkward way that Mu, who was in the audience, assumed I needed to go to the lavatory. In the next scene, all the girls who did not have speaking parts were ranged in rows in front of us, representing the waves of the sea. In due course they ran forward and backwards, a little nearer each time, just like breakers, until they knocked Anne off her chair – thereby proving a point about flattery.

There were quite a lot of outings from the school: to "Tumbling Bay" for swimming – which I learned later at "Dames' Delight" in the University Park – and once to the gas works, a hellish place with huge, ugly structures, clouds of steam and smoke, clanking and hissing noises, coal and coke fragments crunching underfoot, and a pervasive, sour smell. There was a metal staircase winding up the enormous gasometer, and I started climbing up it. After a time I was noticed and a terrified teacher implored me to come down. I lingered. It was rather nice, frightening a grown-up like that. Then I ran down, and was "told off".

The more I learned English, the more I forgot Danish. I would lie in bed trying to count in Danish. More and more numbers vanished. It was like watching holes appearing in fabric, and growing larger, till it had all gone. At home we spoke German. Outside, I felt as if my brain was wrapped in cotton wool: I lived in a blur of incomprehension. It seemed essential to learn perfect English. I collected words and phrases as if my life depended on it. I did not want people to know that I wasn't English, and I was terrified lest I betray my origin with a wrong word. One that gave me particular trouble was *flicker.* The German for the same phenomenon was *flimmern.* Or was that the English? I cudgelled my brains. But as soon as anyone asked me my name, the game was up. "*Gabbi? (*or *Garbi?)* Ooh, that's a funny name. Where are you from, then?" And then the game was up. Of course the girls at school had great sport with my name: "Gabbi's scabby," or: "Gabbi's got the gift of the gab"; or: "Garbi's garbage."

I envied the true English girls with their fluency and their natural patriotism and hatred for the *Jerries,* and wished they could understand that I was a refugee from those same Jerries that their fathers and brothers were fighting, although at the same time I was a Jerry myself and spoke their language. I was deeply ashamed of my knowledge of German. When I went to Devon for a holiday with a German book to read on the train, I wrapped it in brown paper and tried to hide it from the friendly guard and his, "What's that you're reading, then?" – burning with shame and fear.

It all came to a head one day in the asphalt playground at St Denys. There was a desirable wall to bounce a ball against –

Right hand, left hand, round the world and to-back-si – so we had to take turns at this wall. But Eunice Coghill and her friends would not give way, and the argument became heated. Suddenly Eunice shouted:

"You're just a dirty little German rat!"

At this, a gaping void seemed to open under me, into which I was falling helplessly, in floods of tears, unable to do more than gasp –

"And you're an English rat!"

– realising as I said it that a proper English person could not be a rat, like a Jerry, and that I had not only been thrown out by the Germans, who wanted me dead, I was not acceptable to these English girls either, or to anyone, anywhere, ever.

Some of the older girls ran to fetch Sister Constance, who soon stormed onto the playground, her veil flying in the wind, looking more Churchillian than ever; she ordered everyone into their classrooms, stood in front of us, glaring, muscles in her jaws pulsating; made me sit on a chair facing them all; and said:

"I'd like to flog every one of you."

Once again, I fervently wished I could cease to exist, while she harangued the girls, most of whom had nothing to do with the case. She was giving them a lesson in collective responsibility. Finally she insisted on every girl getting up from her desk and coming to me to apologise. It was extremely embarrassing - I felt as if I was a usurper and had no right to their awkward approaches. After all the others had left to go home, Sister Constance pushed Eunice and me - both of us sobbing again - roughly into each other's arms.

"There now," she said. "Kiss and make friends."

Which we both found rather difficult.

As I walked home with my faithful Anne Martin and some other girls, we discussed what had happened, and how difficult it had been for them to find words to apologise. But when I described the event to my parents, they said:

"That's the English way. You see how good Sister Constance is."

"But it was awful! She was being unfair to most of them!"

"But do you know what's happening in Germany? Do you know what German teachers are doing? Peter and Maleen had to go to school, but their homework wasn't taken in; they were not allowed to look into the schoolbooks; on school outings they had to walk in the gutter, not on the pavement; Peter, who was a devout Catholic, was not allowed to enter a church, and had to stand outside the door when the class were taught about the crucifixion, which was considered the first of the Jews' many sins. When the boys came out at the end of that lesson, they looked at Peter with disgust and loathing, as if he personally had crucified Jesus. .... Compared with those Nazi teachers, your Sister Constance is a shining hero."

*

School was a nightmare for Mu when she was small. She struggled to pass tests, had a stammer and bit her nails. Her parents believed that hitting her was the best way to help her over both these problems. But Fe, my father, was a brilliant student, and the apple of his mother's eye. His teacher at school once told her he didn't really need to do any homework - he seemed to know it all already. Her reaction was to move him from that school to the most demanding and prestigious school in Berlin. She herself studied Greek, so as to be able to help him: before breakfast she would take him to a park, where she would drill him. Her ambition for him was that he should be *ein Gelehrter* - a scholar - and he accepted that this was the most important thing in the world, all his life. And he expected everyone else to accept it, too.

No doubt about it: my parents had a disastrous marriage. Each was bitterly disappointed in the other, after the fading of the fine first flush of passion and romance which had made them defy both their parents and their own common sense and get married on Lore's 21st birthday, October 25 1925. Peter was born six months later. Günther's parents bitterly opposed the match and threatened to cut him off financially if he went through with it. He defied them - and they kept their word, plunging the newly-weds into poverty and a life of frequent moves from one pokey garret to another. Their happiness was further clouded by a skiing accident which damaged Günther's knee and left him in pain for over a decade.

Love was strong enough to overcome their difficulties for some years. Günther got a job at the Odenwaldschule, a progressive private school in southwestern Germany, in the Odenwald mountains. My sister Maleen was born in January 1927. The photograph on the next page shows my father, sitting happily in the garden with

My father Günther, with his first two children, Peter and Maleen

his first two children and singing, the model of a contented family man. Five years later the Nazis were in power, and when his wife became unexpectedly pregnant, he ordered her to have an abortion, as this was "no time for a Jewish baby to be born." But she defied him, just as he had defied his parents when they married, and the baby was born on December 17, 1932, nearly six years after her sister. That is how I came into the world.

To Lore, Günther was a superior being, naturally elegant, intellectually brilliant, athletic, beautiful – and she was willing to listen to him and admire him and worship him, very much as Gretchen adores Faust in Goethe's drama. And he must have enjoyed her unsophisticated intelligence, her emotionalism, her willingness to learn from him.

For my father, ancient Greece was almost a religion. He devoted his life to those superior beings, the Athenians, strolling in their groves, debating philosophy and ethics and generally introducing mankind to all those areas which are still identified by the psy's and the phy's and the logy's and the sophy's and the metry's of their electrifying language. The great thinkers. The inventors of democracy. The great artists, sculptors, architects, dramatists, poets, athletes …

I remember him chiefly hunched at his big desk, several books open in front of him, smoking Woodbines, painstakingly reconstructing defective papyri. Working from blurred photographs, he brought all his faculties, his intelligence, his mental self-discipline, his knowledge of other texts, to bear on gaps and holes in the ancient documents, till he felt sure he knew what the missing words were – thus opening another inch or two of that magical territory inhabited by a superior race.

This was not at issue between my parents. What Mu reproached him for again and again was: not having gone to Greece, back in 1933, when he had lost his job because of the Nazis. She urged him to go, to wander with a rucksack in the landscapes and among the ruins of his obsession. She would stay behind with the children; she would manage somehow. Yet he would not go. He did leave her; but he went to Denmark, where he worked with Professor Carsten Hoeg on an edition of the works of the Church Fathers, the Prophetologium. Hellenistic Greek - not Classical!

In Oxford, he worked as a librarian for Mansfield College - coolie work, he called it, contemptuously - coming home at midday and then retiring to bed for several hours. We were supposed to remember this and to come home silently; but we often forgot, and came crashing in through the front door, shouting or talking, and running noisily along the corridor to the kitchen. Then the dreaded reminder would come: his study door handle would rattle, and he would emerge in his long johns and hang over the banisters and shout down at us, Zeus thundering from Olympus. Mu would hurry from the kitchen, wiping her hands on her apron, shoo us out into the back garden, and then return to the battle, yelling back at him up the stairs. All this noise would often get Mrs Brooks next door angrily banging on the party wall, to which Mu would respond with vigorous blows with a broom handle.

Fe felt absolutely justified in demanding absolute silence - even other children playing in the street would be shouted at from his window and told to play elsewhere - because he devoted himself so completely to his real work, his papyri and his Greek authors, till well into the small hours of the morning. Surely we should all appreciate how awful it was for him to earn money to keep us all by working in the library - anyone could do that - but his gifts, his understanding of the Greeks, his insights - these were unique; they cost him dear; we should all be trying to support him in his dedicated labours. It never occurred to him that his was not the only possible point of view; that his vision of himself as a humble labourer in the vineyard of Greek civilisation looked to others like simple egotism.

His servitude to the Greeks made him fastidious; an aesthete. But Mu was rough and ready; and the longer they stayed together, the more they polarised. Fe spent ever longer in the bathroom, enraging

the other members of the household, fixing his metal shaving mirror
to the window to get the best light and balancing on two lengths of
doweling (to avoid getting flat feet) while he shaved meticulously. He
maintained he had delicate skin - unlike the rest of us - and therefore needed his own private bar of Pears Transparent Soap - which
my equally fastidious sister also used, secretly. He found her out
when he spotted some tell-tale suds on it, and so we had another
row. He would emerge from the bathroom at last, his face glistening with Vaseline, with a net cap on his head to press down his hair,
which had a tendency to go fuzzy. At breakfast he insisted on his
ration of butter being kept separate from ours, on a high shelf that
no one else could reach, and his coffee cup had to be warmed up in
the oven, otherwise his coffee would get cold too quickly.

Mu also believed in cleanliness, but in her case this entailed a
great deal of muscular labour, noise, and discomfort. Clothes and
linen were boiled, at first in the copper basin built into a corner of the
scullery, later in a zinc tub on top of the gas cooker, then scrubbed
on a washboard, and finally lugged upstairs to be rinsed in the bath,
where it was not infrequently discovered that some of it had got
singed. Then it was hung out to dry in the garden or, in wet weather,
on string criss-crossing the kitchen. Later it was ironed on a folded
blanket on the kitchen table - cue for more singeing. Trousers were
particularly difficult and often had several parallel creases. - this
might only be discovered just when the wearer was leaving the
house, and to save time she sometimes tried to rectify it on the leg,
pressing a pad of brown paper against one side and the hot iron
against the other, while the wearer gibbered with fear. But carpets
were not ironed: they were washed in the bath and dropped from
the window and manhandled onto the washing line. In the evening,
patches were sewn on, socks were darned. Every room was cleaned
every day with broom, mop, dustpan and brush, buckets of water,
old vests, newspapers, dusters; rubbish was thrust into a sack on
a nail outside the kitchen door, which had to be tipped out on the

As a toddler in Germany. I hope my bell-ringing didn't disturb my father's important research on Ancient Greek philology too much

kitchen floor periodically because some important document, even a cheque, was missing. My father was not amused. "Furor domesticus" he would murmur as he retreated to his study.

While she worked, she sang. She had a clear soprano voice and a huge repertoire of folksongs, lieder, hymns, chorales, Nazi and communist marching songs. This got on Fe's nerves. So that was another trigger for rows. Food was yet another. Mu considered cookery books and recipes a ludicrous affectation. Presumably her only experience of cooking had been in the *Wandervogel* - the teen-agers who hiked in the countryside and cooked whatever they had brought from home over an open fire. What could be nicer than a big bowl of over-cooked and slightly gritty spinach with a hunk of bread, sawn off a loaf pressed against her bosom, and liberally spread with margarine? One did not think about cooking; one needed no recipes; one just *knew* how to do it; so gravy was full of lumps; there were ants' eggs in the semolina, and cakes were sad and soggy, because she had never heard of baking powder. Her gardening methods were equally laborious and eccentric. It would be a silly waste of money to buy gardening tools. A kitchen knife for weeding; scissors for cutting the grass; a shopping bag and coal shovel for cow manure from Port Meadow. Plants should grow and develop freely; a vine that reached the scullery window was invited in and trained along the shelf with the saucepans. From time to time she tried to uproot a stinging nettle or a bramble, with tears in her eyes: was she not murdering an innocent being? Her apple tree seldom bore fruit, though her plum tree did, but only for some years; it was a shame, but their right to life had to be accepted.

*

My early years in Oxford were brightly lit by my friendship with Anne. We lived in a private fantasy world of ships and aeroplanes and all sorts of adventures. We would roam down from her house in Polstead Road, across Aristotle Bridge, to the playground, where the swings became the whirling propellers of a Spitfire we were repairing in mid-flight, which involved my raising my feet and holding on only with my hands when she whistled. Alas, on one occasion I let go with my hands too, crashed down onto the cinders and was rather badly hurt. Or we would go to the railway and place a penny on the rail, hoping a train would flatten it so that it could be used as an identity disc (which everyone was supposed to carry, but we had lost ours). We never found the flattened penny. Near the railway was an abandoned dump of builders' materials, where mounds of gravel, overgrown with weeds, produced a wonderful terrain for exciting games of hide-and-seek, which we played with some boys. But when they started playing football, we were told that as girls we could not join in. We were beside ourselves with fury. As we walked sulkily back along Polstead Road, we decided that there must have been a war at one time between men and women which the men had won, so that now they were the bosses. One day soon, we promised each other, there would be another war, and this time we would win, and then the boys would be the inferior sex. How pleased I am to see that women's football is now an accepted sport! Just occasionally I even see mixed teams – excellent! But too late for me.

Usually we would go across the railway bridge and down onto Port Meadow and tell each other stories of the kingdom it actually was, with the children in charge and the grown-ups having to do as they were told. At times we practised tree-climbing on a willow in preparation for climbing the rigging of a great sailing ship. High in the branches on a windy day we could almost see the heaving ocean waves come rolling across the grass. Once Anne's delicate little sister Clare came with us, and we picked cuckoo flowers and made a wreath and crowned her Queen of the May. If it rained we had to stay in her house. We decided to put on a play. Having never noticed that plays had plots, ours was simply a succession of ideas. One was:

"Autumn comes whistling overhead"

– at which point I leapt off a table with my arms outstretched. Our audience - Anne's mother, aunt, and grandparents - were very polite, but puzzled. We also had a go at cooking, and decided to see what happened if one cooked opposites: sugar and salt; cheese and jam; marmite and honey. The result was such that a certain smell which occasionally reaches my nostrils still makes me feel sick.

Every morning, Anne would be waiting for me at the corner of Polstead Road to go to St Denys. We walked so slowly, stopping to discuss everything we saw and thought of, that by the time we reached "Phil & Jim" (St Philip and St James' Church) we were often late, and we would start concocting our excuses. Anne's best one was: "The clocks on the four sides of the church all said a different time, so we didn't know which one to go by." The reason why they said different times was, of course, our incredibly slow progress round the church.

One day Sister Constance sent for me to come up to her little office. There sat a large woman with a large folder of papers. Sister Constance explained that I was to have my intelligence measured. As an Enemy Alien I was not entitled to sit for the Scholarship which enabled a few girls to go to a grammar school; but this test should have the same effect. I found myself answering a large number of strange questions, such as: could this triangle fit into this square? The upshot was that I had to leave St Denys and enter St Faith's, its sister school in the Woodstock Road, which I hated to do: at St Denys we resented the girls at St Faith's in their pink, maroon and grey uniforms and told each other: "St Faith's girls are stuck up". Now I was to go over to the enemy.

Far worse was the fact that Anne had to leave Oxford, because her parents were getting divorced, and she was to live with an aunt at Twickenham. My friendship with her had meant that the "dark days of the war", the fear of a German invasion, the fear of the Nazis, had meant nothing to me, just as the *Wandervogel* had protected my mother from some of the horrors of the First World War. Now we only saw each other when Anne came to Oxford during school holidays, when it would take us quite a time to get over a sense of strangeness and back into the swim of our symbiosis.

I did have some friends at St Faith's: Jocelyn, a tiny girl with long plaits, and Joy, huge and short-haired, who would invite Jocelyn and me to sit down among the damp coats in the cloakroom and "meditate on the futility of life". And I was still building up my English. At the beginning of one playtime, I heard a teacher ask a prefect to go out and see if it was raining. The girl came back and announced it was "more like a penetrating drizzle". Two new words! I rushed up the steps to see what a *penetrating drizzle* was, missed my footing, and fell with my face on a higher step. In fact I had landed on my front teeth, which left two white marks on the step, and to this day those teeth are slightly chipped. Never mind! I now knew exactly what *penetrating* and *drizzle* meant.

I did not stay long at St Faith's; my father, perhaps remembering his own transfer to a more prestigious school in Berlin, transferred me to the Oxford High School, with its navy blue uniform, which I hated to do: we St Faith's girls resented the High School girls, who always won all the inter-school competitions and were stuck up. Once again, I was obliged to go over to the enemy.

My chief trouble at school was boredom. I had to do outrageous things to make life more interesting. One of my chief aims in life was still to *frighten the grown-ups,* and I remember enlivening a tedious wait for a lesson at the top of the building by climbing over the banisters and dangling over the four-storey stair well. When an anxious, angry teacher ordered me to come back at once, I teased her by moving my hands from one banister to the next for a while, before swinging back onto the stairs. Another time a few of us decided to perform an opera. We were singing loudly while waiting for Miss Tait, the Latin teacher, to arrive. The French teacher next door came and told us to be quiet. Next week she pre-empted us by chalking a message on the blackboard: *PLEASE KEEP QUIET AS THE CLASS NEXT DOOR IS PREPARING FOR AN IMPORTANT EXAM.* We rubbed the message off and continued singing; so when the French teacher stormed in and pointed at the blackboard crying "Can't you READ??" we smiled. Such misdemeanours meant being "sent to Miss Stack." We sinners would queue up outside her white-painted door feeling rather frightened, although in time I was aware that all that would happen once I was in there would be: "Oh Garbi, not again! What is it this time?" followed by a pleasant chat about this and that - my future, for instance, maybe as a doctor - sitting in a comfortable armchair opposite her.

*

I was twelve years old when the Second World War ended in Europe on May 7. Peter was still in the army, in India, suffering boredom and frustration; Maleen had been expelled again from Milham Ford School for the crime of "Looking At Men" - she had a crush on a certain bus driver and used to watch out for him at Carfax - the bus driver probably knew nothing about it - and then went to a fantastic co-educational boarding school in Shropshire run by a refugee, while I remained at the High School. A number of the refugee boys had left us, but one, Kurt Iwnicki, was still with us. A few years older than me, thin and pale, he took an avuncular interest in me (and did for the rest of his life).

Now at last the war was over, and we were all wild with joy. American soldiers in the Clarendon Hotel in Cornmarket set loud-speakers in the windows playing loud jazz and danced in the street. At some point we were in London in the huge crowds surging towards Buckingham Palace where the Royal Family and Churchill stood and smiled and waved. Mu went out in the night when, for the first time in years, the street lights were switched on, and helped herself to armfuls of blossom from trees in front gardens, confi-dent that no-one would blame her on such a day. Now, she said, everything will get better, you'll see. Fe will get a proper job at a university and we will move from here to a bigger place somewhere and we'll have enough money and we'll be naturalised... "We'll get onto the green branch", as she put it.

How wrong she was.

In September, Anne and I, on holiday near Cirencester, where one of her grandmothers lived in a home for clergymen's widows, joined the villagers celebrating VJ Day round a huge bonfire with a small figure of a human on an old chair at the top.

"That's Hiro-Hito," we were told; but, though we had seen plenty of cartoons of that evil little man with huge teeth, we found ourselves unable to cheer when the flames licked him to pieces. We had not then heard of Hiroshima and Nagasaki, and the worst cruelties of the Japanese had been kept from us (though one of our heroes was Mao Tse Tung), but even if we had, our imaginations were too vivid to rejoice in the replica of a human being burnt. Later, we felt the same on Guy Fawkes Nights.

*

Fe did get a proper University appointment, in Manchester - not that it was what he really wanted: ever dissatisfied, he found himself "teaching Greek to the Theology students" (which meant *Hellenistic* instead of *Classical* Greek) "and Theology to the Greek students" - Christianity, that crazed product of primitive desert tribes. However, it was a proper job; only it wasn't with us that he was going to enjoy a more prosperous life.

One day he brought Stella to have tea with us: a woman as tall and thin as Mu was short and plump, much younger, very English, with a somewhat horsy face and glasses and a shy but friendly smile. She had been the producer at the BBC when Fe gave a talk there; they had spent a good deal of time together, and now they wanted to get married. It all seemed so improbable that none of us knew how to react. We ought to protest, to leap to Mu's defence, to hate or scorn or mock Stella; but it was hard to rouse such feelings to someone so gauche and harmless and common-sensical.

So one day, not long after, when I came home from school, it was to be told that Fe had left, for good. Mu wept, and sang the song –

Für die Zeit, da du mich geliebt hast / Danke ich dir schön
Und ich hoffe dass es anderswo / Dir besser mög ergehen.

For the time when you loved me / Thank you so much
And I hope that elsewhere / You will be better off.

It was 1948, and I was fifteen years old. I was devastated. The hole he left in my life was so huge it engulfed me entirely. I tried very hard to hate him, as Peter and Maleen did, but I kept remembering him, and longing for him, and remembering our walks in Wales and swimming at Barmouth, and the hours I had spent with him in the Library looking at picture books of ancient Egypt, and afterwards having to laugh politely at his rather silly jokes as we cycled home; sitting with him, when I was very small, in his study in the evening, on his lap, while he told me the legend of Androcles and the Lion; rushing up to his study to tell him something I felt he ought to know, or demonstrating my ability to stand on my head.

On our evening walks he drilled multiplication tables with me. We tried to speak English – laughed at the absurd mistakes we made, developing a language we called "Refugese"… There was a terrible war on, we were in great danger, we were Enemy Aliens, he spent some time interned on the Isle of Man with other Enemy Aliens, – but until he left us I was sure of his love for me.

To this day I associate him with one particularly beautiful piece of music. It's Schubert's Impromptu in A flat, opus 90, which sounds like a rippling stream, till a simple melody arises in the left hand, redolent of simple happiness, of contentment. But then another deep melody appears, full of longing – of *Sehnsucht* – growing ever stronger and louder till it is overwhelmed by another tumultuous, passionate, *fortissimo* theme which cascades down and finds itself in the rippling stream again.

It reminds me of the stream by "Torrent Walk" at Brithdir in North Wales, where I spent a holiday with him, sometime in the 1940s, during the war, when I was about 10. Just him and me. I remember looking up at him on the bridge when I was in the water, trying to build an island of stones, seeing him looking down on me, smiling affectionately.

I was his favourite. I was much younger than the others and was sometimes able to mitigate the rows that broke out frequently, often culminating in a slammed door and me trotting upstairs after him to find him sitting in his study, his head in his hands, when I would try to reason with him. He and I went for walks and cycle rides together. Once we came to a deep ditch which I couldn't get across. My legs were too short. He lay down across it and told me to use him as a bridge – which I did. In Wales we climbed Cader Idris – at one point I panicked on a steep scree slope, and he waited at the top, talking to me to calm me down – and once we crept to the edge of a vertical cliff, lay down flat and looked down at the lake far below: the wind rushing up sent the loose skin on his cheeks into folds.

But I felt guilty for missing him; it was disloyal to Mu. I told myself that I had been thrown out of his life, and tried to whip up feelings of bitterness against him. After he had left our house, once, just once, when I was walking along the Woodstock Road, I saw him walking along on the other side of the road, a little smile on his face, a spring in his step, quite oblivious to me, and I wondered if I actually existed. For years I was numb, coldly convinced that my existence was pointless, possibly repulsive, certainly surplus to requirements. I could see no point in anything I did and as I developed, thought myself fat and ugly.

*

The other day I found a little notebook in the attic in which I had
written the following poem about my father:

> We are pale because
> We see each other through
> The white ghost of your absence.
> Our thoughts are of you
> As we stare out of our prison windows –
> Adrift, white, distant.
> But we dare not speak of you –
> So we have nothing to say
> And the house is white with your presence.
> I saw you, even,
> beside the bed
> Shivering, white, in tears.
> Something has been destroyed
> If only I could hate and forget you
> Instead of remember, and love.

Chapter 3: *Ecole d'Humanité*

Mu was alarmed at the state I was in, and consulted with other refugee friends. Finally it was decided that I should spend a year at the Ecole d'Humanité in Switzerland. When they were first married, my parents had worked and lived for a short time at the Odenwaldschule, a wonderful country school in western Germany where my father had been a teacher. There, the most advanced ideas not only of education, but of humanity and philosophy were nurtured: anathema to the Nazis, of course, who closed it down and handed over the buildings to the Hitler Youth. Paulus and Edith Geheeb, the founder and his wife, had escaped into Switzerland with some of the members of staff - and with the help of some good Swiss people they had set up this Ecole d'Humanité. Mu had kept in touch with Edith.

How Mu managed to scrape together the money to send me there is a mystery. At that time she was having to call on lawyers to get any money at all from Fe. It was finally settled at £250 less tax as alimony plus 19 shillings and three pence per week maintenance for me - my older siblings, Peter and Maleen, were now independent. And she was working as a domestic in an old people's home for 30 hours a week at one shilling and eight pence an hour. Yet somehow she did it.

So I set out on a long, long journey to a new life - by train to Paddington, then to Victoria to get the boat train to Dover - on the ferry across the Channel - then a long, long train ride through the night to Basel, another train through rolling hills - which grew

Paul Geheeb, known as Paulus

higher and steeper, with more forest, and here and there a tooth of grey rock showing. Then I saw the snow-covered peaks with soft clouds coiling round them. At Lucerne a little cogwheel train took me very steeply uphill through the greenest meadows and woods, with a view down to two lakes, and the sound of cowbells whenever the train stopped. At Brünig-Hasliberg the bus to Goldern was waiting - and with a musical tune warned any others on the slender road slipping through shadowy woods, clinging to the side of cliffs, through tunnels and alpine meadows as it approached blind bends. And stopped near a big wooden chalet - the school!

It was afternoon when I arrived, and the hot sun brought forth a special smell from the wooden walls. A number of children and adults were idly chatting on or near the wooden steps up the side of the *Haupthaus* (the school's main building).-Among them I recognized (from photographs) the founder and headmaster, Paul Geheeb, a radical educationalist known to all as Paulus, looking like an Old Testament prophet with his long white beard and deep-set eyes, and his wife Edith, a stout, friendly woman. Edith asked a girl about my age, Sabine, to look after me. Sabine led me across a small grassy area to the *Turmhaus* - another chalet with a tower: this had once been a holiday centre for a protestant church. We went upstairs to the room I was to share with her, which had an uninterrupted view of the Wetterhörner, the snow-capped mountain.

I dumped my suitcase as a gong sounded. We hurried back to the Haupthaus, where a small boy was banging away enthusiastically at a big gong, and found ourselves in the throng entering the dining hall. We sat at tables allotted to each 'family' - every *Mitarbeiter* had a family consisting of between three and seven *Kameraden* - the words children or grown-ups were not used; anyone who was not a *Kamerad* - a comrade - was a *Mitarbeiter* - a colleague.

I belonged to Paulus' family - along with Piet, the oldest boy in the school, and his Dutch sweetheart, Margot, Elnis from Israel, and Peter from Germany - so I sat at their table. Everyone was talking at the tops of their voices - the noise was deafening. When everyone was seated, Paulus stood up and silence fell while he read a short thought for the day, as he did every day - one I remember was: *Erst wenn sich das Herz ändert sich die Welt* - Not until the heart changes will the world change.... As soon as he had finished, the hubbub started again. One or two *Kameraden* from each table went to the serving hatch to fetch the food, and we could eat.

This school was totally different from any I had attended before. For one thing - it was co-educational, and a number of boys came close to me in a different way from the girls .... And the timetables were different. There were just three one-hour lessons - called *Kurse* - every morning. No tests, no grades, no homework. In the afternoons, we were busy cleaning and tidying and working in the gardens, and had free time to pursue our interests; I would prac-tise playing the piano - for this I had to get the key to the piano from Lüthi, the music teacher, - and I tried to get the rippling runs of that Impromptu.

The groups were small, about half a dozen learners with one adult, and the lessons were informal and extremely stimulating. Maths, which I had always hated, burst like fireworks in my mind when we were considering the question: Is there a highest prime number? Nini, a retired ballerina and literature teacher, opened the world of ideas to me. She made us aware of two modes of being, 'Apollonian' and 'Dionysiac'. Using many examples from literature, art and philosophy, she showed us that we had a choice: to submit to the instinctive, exhilarating, passionate, or to be guided by reason and intelligence.

These alternatives were meaningful to me. I could see that my father was "Apollonian" - intellectual, cool, rational - abandoning us in our emotional turmoil, which was exacerbated by his departure - rejecting us as factors that disturbed his inner harmony, his service of Athens, embracing instead his second wife, the cool, reasonable, English Stella. Years later, when he was successful - a member of the Royal Society - he maintained this surgical removal of us from his world. He made sure that there was no mention of us in Who's Who - only his second wife and their children were mentioned.

The school was extremely democratic - not in the sense of having elections and committees - that would have led to dominating majorities and oppressed minorities - no, in the Quaker sense: problems had to be discussed for as long as necessary until the best solution was found. From time to time we would all gather in the dining hall - from the smallest six-year-old to Paulus - and decide on rules. There were only three: No Alcohol; No Going out at Night; No Fires to be Lit in the Forest. So on my sixteenth birthday, a week before Christmas, I broke all three - celebrating with Sabine and Andreas. With the knitted patchwork blankets from our beds, bottles of wine and matches we set off for the forest.

We were soon drunk. We laughed, talked nonsense, veered from maudlin self-pity to absurd high spirits and back again - and finally felt extremely tired. We stamped out the remains of the fire and set off homeward through the forest. I felt very confident and loudly called to the others to follow me. Why did they hang back? I knew the way to go! Then I stepped off the edge of a precipice and started flying through the air.

I heard someone screaming in the distance. Then I hit the ground. It was a steep slope, and I was rolling down it, ending up curled round the base of a tree. The scream came closer; in fact, it was coming out of my mouth.

Sabine and Andreas came down by a more circuitous route and in due course found me whimpering, still curled round my tree trunk. They got me back to the school and I was driven down to the hospital in Meiringen. I had a broken arm and badly bruised knees. Duly bandaged and plastered up I returned to the school next morning and was staggered to see a knitted patchwork blanket hanging from the top of a tree halfway up a steep slope to a rocky outcrop. I was dumbfounded to see how far I had fallen. Did I have a guardian angel? The three of us went back to retrieve the blanket, and the others shared my feeling of awe when they saw it hanging from that tree. But Nini was beside herself with rage: How could I be so thoughtless as to injure myself just days before a performance! Did I know my lines? And what about my bruised knees - as the Virgin Mary I had to kneel!

Well, duly chastened, I learned my lines, and during the performance of the old Nativity Play I kept my broken arm, draped in the loose sleeve, upstage, with a cushion wedged under my elbow. "I am the servant of the lord", I declared piously, "May it be according to his will." I dropped the cushion so that I could kneel on it. Perhaps because I was still feeling unreal, my performance was deemed to be deeply sincere, and I came in for a lot of praise.

Those who could go home for the Christmas holiday left; on Christmas Eve the rest of us followed Paulus into the forest, where a small fir tree had been decked with candles and tinsel, and he read us the Christmas story. We sang some traditional Christmas songs, and returned to the school, to find an unusually festive meal prepared: each of us got a plate with a silver-paper triangle of cheese, a boiled egg, some fruit and biscuits and chocolate goodies. The fourth candle on the big advent wreath hanging from the ceiling was lit, there was singing and excited chatter.

At New Year the local peasants, in accordance with an ancient pagan custom, hung cows' bells round their necks and, consuming only beer, walked round the villages on the Hasliberg for 24 hours, ringing their bells, to drive out evil spirits - then for the next 24 hours they walked round the individual farms and houses; and for the last 24 hours they entered the houses in the final stages of drunkenness and exhaustion. We were warned that they would come into the school and that we should keep out of their way. As luck would have it, I was having a shower in the basement of the Haupthaus when they entered. I turned off the tap and kept the door locked and didn't make a sound - so they didn't find me.

The snow came late that year, and those that could ski dashed off when at last it was possible, leaving those like me who had never touched a ski before to try to work it out.... Spring and summer had us walking in the beautiful meadows and climbing up above the forest belt to the *Alpenwiesen* where the cows grazed, their bells and occasional mooing making music.

Nini's plays dominated the school: *Die Laune des Verliebten,* Goethe's pastoral verse play, the Nativity play, the *Oresteia* with the dance of the furies, *Thunder Rock* by Robert Ardrey, in which a lonely lighthouse-keeper conjures up the ghosts of a family that had drowned nearby - a gentle tragic love develops between him and the daughter. Everyone was roped in to make costumes, rig up lights, organise or take part in the performances, invite people to come and watch - and a great deal of praise came our way, especially for me, who played the lead in all of them. It quite turned my head to be told that I was very talented and ought to be an actress. Not a doctor.

When I got home, at the end of the year, there was no piano. My father had taken it with him to his new life with his new, English, wife. So I never did get to play the Impromptu - or anything else, really.

Chapter 4: Drama

I had to go back to the Oxford High School for a year and take the A-level exams. But I was determined to get onto the stage, and applied for auditions at RADA and at the Central School of Acting, where I was offered a place. Oxford City's Education Department would not award me a grant for that - but they would give me one to go to university, on the strength of my A-level results. Peter and Mu insisted that I should apply to Somerville College to read English. I got through to the interview stage, had lunch with some high-powered women there, and was offered a place - but only to read Modern Languages. This I refused: English or nothing, and preferably nothing had been my attitude from the start. I wanted to ACT!

I was pleased to discover that someone was trying to start a "Fit-Up Rep" (a repertory company without a home theatre), to tour the villages of Oxfordshire. Soon I was rehearsing *Gaslight*, a Victorian-style melodrama in which I played the part of a wife being driven mad by her evil husband, who terrifies her by interfering with the gas lamps, which grow brighter and dimmer. The husband was played by Jimmy, a cheerful Irish bus driver with very definite ideas of how the stage should look. So when we got to the village halls where we were to perform, it was with a complete set of props and Victorian furniture, which had to be squeezed onto the narrow platforms. Real door and window frames were attached to the curtains at the back of the platform. In the end it was so crowded we could hardly move, and when Jimmy swung round dramatically

One of the studio pictures I used to try and get work as an actress

his cloak would send little tables flying into the audience - which rarely consisted of more than half a dozen little old ladies. That Fit-Up Rep soon folded.

I then set off for London, the heart of Britain's theatrical world. From now on, I was going to be self-sufficient - after all, I was nineteen. First I needed to get rid of my German name - I needed to be English! I discovered that this entailed visiting a Justice of the Peace and asking her to change my name from Zuntz to Henry - the name Peter had been given when he enlisted, as it would have been very dangerous for him to be captured by the Germans with that name. The JP I found was busy baking at the time. She invited me into her kitchen to swear the necessary oaths and fill in the necessary form. That done I gave her five shillings and was henceforth known as Irene Henry, or sometimes Rene Henry, and no one need know I was not a proper British person. I found myself a room near Paddington, at £3.10 a week; next, at the Labour Exchange, a job: cutting sandwiches for the restaurant in Dickens & Jones, for £4 a week. With my first pay packet I paid my rent and bought a copy of *The Stage*. One of the advertisements was for a "Student ASM" - Assistant Stage Manager - at a repertory theatre in Ashford, Kent.

This theatre had opened just after the war. A man called Richard Dale had put his demob gratuity into it. He and his sister Marie played most of the leads. They lived with their parents some way away and arrived at the theatre by car, so they must have been quite a well-to-do family. However, the theatre did not prosper - nor did many of the other theatres that opened all over the country as the post-war wave of desire for a civilised life style broke on the rocks of public apathy - and of the cinema - which was so much more economical than live theatre. In the fullness of time, those cinemas would in turn make way for bingo. Six months before I arrived, the Ashford Theatre had lost three actors, and apart from the Dales themselves there were then only two. Now Richard was recruiting "Student ASMs" like myself in a desperate and slightly illegal attempt to keep his theatre going.

I now learned just what "repertory" theatre meant. Week by week, one play was being performed in the evenings while another was being rehearsed during the day, in preparation for the following week. My job was to paint huge posters for each new production, and assemble all the props required, and to ensure that they were in the right place on the stage at the right time. I was also the prompter, was responsible for "noises off", and for the lighting. And I also played small parts in some of the plays. This meant that I had to buy a set of theatrical make-up - greasepaint - and also suitable clothes for my part. I had no free time. Sundays and Mondays were the hardest: the old set had to be struck, the new one set up, with all its props; then came the dress rehearsal for the new play, followed by the opening night. My pay was pitiful, and the digs, which I shared with Barbara, one of the actresses, were freezing cold.

But after a few weeks, Richard gave us the sad news that the theatre was bankrupt and would have to close. The last play was the world premiere of *Western Wind* by Charlotte Frank. Nobody knew their parts, one of the actors kept going round in circles ignoring what anyone else said so that it didn't make sense at all and I couldn't think where I had better prompt what. At one point they were supposed to change from pyjamas into full evening dress on stage while someone else was turning down the bed; then a man was waiting for a girl who was putting on a silk nightie. Not knowing what to do while he waited he started bouncing up and down on the bed ....

I was shocked by the cynicism of the actors. None of them cared about the art of the theatre, clarifying our understanding of the great life issues, stripped of the dross of irrelevant coincidences, and so on. The audience, sparse as it was, sat there like suet puddings, only reacting with giggles if there was something sexy.

Soon I was back in a bed-sitter in London, visiting theatrical agents and buying *The Stage*. One advertisement led to my becoming a *Mayfair Mermaid*. Once a week a dozen girls met in a public swimming bath and were taught how to spin and surface dive, form circles and lines and loops, and swim in time to waltzes and tangos, by an older, rather vague, easy-going woman called Thelma. Early in June the nine girls selected, myself included, set out by train for Scarborough.

It was a cold, wet summer, but almost every day we had to go for practice in the South Bay Bathing Pool, which was an enclosed section of the North Sea with a tower of diving boards at one end, the top one ten metres high. Twice a week we performed. We dived into the water one after the other and swam in line while the loudspeakers blared out *The Blue Danube* and we moved our arms backward and forward more or less in time to it. Then *Jealousy*, a tango, came on; we swam on our backs to form a ragged circle and, at a signal from Sally, the oldest girl, performed a "water wheel" - disappearing backward under the water and surfacing, puffing and snuffling, in more or less the same positions - whereupon we would hug our knees and swivel round and round: this was called "the teacup". We were not really very good at any of this; in fact the director of entertainment, a friendly, avuncular man who pitied us in that cold weather - "I've got me long johns on today, I have" - told us quite cheerfully that we were the worst water ballet they had ever had.

But Tom Perry made up for it. He, Thelma and a young man called Stan did amazing stunts off the diving boards. The climax, heralded by a long drum roll, came when Thelma poured petrol over her beloved and set it alight, when he would dive. Pictures of Tom, flying down in sheets of flame, featured on posters and leaflets and on the sides of the old van in which the three of them lived. It required perfect timing. If he dived too soon, the petrol might not ignite; if he left it too late - well, dreadful scars on his back testified to the very real danger gentle Thelma put her man in at the climax of every show.

The Midnight Shows - "Night Follies" - were the best for us, as these were in the North Pool, which was heated; moreover, it had underwater illumination. To the music of *One Enchanted Evening*, we plunged into liquid light. As it changed to *The Glass Mountain* we felt fatefully beautiful, slinking through the luminous waves slender as fishes, wild perdition following in our wake. We seldom grinned or winked at each other during the midnight show. There were often a few young men hanging around the exit when we emerged from the "Night Follies", some of whom would shout beerily, while others just stared, probably wondering if these rubbery-looking girls, their wet hair plastered down, could possibly be the nymphs they had been gawping at.

I was living with a Yorkshire woman called Mrs Howard, in North Street. I occupied the back bedroom in her "two up, two down" terraced cottage; she and her 13-year-old daughter Ada slept in the double bed in the front. She was so fat that when she was seated only the tips of her knees emerged from beneath her belly. She had the face of a Pekinese, frizzy grey hair, and glasses. When little Ada went into one of her weeping fits, or got the fidgets, Mrs Howard would roll her eyes at a large photograph of a fireman in full uniform and comment sagely, "She's frettin' for her Dad." In fact, she had never known her father, as he had died when she was born, of a heart attack, or perhaps shock. After all, they had both been approaching 50 when they got married and never expected to have any children. All this I learned in the first two days of my staying in her house: she never stopped talking, her little dog perched quivering on the small amount of lap available.

I done all the cookin' and bakin' for the wedding mesel', 'undred an' fifty fairy cakes I made, two 'undred sausage rolls, and a three-tier cake with all the trimmings, big enough for nigh on sixty guests. Well, we 'ad a lot of friends, both on us.

But some time later she became aware of unfamiliar sensations inside, and went to the doctor, who diagnosed appendicitis and had her operated on, without noticing the foetus in another part of the vast belly. Ada was born six weeks later, to everyone's boundless astonishment, and the father, Mrs Howard's Loved One, dropped dead.

Mrs Howard was extremely good to me. She would wait up for me after the midnight show with cocoa and cake. One evening there were some National Servicemen among the people round the exit of the North Pool as we emerged. One of them shouted: "Hi, good lookin', what's cookin'?" to which the reply was "Chicken!" leading to "Chicken! Wanna neck?" - "Not with you!" giggled some of the Mermaids. Several of the men were following us. "Hurry!" whispered Sally. We broke into a run. I was relieved when we came to my turning and slowed down; but after a few steps, I realised I was being followed. I darted into the first side turning I came to, a narrow alley; glancing round, I saw two of the men in uniform hurrying to catch up with me.

"Hang on!" one of them shouted. "We wanna talk with you!" They were obviously drunk. I started walking faster; then one of them started running - he was trying to get ahead and cut me off. One of them crashed into a dustbin and fell, shouting. Lights were coming on in windows. And I was lost; I had lost my bearings. At last I caught sight of a red pillar box - yes, it was the one next to number 68. In seconds I was pounding on the door. Mrs Howard opened it, glanced along the street, grasped the situation, shut and bolted the door, and took me into her arms. Or would have if her arms had extended beyond her bosom. As it was, she held me by my shoulders.

"There now, don't you fret no more. I've got you. Come and sit down and drink your cocoa. You must never go to bed on an empty stomach, ma loved one always said."

There was a whimpering sound from upstairs.

"They've gone and set off our Ada an' all," she observed grimly. She heaved herself slowly up the stairs. "Don't you fret, our Ada, it's only a couple of drunks. They'll soon give over."

Ada was standing by the window, shivering in her night dress, sobbing and staring at the two men, who were still shouting and throwing rubbish in the direction of the house.

"An' get away from that window, lass!" Mrs Howard exclaimed, pulling the child back to the bed. The men tired of their shouting at last and left, and we went to bed. While my heartbeat slowly returned to normal, I listened to Ada's whimpers next door subside under her mother's growled remonstrances.

Mrs Howard taught me a Yorkshire proverb:

'Ear all, see all, say nowt, eat all, sup all, pay nowt; and if ivver tha dost owt fer nowt, allus do it for thysen.

"An' you'd do well to remember that an' all, lass. Allus look after number one. With our Ada takin' on so, I'm that worried, ah've lost two stone! Two stone! Ah weighed meself in Boots t'other day - ah'm down to fourteen stone! It's worry what makes you so thin."

The season over, I was back in London, once more studying the columns of *The Stage*. The only interesting advertisement was for "Dance Hostesses" at the Cabaret Club. Cabaret! Surely that meant brilliant political satire from stand-up comics, and *avant garde* music! I applied immediately and was duly called for an interview. I found the night club, near Piccadilly, and went in. It looked dusty, tawdry, and threadbare. There was a dance floor, surrounded by a ring of small tables with chairs; there were alcoves with plush covered benches, a piano, a stage - and a tiny office, with a desk and a sofa. Here I met Mr Murray, the club's owner: a large man who half listened to me as I explained that I really wanted to be an actress, but loved dancing, and how interested I was in cabaret, and so on.

"Yes all right, you'll do," he said at last; "we sometimes have customers who want to talk."

I took in that "sometimes". What did they usually want?

"I've heard", I said, blushing, "that sometimes women who work in this sort of place are - er -"

"Well you may sometimes get a customer offering to take you

home. My advice to you is - never accept such offers. Get yourself
a taxi. OK?"

"OK, Mr Murray!"

I got myself an evening dress at an Oxfam shop. Now I spent the
mornings at the club learning the dance routines. The woman who
taught us these was a large blonde, who seemed to be intimate with
Mr Murray. Soon I was being fitted out with costumes - skimpy
green shorts for *Old Macdonald had a Farm*, in which we had to
prance around in various ways to indicate farm animals; frilly skirts
for a can-can, and flesh-coloured body stockings which gave the illu-
sion of nudity, while actually covering us from neck to ankles. After
a week I was deemed ready to start work.

This meant wearing evening dress and sitting at one of the little
tables with two or three other "dance hostesses", chatting until such
time as a customer sent a waiter over to summon one or more of us
to join him. We were then supposed to talk, accept food and drink,
and get them to buy things for us - huge teddy bears, boxes of chocolates, bouquets of red roses, Black Sobranie cigarettes, which scant-
ily clad girls with trays hanging from their necks brought round
from time to time. Most of these gifts were handed in at the end of the
evening to be sold again next day. When the pianist started playing
These Foolish Things we had to excuse ourselves and go backstage
to change for the floor show, which happened twice every evening.
It would start with us all dancing round together; then a contortion-
ist would tie herself in knots, followed by another group dance, then
some more acrobatics, and so on. Afterwards, back in our evening
dresses, we rejoined our gentlemen; or sat chatting.

I got to know the women quite well. They were essentially pros-
titutes. Each had her own lover - or pimp, perhaps - and in a sense
was faithful to him, despite being promiscuous for money. They
were very interested in sex. One girl, Yvonne, tried to put into words
the sensation of "coming" - orgasm: "It's like as if something was
being pulled together inside you. I only gets it with my Joe, not with

nobody else". Another, Iris, was very pretty and a brilliant dancer but completely over-sexed. She saw sex in everything - any round or cylindrical shape, even bread rolls, made her think of copulation. Once she described how she and her boyfriend had been trying to redecorate their flat, but made little progress as they had to keep stopping to make love again.

After a few weeks, Mr Murray summoned me to his office. He had noticed I was still wearing the same evening dress. Why didn't I get a new one?

"I can't afford one - on £4 a week."

"Why - haven't you been paid to go home with one of the customers?"

"Mr Murray! I promised you I wouldn't do anything like that!"

"Well, you know, it's very bad for you not to if you want to -"

Deeply dismayed, I struggled back to the digs through the last of London's celebrated pea-soup fogs. It was thick and yellow, and so dense I had to grope my way along walls and fences, and still crashed into lamp posts and pillar boxes. Even indoors, I could hardly see across the room, and if I ran my hand across my forehead my fingers were smeared with an oily black substance. It lasted for days, and life in London virtually stopped until at last it lifted again. This, added to my sense of shame at the sordid life I was leading, made me eager to accept an invitation to be an ASM at the Tudor Theatre, Bramhall, which had advertised in *The Stage.*

A few years later, the Cabaret Club became famous because one of its dance hostesses, Christine Keeler, and her friend, Mandy Rice-Davies, were sharing their favours between members of the British Defence establishment and, simultaneously, members of the equivalent Russian one. Known as the Profumo Affair, it was headline news for quite a long time. But by then, I was elsewhere.

*

Nowadays Bramhall is a district of Stockport, Greater Manchester.

When I arrived there, in January 1953, the theatre was still a cinema. Now another idealist, rather like Richard Dale in Ashford, wanted to bring live theatre to the people of Bramhall, and the local paper, the *Stockport Advertiser,* was supporting him.

I found digs, and went to see the last film being shown in the cinema - *Wuthering Heights*, with Laurence Olivier as Heathcliff. On my way back to my digs I came to a telephone kiosk and idly looked at the phone book. Zuntz was always the last name on any alphabetical list - though we had all got rid of that embarrassing name one way or another - but I had learned that the last name in the New York phone book was ZYZ! Intrigued, I had made a habit of looking at the last name in any list, and I did so now.

It was Zuntz.

On the spur of the moment, I dialled the number: Chinley 1. His wife answered.

"Hello - I'm Gabi."

"Garbi?" she squawked.

"Yes. I've just discovered your number in the phone book. I'm at Bramhall. Must be quite close."

"Wait a minute. I'll get Father." She always called him 'father.'

Father! So they had children, and she was in the habit of referring to him as Father - or *Farvi* as I learned later - but for me, he was *Fe.*

There was a long pause. Finally she came back. "Father says could you write a letter, please, and explain where you are and what you're doing and so on. All right?"

"All right."

I copied the address from the phone book and went back to my digs, feeling quite dizzy. I saw him with my mind's eye as I had seen him when I was a child. I remembered our close relationship - different from the others in the house. I remembered how when I was little I had rushed up to the study where he sat at the big desk with all the books he was referring to propped up on it and climbed onto his lap, knowing I was welcome. I remembered looking up from the stream near Brithdir - Torrent Walk - where I had been rearranging some rocks to make a little waterfall - to see him looking down and smiling benevolently - and how we had laughed together at the mistakes we made switching from German to English...

... and then that devastating day when he had moved out and I saw him, walking on the other side of Woodstock Road, with a little smile on his face - and he ignored me - he was leaving us, he was to marry this English woman and move to Manchester -

I did see why the others resented, or even hated him. His selfishness was extraordinary. His weekly butter ration had to be cut out of the family allowance and kept separately, on a high shelf which no one else could reach. At table in the kitchen his legs might collide with Peter's and he would demand that Peter should keep his under the chair so that he could stretch out his. Confident in my special relationship with him I did try sometimes to make him see reason. He was cruel to Kurt, who had come to England alone with the "Kindertransport" and lived with us and was my foster-brother. One day, without any preparation, he said Kurt had lived with us long enough and should move on. I followed him up to his study and tried to make him see how monstrous this was - Kurt had nowhere else to go and was then a teenager - and Fe did come down and shifting his feet self-consciously said Kurt could stay...

I ask myself now - 70 years on - what made him so extraordinarily blinkered in his egotism. Just after I was born the Nazis were in power - and we were half Jewish - filthy Jewish blood was contaminating the Aryan blood in our veins! And so we were insulted and humiliated - and knew that far worse was to come: we needed to get out of the country! As I mentioned, Fe was lucky enough to go to Denmark to work on a *Prophetologium* (a study of the words of biblical prophets) with a Danish Professor, Carsten Hoeg; but he did nothing to help us - Mu and Peter, Maleen and me - a baby - to escape: Mu had to make her way somehow to see him and ask him to deal with the authorities. She told me later that when she had located him - with some difficulty - all he had said was, "I'm glad you've come; now we can file for divorce." Why was he so callous?

I think he must have regarded himself as a kind of aristocrat - a member of an intellectual aristocracy. So different rules of behaviour applied to him. Different from other people because of his intellect and musical talent (he was an excellent classical pianist). And because of his insight into - empathy with - the civilisation of the Greeks. "Where did they come from, these Greeks?" he asked me once, "with their slender ankles and wrists, the nose and forehead one smooth shape, so different from the half-starved dark tribesmen around the Mediterranean with their superstitions, scrabbling for possessions - and here were these tall, fair haired Aryan Greeks, founding cities and establishing democracy and creating noble temples and theatres - where did they come from?" - "From outer space?" I suggested - and he smiled.

Now I sat down to write my letter, telling him that I wanted to see him again; that I had never understood why he had abandoned me without a word, after we had been so close; that I was often depressed and at a loss ... that I didn't see any prospect of success in the theatre for myself ...

He replied, in writing:

Thank you for your letter. It gives us hope that a meeting with you need not end in emotional upheaval as in the case of Peter.

Peter had visited them at some point uninvited and had been admitted, reluctantly, as some other guests were expected. Peter had been introduced to them as a friend. No one was supposed to know that Fe had been married before or that he had a previous family; but the guests commented that Peter's appearance was extraordinarily similar to Fe's, and so the cat was out of the bag. Then Peter lost his temper and told them all roundly what he thought of this concealment - or denial - of his existence, and of Mu's, and all of us. But now I had been invited to spend the weekend of his 52nd birthday - January 28th - with them ...

So, about the time when the inevitable announcement came that the Tudor Theatre, too, was bankrupt and would have to close, I made my way for the first time along the narrow road - "unsuitable for motorists" - to the village of Chinley and the lonely house called Newstead. I found Stella struggling to cope not only with a sick child - their son Carsten had polio - and a new baby, but also with Fe's insistence on the primacy of his needs: like the absolute silence when he was having a nap, or playing the piano, the really hot coffee, the really good food ... Some time was set aside for conversations with me.

By now I was disillusioned by the theatre, and felt I should do something positive with my life. The old dream of running an orphanage - with Mu - came back; or to be a doctor; or a social worker ... Certainly not, said Fe. Social work and so on was a fine thing to do - but the likes of us should devote our intellectual gifts to higher things. I stayed at Chinley quite a lot, being a sort of au pair for Stella. I accepted his never-ending complaints about their lack of money, never having enough for a holiday - about the extra work caused by Carsten's recurrent ill health, about the thankless task of teaching mediocre students and reviewing third-rate books - and in between he doled out advice for me. In the end I decided to go to university - the memory of the Grecian façade I had noticed while walking past University College London was quite enticing.

By March the Tudor Theatre was a bingo hall and I was back in Oxford. In the months and years that followed, my renewed but strictly circumscribed relationship with my father did, probably, heal the deep wounds the divorce had inflicted, and I was not as distressed as Peter and Maleen and Mu. I tried to build bridges for them; the vehemence with which he rejected them seems extraordinary. I had tentatively suggested he might send a card to Peter for his daughter Claire's birth in December 1953. His response –

... Your suggestion re your brother, I suppose, must have come from some sudden whim; otherwise you would have recalled our long talk on the matter. I wish him and his dependents the best - and there

it rests. The sphere of instability, insincerity, resentment, cruelty - lies behind us and shall never touch ours again. That's final. Be realistic ... You know that you are welcome here, and more than welcome, for your own sake, and for that only. ... We will not be drawn into what is the very negation of the life, and lives, we are building up.

It seems incredible that he never faced the fact that he himself was the cause of the "instability" - that the "cruelty" was his. Kurt, my foster brother, once made his way to Chinley to see him - and perhaps to make bygones be bygones - and was left standing on the doorstep, in the rain, and had the door shut in his face.

I felt guilty for being singled out and being admitted to his "sphere".

Nearly forty years later, in March 1992, he tucked a scrap of paper into a letter he sent me which read, in German: "To respond to a wish that has been expressed in many places, I put into my obituary for the British Academy a reference to my first marriage and offspring. The same I'll add to Who's Who - if I should live long enough for the next issue, which is unlikely."

In fact, he died less than a month later. Still - better late than never? His British Academy obituary, 30 pages long, may be viewed online. All three of the children by his first marriage are mentioned, though Mu is referred to only as "his wife".

As for Who's Who, a recent internet search by my son turns up the following in its sister publication for the deceased, Who Was Who:

Zuntz, Prof. Günther

DrPhil (Marburg); FBA 1956

Dr. Leo Zuntz and Edith (née Bähring); m 1947 Mary Alyson Garratt; two s one d, and one s two d by previous marriage; died 3 April 1992

So there we are, Peter, Maleen and myself: "one s two d." And again Mu is left strictly anonymous. What strange wrestling in the heart went into this reluctant compromise, I wonder? Then again, Mary's children are also reduced to cyphers, and it is a very short entry indeed.

5: University, CND, David

So I entered University College London - "the godless institution of Gower Street" - founded in 1826 as the first explicitly secular university in Britain - with the fully clothed corpse of Jeremy Bentham on a chair at the top of some stairs, to read German with subsidiary English. In those enlightened days I did not have to pay a penny for my tuition, and even received a subsistence grant. I found a large bedsitter at 131 Mercer's Road, in Tufnell Park, with a friendly family called the Stanleys who would quietly leave a plateful of home-made scones in my room for me to find when I came home. And there I lived for some five years.

During my first year at UCL I had to learn Latin, Anglo-Saxon, Middle English, Old High German, Middle High German - and I was reading Milton, Dryden, Spenser, Dr Johnson, Shakespeare, Virgil, *Sturm und Drang* literature, and books on stylistic analysis. I tried to get involved in college dramatics, and joined the swimming team - but as usual, I felt like an outsider, this time not because I was a German in an English school, but because I had not come straight from school, and was about two years older than the other students. I also felt guilty because I had an unfair advantage - being bilingual. I tried to keep my German origin secret.

The German Department was not located anywhere near that noble Grecian portico but in some grubby disused warehouses called Foster Court. Here a charming Professor Forster led a team of mostly quite young men - one being a German called Willy Schwarz whose

David playing the flute and showing off his dress sense

English was almost incomprehensible - and one formidable woman - 'the Wilk' - from her surname, Wilkinson - teaching and lecturing mostly to young women and a tiny minority of male students.

One of them was David Gill, tall, slim, brown-eyed, rather shy and gauche. He and I shared many interests, cultural and political. Our first conversation, in the library at Foster Court, was about Nietzsche's poetry, which we both loved. David wrote extremely good poetry himself. He was the first man I had met who was genuinely, naturally *kind* - not absorbed in his inner life, he regarded others with interest and good will - and literature, the arts, politics with quite acute insight. And he wrote *real* poems. He was a year ahead of me in the course and left to do his National Service.

I got a first class degree, and on the strength of it I was given a studentship - slightly more generous than the undergraduate grant - to do research. I chose a medieval topic and was immersed in Gottfried von Strasburg's *Tristan und Isolde* and the language and set phrases of courtly love. Unfortunately, I was also obliged to read boring books about it - by German 19th century academics - and came to detest academic work. I was expected to produce four copies of my thesis - so I used carbon paper in my typewriter, a very difficult and exasperating job. For one thing, carbon paper was very difficult to handle, and for another, every ten pages or so I would find I had put the carbon paper in the wrong way up and have to type the entire page again. Finally I got four copies bound and submitted them correctly, and in due course presented myself to a tableful of professors to defend it.

"Where are the footnotes?" demanded one of them. I explained that I included all information in the text. "What!" he expostulated. "Can't have a thesis without footnotes." Then another said, "This bibliography's no good. Look - here you put the date of publication *before* the place of publication - and here the place before the date! That won't do. You'll have to do it again. Sort out your bibliography. Get a decent set of footnotes."

So during the following year I dutifully extracted bits of text and fitted them into the bottoms of pages as footnotes – regularised the bibliography – typed the whole thing out again – four copies – got them bound again and submitted it again – and so at last I got my M.A. I don't suppose anyone ever read it. It was a complete waste of time. It left me with a deep dislike of academia.

But I discovered something else: I liked teaching. I was able to augment my studentship by teaching German to a large class of students. I prepared my lessons carefully, as I had prepared my parts when acting; established a rapport with students, galvanising their minds, watching the light of comprehension dawning in their eyes. Real pleasure!

*

In 1958, one day in February, I received letters from my father and from my brother (who were not on speaking terms with each other) each of them containing the same article by J.B. Priestley entitled *Britain and the Nuclear Bombs* cut out of the *New Statesman.* In it, Priestley argued that the monstrous danger posed to the whole planet by these weapons must be averted, that the bombs must be disarmed, and that Britain was ideally suited to lead the world away from the nuclear holocaust. Compared with the USA and USSR, our nuclear arsenal was insignificant anyway. We could well afford to get rid of them, without affecting the "balance of terror", and point out that we were much safer without them, as no one would want to launch a "pre-emptive strike" (as they might now, to prevent our nuking them). Moreover, we could invite the two Great Powers to use any inspection methods they might want to try out to ensure we really had dismantled all of them, since the difficulty of "verification" was always brought up as an argument against nuclear disarmament.

But why did the Bomb exist?

In the early twentieth century, scientists in many countries began investigating the nature of the atom. They discovered that split-ting the atoms of uranium led to a release of immense energy. This could be harnessed - electricity could become freely available. But it could also be used for destruction. Believing Nazi Germany was developing a nuclear weapon, the American scientists accelerated their own research and tested the first atom bomb on July 16th. But too late - Germany had surrendered on May 8th! Hitler was dead and gone! Never mind. Research and development continued; there was still a war going on, against Japan. So the next test - a real, live one - came on August 6th, when a uranium bomb was dropped on Hiroshima - a good place to test because it was still fairly intact and had not been devastated by incendiary bombs, unlike most Japanese cities, so now they could scientifically measure the effect. And three days later a *plutonium* bomb was dropped on Nagasaki: useful to compare the two types of bomb like that ... interesting ....

The lucky ones were the ones who were killed immediately. Others were blinded by the light "brighter than a thousand suns" -

... burnt to ashes in the heat ...

... the heat flash caused instant burns - skin melted - skin and flesh hanging down -

...burnt beyond recognition ...

...hair loss led to baldness...

...nausea, bleeding gums for months ...

... wounded by the collapsed buildings...

...dying of thirst ...

...cancers caused by the radio-activity ...

Learning of such suffering, almost eclipsing the horrors of the concentration camps, we thought everyone would say: "This must never happen again".

But no. On the contrary, more and even more terrible *Weapons of Mass Destruction* were designed and manufactured. The Labour Government of 1945, which created the wonderfully humane National Health Service, did also start making inhumane atom bombs. Then France joined in, Russia, China, India, Pakistan, North Korea ... Israel ... and NATO countries accepted American nuclear weapons in their territories. And new ways of "delivering" them were designed - rockets - Inter Continental Ballistic Missiles (ICBMs)... They were always called "deterrents" - "we've only got them to make sure no one can attack us with them". How so? "Instant Retaliation. You hit my dog, I'll hit your dog. If you KNOW that, you won't hit him. Will you? But you've got to be convinced that I will ..." Ever more brilliant science was used on all sides. Now everyone who has the equipment is able to detect if a nuclear weapon has been launched anywhere in the world - and instantly - almost automatically - one of *ours* will be on its way to hit *yours* in its flight before it has even got into our air space! Wonderful! Rather expensive, but the taxpayers were happy their money was so useful - pity there wasn't enough left over to feed the hungry, heal the sick...

I was completely convinced by Priestley's article. So, when I saw a notice on a College notice board about a plan to march from London to the Atomic Weaponry Research Establishment (AWRE) at Aldermaston, I wrote and told David about it, and that I would want to join this march. He was then still doing his Military Service, but wanted to join me, though he might get into trouble.

So on Good Friday, 1958, we joined the crowd in Trafalgar Square, and after listening to some speeches we set out on the march. We got as far as West London and spent the first night on the floor under a grand piano in somebody's house. When we woke up the next morning, it was snowing - the worst Easter in living memory. Nobody will want to go on the march in weather like this, we thought, so we had better go. Obviously hundreds of other people thought the same .... As we marched, we were cheered along by bands playing jazz at the roadside - or by singing

> *Oh when the saints, oh when the saints*
> *Oh when the saints go marching in*

> *I wanna be of that number*
> *When the saints go marching in -*

and

> *Gonna lay down my sword and shield*
> *Down by the riverside, down by the riverside*
> *Ain't gonna study war no more*

and other songs that grew very familiar. We marched great distances, and to be honest, it wasn't fun. My feet ached, I got blisters, I longed to stop - as we did, eventually: good people in Slough and Reading fed us and organised sleeping accommodation for us. Once this was in a primary school: one had to bend down to reach the little wash basins, and the tiny children's toilets were like open crocuses. There was some hostility from bystanders, especially in Reading, but in general, people looked at us with astonishment. Even tabloid newspapers grudgingly admired us for turning out in such awful weather - it was cold, and the snow gave way to rain.

Our home-made banners read

BAN THE BLOODY BOMB!

Use H-bomb money to feed the world's starving kids!

OXFORD (along with many other towns and villages) **SAYS NO!**

WORLD IN PEACE AND NOT IN PIECES!

1. Hiroshima. 2. Nagasaki. 3 ?????

I WANT TO LIVE!

LET BRITAIN LEAD!

There were many others, and simple round placards with the symbol of CND - the Campaign for Nuclear Disarmament. Known today as a universal symbol of peace, the design was based on the semaphore signals for C, N and D - and the circle round it - an unborn child... Some big banners showed lurid pictures of the mushroom cloud, and children's faces.

With David on the 1958 Aldermarston march

For hours we marched through open country. From the top of a hump-back bridge we could see the unruly line of the march stretching in either direction, like a vast, shabby snake with litter stuck to its back, rippling slowly between the hedges; one after the other, the banners rounded a distant bend. There was no one there to see us except a few birds.

At last, very tired, very footsore, we got to the village of Aldermaston, and walked on, past the huge base, the grim security fence, the queer buildings and structures and pipes, the odd mounds and hummocks inside, the gleaming metal, and the serried ranks of police, till we got to the gates - a motley, weary, shabby crowd. We read the warning notices about police dogs and electrified fences and felt cowed by the vast, impersonal, efficient autonomy of it all. Later, in Falcon Field, we listened to speeches before setting off again for the comforts of civilisation. But as we came past AWRE - again, David touched my arm and pointed. There, behind all the security fencing, sat a group of rabbits, munching grass and flicking their ears. And we were reassured - to some extent.

That was the first of very many demonstrations. And we wrote letters to politicians, and to newspapers - surely the simple logic of our argument would convince them. We went to meetings. For years we ran Oxford CND, published a newsletter, plotted eye-catching and significant demos, attended committee meetings. But all the time, things got worse and worse. France got her Bomb, then China, and Israel, and India and Pakistan. And Britain, who could have led the world away from the nuclear abyss, keeps up its "deterrent", its city-killer missiles ever ready on our patrolling nuclear submarines.

David wrote poems - such as

HIROSHIMA TREE

It was a sudden tree.
Bright blossoms churned the sky

as children with packed lunches
started for school.
They'd never seen (or heard)
a tree like that before.
Their Natural History books
showed no such tree:
a tree whose coiling roots
tore out a city's heart,
whose trunk was a volcano
of bricks and glass and bones,
whose blossoms liquefied the eyes
of those who turned to see.

In 1958, David and I got married, and lived more or less happily most of the time ever after. David was still a Christian at that time; I was not, but had no strong objection to a bit of Christian mumbo-jumbo if it made him and his parents happy. Wytham Church, in a village just outside Oxford, appealed to me, so one weekend when he came to visit me in Oxford we cycled out to the village and called on the elderly vicar. He appeared to have no experience of marrying two people who did not live in his parish; he would have to consult "the bishop's surrogate on marriage". In due course he informed us that the ruling was that I would have to sleep in the village three nights and leave a suitcase for a week. I therefore knocked at the door of a particularly attractive farmhouse in the village and asked if I might sleep there for three nights... The farmer's wife was a bit puzzled but raised no objection – nor to my leaving a suitcase for a week .... So the great day came, David's parents and his sister and a host of uncles and aunts, Mu and Peter, his wife Brenda and little Claire, and Prof. Maas, assembled for the service. One uncle played the organ while his wife worked the bellows: as we turned from the altar to leave the church, her posterior was rising and disappearing behind the parapet of the organ loft. Afterwards there was cake and wine at Beamsend - and then we departed for a honeymoon in Wales.

A couple of years later, our first child was born: Thomas Paramor Gill, or Tom for short. His slightly unusual middle name was our way of preserving the maiden name of David's mother, Marjorie Paramor. She was one of five siblings, but the women changed their surname on marriage and the men were childless, so this old Norman surname was in danger of extinction in our family.

I had read an article in a magazine saying that pregnant women who smoked tended to have easy deliveries, so I carried on smoking - a habit I had got into in my cabaret days - never thinking that these "easy deliveries" might be caused by stunted babies. I paid for my sins: Tom was born a fortnight late, after three agonizing days of labour, and was the heaviest baby born in Portsmouth General Hospital in the year 1960.

By this time David had got a job teaching at Bedales, a progressive private school in Hampshire, and we were living near the school in a small village called Steep, near Petersfield. We were very happy - in complete harmony, not only about politics, but about life in general. I admired him - I realized that his poems were the real thing. For instance -

OFF-DAYS

Did they always leap out of bed in the morning
Those discoverers, harrow their historic beards
Do fifty press-ups in the tilting cabin
Then strut the deck, a rolled-up chart
Of unlabeled continents under their arms?
Did they greet that all-discoverer, the sun,
As if it wasn't just another Monday morning
But a day of profound revelations?
Could they always have looked ahead

As rigid as bowsprits,
Craning forward, shading their eyes in the immortal pose
Of the vigil on the bridge?
Did Vasco da Gama never oversleep,
Forget to up anchor, spend a lazy day
At cards, or fishing for squid?
And how many times was Mungo Park
Alone
On the Niger
Pissed off with exploring?

My admiration was confirmed when Chatto and Windus included two volumes of his poems in their "Phoenix Living Poets" series. *Men Without Evenings* was published in 1966, followed by *The Pagoda* in 1969. Other poets in the series included Robert Conquest, D.J. Enright, John Fuller, Norman MacCaig, Laurie Lee, John Silkin, Edward Storey, Adrienne Rich and Ann Sexton. When we were married, I imagined we would be quite famous, part of a literary elite of successful poets (and their partners) with new selections of his poems appearing from time to time and being discussed in serious publications. But David never published another book with a conventional publisher, although he did publish many poems in prominent poetry magazines. After a while he got bored with rejection slips and preferred to put together selections of poems and get them printed as little chap-books or pamphlets by our local printer, Parchments – sometimes with illustrations by his sister Margaret, or Nic Cottis' wife Sally – and give them to friends and relations.

Chapter 6: Nyakasura

The hills roll up to the mighty Ruwenzori mountains. If you stand on their flanks by one of the headlong streams or waterfalls and look down, you see the curved hills, shaggy with twenty-foot deep elephant grass on their lower slopes, shaved to a tawny pelt by the wind at the top, and valleys like craters, often with lakes at the bottom. At one time all this land must have bubbled like boiling porridge.

Here and there you see oblong patches of cultivated earth framed by piles of weed; and further down there are endless banana plantations, their great green leaves stirring in the breeze. If you follow one of the damp black paths that run like tunnels under those green wings you find, here and there, a mud hut thatched with a mop of brown banana fibre, full of muddy children and their parents, and shrieking goats, anxious hens and cows with astonishingly long horns. But move on and the deep silence of the banana plantation will close over your head like green water.

From time to time the plantation is alive with whispers as the wind stirs the leaves, and suddenly with a roar the rain comes pelting down, ripping the banana leaves to ribbons, pouring through the thatch roofs, whipping the mud to chocolate pudding, transforming paths to rippling streams as the storm strides across the hills and batters itself to death in spasms of lightning on the mountain slopes.

The people do not fear the storms; nor the earth tremors that sometimes rumble underfoot. They fear the spirits of those imperishable conquerors of long ago who kicked cliff faces and split them, drank the milk that still drips from the breasts of rock behind the waterfall, and one day marched into one of the lakes, and built a castle at the bottom whence they send out giant birds to steal small children to eat. Sometimes they wander about in the night, hooting in their incomprehensible language. Also the people fear the spirits of their departed forebears who will suddenly take offence. They never know what careless act, or word, or thought might offend those spirits and induce them to afflict the family, or their animals, or the crops, with sickness. Only the witch doctor can find out how they have been offended. In exchange for a goat or so he will utter his magic incantations, sprinkle his potions, and remove, deftly, a whole banana from under the sick man's skin (no wonder he suffered so!). Sometimes misfortune is brought about by an enemy who is still alive, and then vengeance is called for.

Then life can return to normal. The women bear large numbers of children and, tying the youngest surviving one on their backs, spend their mornings tilling the soil, their afternoons cooking and their evenings watching the men assembled round a huge gourd of banana beer, singing and dancing. From time to time they fight a neighbouring tribe and return, if they were lucky, with new cattle and wives; if not, some of their wives and cattle may find themselves with new owners. All according to accepted rules. Babies often die, and then an orgy of drunken weeping will sweep through the neighbourhood for three days and nights, tailing off in singing and peace. Whatever happens, the bananas keep sprouting and producing their fruit, and so life goes on.

Into this green Ugandan land came, almost 100 years ago, a retired British Naval Officer called Lieutenant Ernest William Eborhard Caldwell. He had left the Navy for health reasons. A member of the Christian Missionary Society, he had been teaching at Buddo School, in Kampala, but decided to found a school of his own, where his own ideas could be put into practice, using his own wealth. Several boys at Buddo came from Toro, the kingdom in the West of Uganda, and inspired him to found his school there. One of them, D.K. Baguma, wrote a history of the school and its founder, the source of much of the following information. He describes Caldwell – always referred to as The Founder – as being extraordinarily talented in all practical fields, and mathematics, but also extremely shy and taciturn, and with a passion for work. The school he founded in March 1926 took over the buildings of a Central School which had closed. But the Omukama, or King, made available a site formerly occupied by a mill, by the river called Nyakasura, and at weekends the boys would join the porters clearing the bush and building dormitories, classrooms, a chapel, and other buildings on that site, using mud and wattle, palm tree trunks, banana fibres and papyrus reeds. Amazingly, by July 14th 1926 it was possible for the school to move there.

By the time we got there, in 1962, the school was well established as one of the leading secondary schools in Uganda. The headmaster – he was the fourth – was the Reverend Everard Perrens.

Why were we there?

We had been so well suited with our position at Bedales, a progressive boarding school in Hampshire. We had a small house, a two-year-old child, agreeable neighbours and colleagues, fellow campaigners against The Bomb, in a lovely part of the world, and we were in danger of spending the rest of our lives there ... but we must see more of the world and do something useful and meaningful! And when the report came that the Atmospheric Nuclear Tests that were being perpetrated deposited the least amount of nuclear fall-out near the equator, we started looking for places where we and our son Tom would be in least danger. An advertisement for teachers in Uganda led to interviews where we were assumed to be good Christians (we were agnostics, actually) and given the address of Nyakasura School, which needed an English teacher. In due course we boarded the *Kenya*, British India Line, a huge ship, where we

had a First Class cabin, and our first taste of upper class living...
and of colonialists.

As you approach the First Class Dining saloon (I wrote at the
time) *the head waiter pulls open the swing doors and you plunge
into the air conditioned coldness. The square white tables are laid
with lots of cutlery, and there are plastic flowers on each. Spaced
very regularly among the white squares stand the Goan stewards, each poised to leap forward and pull back a chair as a passenger approaches his table. The head waiter - a white man - prowls
around throughout the meal, his gimlet eyes darting to and fro
behind his glasses from plates to waiters - he is obviously longing
for a mishap. At the slightest clatter he leaps forward hoping something has happened to justify his existence. The handsome brown
waiters, very courteous and attentive, ignore him completely. Tom
has to go to the children's dining room an hour before the adults are
fed. The two stewards who serve there both look so melancholy that
we think it must be a punishment to work there. This is plausible
as bedlam reigns at every meal as mothers tried to coax their children to eat. There are three cooked meals a day and the children are
expected to eat three courses at each. No wonder they push their food
around on their plates until it looks revolting and is finally taken
away by one of the stewards. Perhaps they look so melancholy as
they throw the food into the sea because they remember hungry children elsewhere ...*

*Most of the passengers are returning after home leave, "old
hands", and soon we are having things explained to us. "Give an
African a shirt, and he won't know what to do with it. Sell it to him,
even if it's only for sixpence, any laughable sum, then he'll value
it. Give it him, and mark my words, he'll go and sell it. Make him
give you something for it. Mark my words: never give the African
anything." We are always being told about this* African, *an incredible being, completely amoral, a thief, a burglar, and diabolically
clever, yet at the same time abysmally stupid, idle, childish - but*

also a rogue, dangerous, a Politician. "If you happen to knock an
African down with your car, don't stop. Drive on. Go to the nearest
police station and get it sorted out there. Otherwise a mob may come
along and, well, maybe not hang you from the nearest tree but beat
you up. This chap was driving along and he saw this African who'd
obviously been knocked down, so he stopped and got out - all these
Africans just standing there, not doing anything - and they beat him
up. Simply because he was a European and another European had
knocked him down and driven on."

"Even after they've been with you for years and years, your own
servants may suddenly turn Mau-Mau. There's no gratitude in
them." "I will not stay in the country if Kenyatta comes to power.
I consider I still have some pride. I will not pay my taxes to that
disgusting old man. What has he done? He's been convicted by the
High Court of being associated with Mau Mau, hasn't he? The man's
a criminal. He's a disgusting old man." "I had this boy -" said a
South African living in Rhodesia - "oh, they always forge their references, or use someone else's, or else their papers have just been burnt
in a fire - so anyway, I said I'd give him a try. My dear, I don't think
he'd been in a house before! He was terrible! One day we were having
supper; he had served and gone out. I decided I wanted another
potato, so I rang the bell and told him and do you know, he simply
stretched out his hand, put a potato on a spoon, wheeled it through
the air and slapped it down on my plate. I sacked him on the spot. Oh,
boys and babies, it's all we ever talk about. You can't imagine how
stupid they are. A friend of mine was giving a dinner and there were
tinned peaches for dessert, and the boy simply opened the tin and
brought them in like that. She told him to take them out of the tin and
bring them in on a tray. So he simply poured them out on the tray!"

"The African smells - oh, terrible. It's not their fault. I had a boy
once, he was quite clean, but he smelled awful so we had to get rid
of him." "Once I had one who would never knock at a door. Once he
burst in when I was quite nude. Of course I screamed and screamed

and put a blanket round me and said I would - kill him if he didn't knock. So after that he always knocked at every single door he went through, you know, and it drove me mad..." "What you pay them? Well, it depends on their experience - £2 or £3, and then you tell them you'll give them a rise every six months, say ten shillings, until they're earning perhaps £6 a month. That's high. Then you tell them their wages won't go any higher but you'll give them a bonus every six months; but you can cut this bonus if they break anything or do something wrong. You're forbidden by law to cut their wages. But there's no legal minimum wage..."

"There's a small beach by the lake where we live. It's very pleasant. We take the children there for picnics and to paddle in the water - there's no bilharzia there - the only lake in Rhodesia where there isn't. And all of a sudden these dreadful Outward Bound boys will come and practically jump over our heads into the water -. The place is ruined now that they keep their boats and things nearby. The idea is to toughen them up or something. It's really stupid. They teach them things they knew long before the White Man came -. These little men with glasses come out from England and put their arms round the Africans' necks. Of course the Africans roll their eyes and don't know what's happening..." "I had a director once, quite a nice chap really, but he tried to climb onto the Nationalist bandwagon. For instance when they went on safari and his wife made some sandwiches he would actually give them to the boys! You can imagine their faces when they tried to eat these dainty little sandwiches! He was quite out of touch of course - a Professor in England and came straight out to us. He was brilliant on the research side but they're all the same, these people, like Reverend Michael Scott. I heard him once. I think he's probably quite a good man, but now he'll simply back anything African. Look at Hastings Banda! Look at what he's doing in Malawi! Rhodesia now, it's all messed up."

Life on board involved a lot of mammoth meals, and drinks, and conversations. At 12 o'clock the band would strike up and we would be singing songs like "She'll be coming round the mountain when she comes ...". A Sports Committee organised dances and fancy-dress competitions and the like. But one morning we saw a hazy mountain smeared with white - Gibraltar! We joined the long queue of passengers squeezed out like toothpaste along a steep gangplank to a small steamer that took us towards the Rock, a colossal grey pudding with trees instead of jam trickling down its sides, and cubist houses at the base. We disembarked at a small jetty where taxis were waiting to take people on a Tour; but we walked up with Tom in his pushchair through narrow streets and past flats festooned with brilliant washing billowing from lines stretching from windows to the rock face opposite. We patted a donkey pulling a rickety cart with a few vegetables and the bony animal lifted his nose and began to bray honkingly, deafeningly - people held their ears and we fled. It grew intensely hot till we reached the Moorish Castle and looked down at the town.

Our next port of call was to be Port Said.

"Go ashore in Port Said? And pay good money to Egyptians? Never! I trust you've posted all your letters in the ship's box well outside the thee-mile limit, otherwise they'll cost you a shilling and four pence instead of sixpence and you'll have the pleasant thought of all that money clinking into Nasser's pocket!"

Our mooring was alongside the main street of the town, and dozens of small boats with brightly coloured goods came darting out towards us like wasps to a pot of jam.

"Pour boiling water into them. No - molten lead, then they'll sink as well!"

Little brown boys came swimming and spent the next few hours treading water and diving for pennies. Boats came out and the Arabs were upon us! They were selling large pouffes, Turkish shoes, plastic camels, jewellery, carpets, wooden plates inlaid with mother-of-pearl. Models of Queen Nefertiti formed the knobs of sword sticks, fly swatters, shoe horns. Young men stood in their boats shouting, their heads thrown back, while older men at the oars casually pushed aside competitors' boats: "Vat you vant? You vant rocking chair? No? Vant shoes? Vant vallet? Vant suitcase? Vat you vant? Vant a camel? Vant a man? Vant me?" Ropes were slung up to prospective customers, and soon rolled up rugs, camel seats, pouffes, each accompanied by a basket for the money, were hauled up. Then the haggling began.

"Three pounds."

"Thirty shillings."

"Vot? Is a big, is a beeg von! Hey, mister, vait, no send back! Vot you vont a leetle one? Here, two pounds."

"Thirty shillings."

"Meester, is impossible, vot you vont, you vont I cut my throat? All right all right" - venomously, as he hauls down his thirty shillings.

We ran the gauntlet of the pier ("Vant bracelet? Chip! Very chip! Bargain! Vant camel?") and at the dock gate a melancholy look- ing man attached himself to us and insisted on being our friend and guided us through baking streets. He introduced us to a fat jolly man in a battered gharry with a battered horse who drove us around for half an hour, Tom, pushchair and all. Talking volubly in broken English he showed us the flats Nasser (whom he reviled) had had built on the sites bombed in 1956, as well as schools, and the bazaar - a long, narrow street with an acrid smell, washing hung out on wooden balconies, stalls with rubbishy plastic goods, fruit swarming with flies, bundles of enamel cups on the pave- ment, wooden chair frames which a man was beginning to uphol- ster, while another was stuffing mattresses on the pavement. There were crowds of people - when we returned in the evening people were having their hair cut at 10 pm, having their photographs taken, shish kebab was being roasted on open braziers; scholarly looking men in night shirts were playing cards at cafe tables, and there were children everywhere - a six year old was pleading with a slightly older boy who sat on the pavement, his head buried in his arms in an attitude of despair; two were rummaging in a pile of refuse; a bunch of boys in a stunted tree were watching an open air cinema on the other side of a high wall. We saw practically no women, and those we did see were all dressed in black, like nuns, with veils on their heads and often over their faces, too.

As we moved down the Suez Canal the heat grew quite unbearable, and there was nothing to see except yellow sand, heaped high by the side of the canal by rusty dredgers worked by dirty, piratical-looking men who put up bits of sacking to give them a little shade. The Great Bitter Lakes were lovely to look at - a hazy blue with golden spits of sand stretching into them. Then came the Red Sea and the heat grew yet more intense - what a relief to get into the air-conditioned dining saloons!

We reached Aden in the evening; it was festooned with lights. It is a free port and there were fine shops at the front, selling photographic equipment and the like, tax free and therefore very cheap. Unlike Suez - there was no soliciting; the men in the shops were not anxious to make a sale. But further inland we were confronted with squalor. Men and boys were lying on crude bedsteads on the pavement - or on the filthy pavement itself - trying to sleep; others stood drowsily by stalls making no effort to sell their melons, their beaded belts, their caps - only a little boy showed some salesmanship, running up from behind a heap of sandals calling "Sandals, sandals, cheap at half the price!" Looking into a house we could see an old woman sitting alone in an empty room - no effort had been made to make these homes pleasant, though they had electric light and fans. Wretched goats, their udders tied up in sack cloth, swarmed around on broken hooves eating anything the human scavengers had left, which was usually nothing but paper; a herd of goats crowded under a cart; a beautiful kid lay on the asphalt beside his mother. Thin cats prowled. Among all these animals stalked the Yemenis, tall, handsome, very dark, slim, and upright, - again there were no women to be seen; an old bearded man sat on the ground under a lamp post, his back straight, a fat book open on his knees. Yemenis filled the ranks of labourers in Aden. I was looking at a young Adonis sitting as if in a trance by a tray with a few bananas when a queer noise drew our attention: it was a man about three feet tall with an outsize head; he came waddling after us making a queer singing noise. We hurried away, and he started scolding – the Yemenis standing around laughed and called out to the dwarf. As we half ran through an alleyway towards the front two men came towards us, their arms round each other; a beggar sat immobile by the roadside, one broomstick arm raised with the hand flat, palm upwards. A small, beautiful boy ran up with two long strings of beads, asking for a shilling. We refused, and he moved off sadly.

We learned that two or three miles from the old Aden is the new, with dual carriageways past blocks of modern air-conditioned flats. These are for Europeans only, i.e. for servicemen and their families to be moved from the base in Kenya when we would be kicked out of that colony.

The temperature dropped by ten degrees as we came into the Indian Ocean; we met the monsoon at 5 am, and woke to see waves like small hills rolling by – the sun caught the spray beside the ship and rainbows leapt up and disappeared. The ship was like a living thing breathing deeply under us. We found ourselves toiling uphill one moment and slithering down the next. Standing near the front was like being on a slow rocking horse as the prow rose above the horizon and then dropped far below it.

We disembarked at Mombasa and after a good day on the beach got on the train to Kampala, where we spent the next two days and nights in a small compartment with our nine items of luggage: this was First Class, all formica and stainless steel. Tom had to be taken for endless walks up and down the corridor, so I got to know the train from end to end. There were two public toilets, one European Type and the other non-European Type – a hole in the floor. The first thing that hit you in Second Class was a smell as of a henhouse. These were old, wooden carriages, battered but not too bad. There was a tap for drinking water in the corridor. All the passengers here were Indian, doing nothing all day, lying on their own mattresses and blankets on their seats. There was also one carriage for Africans; that was fresh and clean, there wasn't the same air of listlessness as among the Indians.

The Rift Valley was more like a vast plateau than a Valley. Seven thousand feet up, it was mostly very rough grassland, dotted with small trees and bushes; hills and mountains on the horizon. Here and there were little circular huts with conical thatched roofs, and corrugated iron one-room sheds. There were lots of flowers along the railway track. The train rose from the Rift Valley and crossed the Equator at 8,000 feet: it was cold! The land still looked wild and unkempt, but the vegetation was lusher, dense woods clambering up the steep valleys and gullies. Saw a gaunt figure stride across a hill, a sack over his head like a cowl, to a small group of huts, isolated from the next except for a hair thin mud path; children minding goats and cows; women bending over fires, babies on their backs. Enormous empty spaces. But here and there were townships, factories, asphalt roads.

Then we were hurtling down into the "spinach green" land of Uganda.

In Kampala, we met Jim and Anne, the couple we were replacing – they were moving to another part of Africa. They told us a bit about the school, and about the house where we would be living: a relatively old one, a little way from the rest of the teachers' houses; quite big, with a water heating system possibly dating back to the Founder, consisting of an oil barrel embedded in a concrete structure outside the house, with pipes leading into the bathroom. Also Anne had been teaching some of the local children, who might expect me to continue.

We bought a car – a Ford Anglia – and drove the 200 miles to Fort Portal. The asphalt road soon turned into murram, a reddish clay.

Crossing Lake Victoria with Tom, Nick and the Ford Anglia

From the town we drove another five miles or so to Nyakasura, and arrived at the headmaster's house, where we were to stay the first night. Everard Perrens was a slight man in his fifties, diffident, straight-forward and devout; his wife Joan was practical, cheerful, and welcoming. Next morning six or eight humble men hung around the house, and when I came out said "jambo" (hello) and hardly dared to say they wanted a job. The Headmaster told them to come again tomorrow and we wooshed past them in the car to our house. In the event none of them was lucky. Joan advised us to take Petero, whom she had engaged to help while we stayed with her for a few days.

The house was a huge bungalow, with a small upstairs room above the garage. Each step, each breath re-echoed round the lofty ceiling, into roomy alcoves. The garden was as big as a park, and soon we had a "shamba boy", Christopher. Across the expanse of hummocky, weedy lawn he would push the lawnmower, hour after hour, perspiration splashing off his forehead, his mighty limbs plastered with grass cuttings, and an enormous smile breaking across his black face if I waved to him. We had long, earnest conversations.

"Christopher."

"Memsahib?"

"This tree."

"?"

"This tree, look. It's dead, isn't it?"

"No understand."

"This tree - finish?"

"AAH! Tree finish! No. Not finish."

It was a small broken poinsettia. Christopher simply rammed it into the round - and it grew and flourished! We realised that the land was amazingly fertile.

We soon became familiar with Fort Portal, the capital of the kingdom of Toro. The palace of the King, or Omukamo, was on one hill, the Anglican cathedral on another. The town below them consisted of three streets of small single-storey Indian shops or *dukas,* with African men working on treadle sewing machines on the pavements outside – they cut cloth spread out on the ground without a pattern and stitched garments, making them up as they went along. Men and women wearing huge brilliant cloths draped gracefully around them sat on small benches facing them, waiting for their garments. The main shop was Bhimjis, as we soon learned. Bhimji had a monopoly of just about everything – groceries, medicines, floor cloths, oil paint, bread, newspapers, equipment for mountaineers climbing the Ruwenzoris, transport to and from Kampala. Some way away was the market where men, women and children squatted behind bunches of bananas, neat little piles of custard apples, passion fruit, tree tomatoes, familiar vegetables like peas, carrots and beans, and fruit such as pineapples and paw paws, all grown locally. Elsewhere, two young men, armed only with metal shears, a soldering iron, and pliers, made nice but smoky lamps out of empty tins; another made sandals out of old car tyres; an old woman made elaborate bracelets out of beads. People wore kanzus – long gowns of cotton – or ragged shirts or skirts – and amazing battered hats.

On the other side of the mountains was Bundibugyo, capital of Bwanda. We drove there one day, down a twisting road and through a part of the Ituri Forest, most of which is on the other side of the border, in the Congo. Trees, some 30 feet high, rather scraggy, close together, were draped with lianas, twisting and looping and coiling round branches like big snakes; some slighter convolvulus-like plants draped whole trees in a tent of leaves. Then the road twisted up again and we got wonderful views across the endless Congolese plain, with the Semliki River twisting across it like a shining ribbon, and the Ituri forest, blue-green-grey, almost like the sea. Steam drifted over the hot springs, and smoke from the grass fires, that left curiously shaped black patches on the flanks of the mountains; some were already showing the green of new grass and of cultivation. Little houses clung like mushrooms to the steep slopes; water fell down the clefts.

Bundibugyo was a more modest town than Fort Portal: a few cement houses scattered along the road, and an Indian shopkeeper with a few men working treadle sewing machines outside. On the way back, we came to a group of pygmies by the roadside, ugly little people in dirty singlets wanting us to buy their bows and arrows, which they pushed into the car through the windows, into our faces; there must have been a dozen arms waving around inside the car.

The first day we were in our house, a gaggle of children stood in the garden, chorusing "Hello Madamu welcome" when I emerged in the morning.

"Hello! What do you want?"

"Please Madamu, we want *sgool*."

So these were the children Anne had told us she had been teaching. They assumed I would too! - A Nyakasura schoolboy appeared - a very agreeable sixth former called George. He had been teaching them in the holidays. I asked if there was no local school for them to go to. There was - but there were fees, a few shillings a term, and they had no money. Of course I said I would try. After all, with Petero doing all the housework, and Christopher in the garden, there wasn't much for me to do. The room above the garage could be the school room. David painted a blackboard on one wall.

But I knew nothing about teaching children, and in a foreign language! So I went to the Bookshop in Fort Portal and bought some teachers' books for English - and Arithmetic. I studied the books while increasing numbers of children milled about in the garden all day, playing with Tom, and his toys, climbing onto the water heater and drumming rhythmically. I learned the names of some of them. The smallest was not much bigger than Tom - Rubego, a tiny fellow with no front teeth who was always plaintively demanding "Water, madamu", and asking for rides in Tom's push chair; Kajusi, a pretty, bright little girl, and her brother Bagonza - which means "love" - Sabiiti, who looked like Yul Brynner with huge swimming eyes and puckered brow, and big, ragged, intelligent Bene, the shamba boy Christopher's younger brother.

I said I would start teaching the day David started teaching at Nyakasura. The evening before, I decided to teach Petero on his own, putting some of what I had gleaned from the Teachers' Books into practice.

"I am Mrs Gill, you are Petero."

"I am mississi Gill, you are Petero," he beamed.

"No. You must say *I am Petero*, I explained, and drew a diagram.

"Yes," he smiled. "I you are am Petero, you - Mississi Gill."

Beads of perspiration stood on his brow as we progressed to "This cup is blue, that cup is white"; at last we had a rest and I asked - with the help of a dictionary, why his *omukazi* (wife) wasn't *hano* (here). I had asked him to bring her, but as so often, the smiling "Yes" had masked complete incomprehension.

Next morning, just after eight, the children came - hordes of them it seemed, all over the garden. George came and got them all to call out their names. Then we played ball. It was completely chaotic at first - they got so excited they could hardly catch the ball. Next, I divided them into two groups, A and B, and sent the smaller ones into Tom's room to play with his toys and draw pictures on shelf paper while the "big ones" came upstairs with me. I asked each one his or her name, guessing the spelling of each - Bene, Bagonza, Kajusi, Sabiti, Nyendo - which I wrote on the blackboard, then each one had to copy it, first on the black board, then on a small card which I pinned onto them. It had seemed such a good idea, simultaneously finding out what their names were - and whether they could read and write; but *Nyendo* dug holes in her card, the others were barely legible; only Bene's was right. However, I hadn't realised that children who are not getting personal attention relapse into chaos. The group down in the playroom got wilder and wilder; soon they were rushing around all over the house. So I sent the ones who had their badges on down and fetched the "little ones" upstairs.

I gave each one a piece of card and a pencil and tried to get them to draw straight lines to form a grid. They had to take turns with the ruler - those who were waiting rolled around with their legs in the air chattering … .

Then they were to write the numbers 1 - 10 in the squares, copying what I had done on the blackboard. They were to do sums, adding 1. They produced answers like this:

2+1=9

13+1=9

4+1=9

5+1=28

I simply couldn't understand what was happening in their minds. I gave out beans; they were to place the right number of beans in each square. This was to get them numerate - *three beans take away two beans leaves how many beans?* - but they kept running out of beans and asking for more - till I realised they were *eating* them. Two of them - tiny Robego and huge Nyakairu - were extremely naughty, rolling around on their backs and singing. The class ended in chaos - yet little Birunga had never taken her big shining eyes off me and had whispered the right answers in my ear; and Byaruhanga had stood proudly in front of the class reciting the days of the week in English. Now they were to go down and Group A was to come up again. Tom came with them, enthusiastically scribbling on the blackboard, and making them all laugh by mimicking me …

I persevered for some time, and more and more joined. Everything that happened was unexpected. Children started writing everything upside down, or in mirror writing. To teach them the names of colours, I gave out crayons and told them to colour squares in their exercise books and write the name of the colour beside it. There were battles fought over the crayons! Each one, in turn, wailed "Madamu, no white!" and had to be shown that the paper was white.

We had a Sports Day, when I divided them into two teams, X

and Y, and tried to get them to run relay races - physically moving half of each team to the other end of the lawn, giving the leaders a stick and trying to explain the system. The first race was chaotic. I explained again, and got Bene to translate; now 80% of them understood. The second race was better; the third seemed to be fine - till Bomero dropped the stick. Instead of picking it up and running on, he turned on Tibe, who had handed it to him, furiously, shouted and stamped and waved his arms around and scowled, while the other team romped home and his own yelled at him. I took Bomero aside and tried to explain the Team Spirit to him. He smiled, quite shyly, not, I suspect, because he understood me, but because he was embarrassed at being so close to me. Then I started shooing them away, but they clustered round the porch and I realised they were probably waiting for drinks. I got Kajusi to help me fill beakers with orange juice and hand them out - but there were only enough for one between three. The kitchen door was like the Black Hole of Calcutta, with imploring hands stretched up trying to catch the beakers as we passed them to those whom Kajusi deemed deserving. Soon there were shrieks of rage: Nyakairu had drunk a whole beakerful. There was no more - just a little water in the filter.

Finally I thought the day's school was over and had settled down indoors - the children were still milling about in the garden - when there was a blood-curdling shriek. I ran out, and there was Rubego, on one leg. He pointed venomously at another boy. "Where does it hurt?" I asked. He thought for a moment, then pointed at his ankle. I led him solemnly into the bathroom and dabbed some calamine lotion on it - calamine lotion was to be my remedy for bruised toes, blinded eyes, sobbing souls - .

It really was getting to be too much. The children were in the garden from 7 in the morning, and stayed on after their lessons till 6.30 in the evening. There were 28 of them. The chief attraction - after Tom - was the big tree in the garden: they were swinging on the branches till Bene and Kajusi had a bright idea: they brought strips of banana fibre and tied the ends of two branches together so that they could sit on them and swing. Tom stomped out to them, very European with his fair hair, and was immediately swept up by Kajusi who tried to go on the swing with him - but he objected: all day his good nature was in conflict with his desire to do things for himself.

The lessons were going quite well, now that I knew them individually and their abilities and limitations. It was a joy to see them lying on their fronts and each struggling with something: Nyindo trying to write M and George taking the big step from 109 to 110 while Bene and John solved problems like 1/2 + 1/4, or 3/4 + 3/8 with the help of strips of folded paper. But I realised that they ought to be in proper schools. Many had had some schooling - even Nyakairu had picked up a lot of English words and could write numbers and letters without having the least idea what they meant - and the girls - Kajusi, so pretty, graceful, and bright, and Rose, warm and kind, and the rest - did round dances, where all sang:

Kabaina kabaina wakame wako

Ti, ti mutiti wa

and clapped and took turns to be in the middle, - "washing" - "shaking hands" - rhythmically - which they had probably learned at school; so I wondered what had happened - had their parents been unable to continue paying the fees?

I talked with Mr Rubombora, the Toro director of schools, and learned that many schools were half empty, with only twenty odd pupils in the classes instead of forty; the World Bank had recently refused a loan because there were four thousand vacancies. I told him I wanted to send my children to local schools; would there be places for them? Yes, if parents paid the fees. Might I be able to join a school and help with teaching, in exchange for free places for the children? No. I would be better employed teaching in a girls' secondary school. The parents could easily raise the money for their children's education if they wanted to - but Batoro men were renowned for their laziness.

I called on some of them with Mr Rubombora and the children. We walked round the knoll of the hill, past a large patch of sweet potatoes, then a young banana plantation; a herd of sheep and goats – and a herd of the local Ankole cows with fantastically long horns. We came to Rose's home – a concrete house with a corrugated iron roof behind a hedge of Angels' Trumpets. Her sister was sitting on the grass in front – a plump young woman wearing a necklace and bracelets and two cotton frocks – one torn to reveal the one below – with four of her children. Her husband was away in Bwemba … . Her tall, elderly mother came out. Through Mr Rubombora we learned that she had gone to Kampala to work and earn the money to build this house. They only had enough food for the family to live on – they could not grow more. The wild pigs destroyed everything – sweet potatoes, ground nuts. They had dug ditches to keep them out but the wily creatures filled in the ditches and crossed over. In two years they would be able to pay for Rose's schooling, because by then the young bananas would bear fruit. Till then they had nothing. The dress Rose wore was a present from Anne; otherwise she would have been in rags, or naked. Balinda's father was a big, strong, handsome young man with bloodshot eyes – he spent all his money on drink. He had recently lost his job as a houseboy. Sabiiti's grandfather, humble, stooping, dressed in tattered rags, revealed that his daughter had simply left Sabiiti with him when she went off with another man; he had no money, just grew enough food for their use. Begumya had no father.

So it seemed to me that the children would have to raise the money for the school fees themselves. There was no point me paying for all of them as we were only going to be here for two years; they had to become self-sufficient.

It was getting dark; the mountains were swimming, as some poem has it, like great birds on the pool of darkness. One by one the children said "Goodbye, Madamu" and slipped away to their dark homes as we approached the lights of Nyakasura and heard the thumping of the generator.

Next morning I instituted the Tins System. I put tins, one for each child, labelled, on a shelf in the pantry. Every time they earned some money, I would put it in the tin, until there was enough for the school fees. They could earn money either by selling me things, or by doing some work. Matara brought two eggs, so I solemnly put 50 cents in his tin. Kaheru brought some carrots, 20 cents in hers. Then the "work" began. The children had been wiping their muddy feet on the white walls of the house. Now I set them to scrub them clean, using Vim and scrubbing brushes. I had to stop them scratching the windows with Vim. I gave them rags and a bucket of water. Soon they needed more water, so I showed them the tap in the "servants' quarters", which filled them with wonder. Remembering the little processions I often saw going to collect water from the stream, I was not surprised when they went mad, turning on the tap when there was no container under it – water was soon cascading down the steps and across the forecourt.

A favourite job was cleaning the car; unfortunately they also cleaned it inside, and it took a long time for the seats to dry out so that we could sit on them. I got them to dig up a patch in the garden and grow vegetables from seed obtained from Bhimji. When the lettuces and carrots were big enough I sent them to teachers' houses to sell them – but if no one wanted to buy them, I ended up buying them all myself, dutifully placing money in the tins. This went on for some time, until there was enough to pay the school fees, and I declared my "school" closed. I started teaching in the local school for nurses – and then our second child, Nicholas, was born.

I got in touch with Oxfam, and asked if they could supply clothes for these ragamuffins. Soon a big boxful arrived, and I spent an afternoon distributing them. The truth of the German saying, *Kleider machen Leute* (clothes make people) was borne out: they all looked lovely in decent clothes.

Children getting Oxfam clothes

Kajusi and Bagonza spent a lot of time in our house, cutting things out of newspapers for a scrap book, playing with Tom. Bagonza was a thin, graceful boy with large, melting eyes, musical - he could spend hours playing a little Baamba harp - and he was a good drummer. He was intelligent, but indolent; he used his intelligence to find labour saving devices. He was the only one who discovered the multiplication tables on the back cover of the exercise book, which helped him doing sums. Kajusi, his sister, was a bright, pretty little girl. She was always teasing Christopher, the big *shamba boy* - but in the nicest way; she would chat with him for hours, but she would be helping him with his work as she did so. She knew I wanted to learn Rutoro, and would tell me words and phrases. Once, I was disinfecting a drain. "What is this, Madamu?" she asked. "This" I said slowly, "is dis-in-fect-ant." - "Oh," she said. "Kwa Rutoro: Jeyes." I laughed, and she smiled, uncomprehending, but pleased to have amused me. She smiled a lot.

Uhuru - Freedom - was the word for Independence from Britain, which was to begin on October 9th, 1962, and Nyakasura made preparations to celebrate it. Shields were painted in the national colours - black, yellow and red; banners were draped across the main building; hundreds of balloons were blown up (and many burst); a triumphal arch was erected across the school road; lights were put up; a bonfire was lit. Fort Portal was adorned with thousands of flags; roads were closed as arches were erected across them. We bought a stack of small paper flags, for my school was not to be left out of the celebrations. David helped boys stick the flags on sticks; I helped Kajusi and Nyindo to make toffee; the other children were rushing around excitedly. Finally I drove them out, telling them to come back at three. At two they were all back again. David had borrowed a big drum from one of the teachers; Bene and Sadiki sat astride it back to back and pounded the two ends rhythmically - they could get six or seven different sounds out of it - and little Bagonza started dancing, like a wild devil, his red shirt flapping round his knees, his eyes flashing as he leapt about on his thin legs; Big Bagonza swayed voluptuously till he noticed that I was watching him when he stopped, overcome, and giggled. I called Kajusi and we prepared the feast under the big tree - cake, biscuits, toffee, smarties, bananas, orange juice and milk. Sudden silence as they fell to. When the last crumbs had been eaten, I gave out balloons and then the flags, and David got them to line up and march round and round the lawn while he blew *John Brown's Body* and *When the Saints Come Marching in* on his recorder. Strange children gathered at the entrance and watched.

So we participated in the birth of a nation.

Around the same time, we had a birth of our own. Our second child was born on June 23, 1963. It was a fairly straightforward delivery, but only after a gruelling three-hour drive over bumpy roads from Nyakasura to Fort Portal. It was a boy, and we named him Joseph. Only some months later did we suddenly feel that it wasn't right - and we renamed him Nicholas Makepeace Gill. "Makepeace" reflected our pacifist ideals. It was also the middle name of William Makepeace Thackeray, one of David's favourite novelists.

*

After our return to England in December 1964, we went on paying school fees for Kajusi, Begumya, and Bene, and received letters from them. Kajusi wrote:

Dear Mdm. Dear Mrs Gill,

I am very pleased to have this short time to talk to you first of all let me greet you how are you dear? How is Tom and Nicholas? We are all very well. I think Tom is a very good boy. Please I want to see Nicholas and Tom, please come to Nyakasura, oh dear I want you all to come back here, every day I think of you and Tom and Nicholas and Mr Gill. My darling let me stop here, I have no time, bye bye. My mother and sister Kakwini are greeting you and your children. Yours Mary Irene Kajusi.

But as the years passed, the news got worse, especially for Kajusi. She had a son in 1973, but she was mentally ill after his birth. She wrote - on January 6th 1981 -

I had been ill for seven years. I suffered from mental illness and I was taken to Butabika hospital. My first attack started after delivery. Since then I had been having treatment at Kabarole mental hospital. Even now I'm getting tabs from there.

My first born is eight years now; he is going in P2. The next is four years, they are both boys. My mother is the one who looks after them. ... My brother Bagonza died now it's two years ago. ...

*

Some 30 years later, in December 1993, we went back to Uganda.

Uganda had been through hell. The happy optimism of "Uhuru", the celebrations on that October day, had turned to despair as civil war broke out. The Prime Minister, Milton Obote, called in the army to assert his power, promoting one Sergeant Idi Amin to lead it - soon having to flee into exile in Tanzania while Amin assumed dictatorial powers and massacred Obote's supporters and tribesmen. Amin was in power from 1971-1979; he expelled thousands of Asians, who had lived in the country for generations, and allocated their businesses and properties to his friends - who lacked the training and experience to manage them. The result was an economic crisis with hyperinflation; foreign aid money was used to buy weapons. Amin dreamed of ruling the whole of Africa, and invaded Tanzania. His forces were soon driven back by the Tanzanian forces and the Ugandan exiles who were there with Obote. Amin was finally driven out - and into luxurious retirement in Saudi Arabia - in 1979, and elections brought Obote back into power. He was opposed by the National Resistance Movement, led by Yoweri Museveni, and the civil war - the "bush war" - that followed caused terrible suffering for years, until 1985, when Obote was toppled and the NRM overran the capital. Now Museveni was sworn in as President; he promised to establish democracy. But the monstrous brutality of the "Lord's Resistance Army" in Northern Uganda defied all attempts to stamp it out. And by this time, the AIDS epidemic was rampant.

Museveni had been in power for some eight years when we decided to go back for a three-week holiday. We contacted Nyakasura and received encouraging replies from the current headmaster, Henry Mehangye, and his wife Idah. We travelled by air to Entebbe, where we got our first taste of inflation when we exchanged our money for Ugandan shillings: 1000 Uganda shillings were worth about 60p, and were handed out in bundles the size and shape of bricks....We drove into Kampala in a "taxi" - a minibus - past the shores of Lake Victoria and pleasant little houses with their banana trees and vegetable patches and goats and babies and hard-working brightly attired women and ragged, idling men, and into the slums of Kampala and on to the Hotel Rena on Namirembe Hill. As we were carrying in our luggage, a whitish car came hurtling down the hill, hotly pursued by a police pick-up. Several uniformed policemen were standing in the back, shooting wildly in the direction of the car. The people in the road flung themselves down on the ground behind any parked vehicle, or wall, or heap of rubbish they could find, and spent the next few minutes visibly saying "phew" to each other....

Next morning we took the bus to Fort Portal, and so we got back to Nyakasura, after 30 years away.

What had changed?

The buildings looked shaken and shabby, and in fact they had been neglected during the years of misrule and civil war - windows were broken, roofs leaked and damaged ceilings and paintwork; anything that could be stolen had been stolen: not only lights, but switches, and the wires had been pulled out of the walls. Gardens had been abandoned; there were hens everywhere. The early 60s, when we were there - "Obote One" as it is often called - was looked back to as a honeymoon period. Things deteriorated rapidly even before the horrors of the Amin years – which were followed by the horrors of civil war.

"Our" house still stood at the end of the avenue of Jacaranda trees, their blue blossom carpeting the ground. It was now inhabited by Ndora – an Old Boy, now the Deputy Head, and his wife, who was also a teacher. They had eight children – one an AIDS orphan they had adopted – and work and a large family made him seem careworn. He was a practising Catholic, but refused to go with us to see a waterfall and caves on the grounds that they were the abode of the Bachwezi, the mythical early inhabitants. He said that some years ago some of his small children had been frightened by owls hooting in the night, so he had thrown a stone into the trees to frighten them off. "Now I have diabetes", he said. I laughed, thinking he was joking, but he shook his head forlornly.

We were anxious to see as many as possible of the children we had got to know through my "school", and others. We had been writing to Bene, or Boniface Kasaija as he wanted to be called, the biggest and cleverest of them, and he had written in reply, with information about some of the boys David had been teaching. Now we met him – he was very tall and thin, with extraordinary gangling movements: his legs did not always obey him, a result, he said, of a stroke some years before which had paralysed his left side for a time, and at times he was doubled up with pain from a peptic ulcer. He was 43 years old, and the father of two small girls, by different mothers – one of whom had died, the other living nearby with her parents. He had no wish to marry her – "it was only a casual affair" – but he was paying school fees for both girls. I met the younger, Goretti, aged about 11, with Bene's unmistakeable nose in the middle of her pretty face. At first she was rigid with shyness, but soon she thawed out and was lively and cheeky and good fun. Her school report was bad; she was truanting a lot. Bene wanted to get her into Nyakasura Primary School – a fairly recent innovation – and intended to coach her himself. He was a teacher himself now at a nearby Senior Secondary School, but unqualified, and in danger of being "retrenched" – the IMF having decided there were too many public servants in Uganda and insisting on "retrenchment". Already teachers' pay was so low that most of them had to take on two or three jobs – meaning that they did none of them properly.

Bene was living in a tiny mud hut with his mother, who was over 80, gaunt, with few teeth, but lively and interesting. She refused to believe that a black man could be a proper priest or a proper doctor. Luckily there was an American priest on the staff at Nyakasura and he was kind enough to come and hear her confession, despite knowing little Rutoro, and give her Holy Communion. The nearest white doctor was at Virika, on the other side of Fort Portal, and another of the old lady's foibles was a flat refusal to enter any kind of vehicle. So the strange symptoms she described to us, flinging her dress up over her head to show us her stomach, in which something that felt like an unborn child was moving about, and her breasts, which she said were becoming more like a young girl's – these strange symptoms remained untreated. Mindful of certain Old Testament stories, I asked Bene if she could possibly have conceived, but he answered: "No. My father died soon after I was born, and she has not misbehaved since then."

Since their house consisted of one room, with just a few waist-high partitions, they could have few secrets from each other. The mother's corner had a bedstead with a few mats on it, and often an open fire on the ground, the smoke escaping through an unglazed window. She sat on the ground very near it, and from early evening shared her space with the hens and the goats, and Bene's bike. His school books and papers lay in slippery piles in the opposite corner. The third corner was full of bricks; in fact they were stashed up all round the hut. One of Museveni's schemes to improve the nation's housing was to get people to make their own bricks of murram. Bene described the method enthusiastically. His first batch looked pretty crumbly, but he had got the hang of it and the most recent ones looked quite good. In fact brick-making was going on wherever we went, with temporary kilns smoking and stacks of bricks for sale at the roadside, or being used to build houses. That was what Bene wanted to do with his; but he was up against his landlord, a Pentecostal Bishop, who had bought land in the area and was trying to remove the sitting tenants. He had forbidden Bene to replace his "semi-permanent" house with a brick one. Bene was considering taking him to court.

The fate of "semi-permanent" structures was demonstrated by his brother Christopher's house, a few steps from Bene's and his mother's: a pathetic ruin. Christopher was in prison, serving an eight year sentence for rape - rape of a ten-year-old.... Bene was not convinced of his guilt, and remembering his good nature when he was our shamba boy, it did seem strange. The old mother grieved: would she live to see him again?

Kajusi's fate was as awful as I feared. A letter from a later Nyakasuran wife described how she had employed her, and also her son Mwesige, in 1988; but after a fortnight, Kajusi had failed to come, and when she had visited her and her mother Janey she had found her lying on the mud floor, dirty, tethered to two stakes at hands and feet. When sick she became totally irrational and violent, using bad language, tearing off her clothes, rushing dementedly through the bush, and had to be forcibly restrained. She spent years in the mental hospital, appeared to be cured, and had a second son, by the same man - she didn't live with him because he had another wife, the same situation as her mother's; but she went mad again, for 18 years, and on bad days was in danger of harming herself and others and had to be held down by force. Her medication was a heavy sedative, but there was little medical help for her. I knew from letters she had written to me that she had periods of sanity. She had died in 1991.

We visited her mother Janey in her nice, neat house; she told me, through Bene, that her madness was first recognised as such by a doctor during her first pregnancy, and that she had died because "the blood had risen into her brain". She was buried near the house. It is hard to believe that such a dreadful fate was waiting for the charming, lively, friendly child we had known. Could the pregnancy have been the cause? Had she been raped?

Another person we were keen to see was Petero, our "house boy". We had kept in touch with him, and his granddaughter Tibananuka penned an impeccable English translation of his words – he was illiterate:

I am very glad indeed to see that I have been given this time from GOD to write a letter to you. … Anyway I still remember you every time, every day, every minute. … The school fees for my children, I have got a banana shamba so I have to pay the school fees for them. E. Tibananuka has been promoted to Primary four and her work is promising that she is working hard and she loves netball…

We knew that after our departure his wife had had a large number of children, but that he had not been working for wages for many years. So we expected scenes of great poverty and hardship.

Far from it. We met him on the road by Bukuku market – thin and smiling, slightly grizzled – and he led us through fields of grass where a few goats and cows were grazing, patches of banana or matoke, interplanted with beans or cassava, across little streams separating fields of maize and yams – and this was all *his* land! He was a Lord! He had made the most of the modest salary we had paid him. We came past several little houses: one was his eldest son's; another was his sister-in-law's, and so on; and behind each, on the neatly swept black earth, sat small, peaceful children with glistening eyes. Finally we walked along a straight, well-swept path under banana plants, with a few flowers at the side, to Petero's own house: a neat mud hut with a corrugated iron roof, divided into rooms by six-foot-high walls.

On these walls there were various messages in English. One was a poster which showed who exactly goes to hell: people hurtling down into an area of skulls were waving banners saying "child abuse", "sodomy", "gay rights", and so on. Another was the careful work of a primary school child, who had used green and black pencils to write "Home is the Nearest to Heaven on Earth." Indeed, surely this home of Petero's, with its well-tended plots, with his clan members all living near together, largely self-sufficient - this must be the African Idyll.

A similar estate belonged to Mr Mwosi, who had been the bursar at Nyakasura. Again, there was a long walk through fertile fields to reach his house. His sitting room was bright pink; his wife's kitengi dress was the same colour. Both of them frequently offered up prayers - for our coming, for our food, for our family, for our departing, for our next journey. "Until I was saved," he said, "I had two wives, and each of them gave me ten children." All this vast family seemed to be there - the youngest daughter, aged about 16, sang and danced a spirited song of welcome ("Wel-o-come, wel-o-come dear visitors") with her small nephews in the small amount of space available.

Bene had written to ask us to donate books to Kihembo School, where he was teaching, which we had been glad to do. Described as a "Third World School", because it had no amenities like electricity or water, it had been started with great fervour by some Seventh Day Adventists, who built it with their bare hands on a hillside with a stunning view across to Kabarole Hill and the Ruwenzoris beyond. (The round palace on Kabarole Hill, built in the early 60s, had been looted and burnt; a new palace of more conventional design was being built near it.) The idealism of the director, Mr Ndyanabo, his teachers and governors, was palpable: they were out to educate heads, hearts and hands, just like Pestalozzi. Now Henry Mehangye took us to the school, and we were guests of honour - it was quite embarrassing. We were solemnly shown the Laboratory, a modest mud and wattle structure with a few test tubes and Bunsen burners linked to a large gas bottle by pipes let into channels in the cement floor; then the wood and metal workshop; some ordinary

Kajusi with my son Tom

classrooms - earth walls, windows without glass - the kitchen, library and dispensary. This last was managed by Mrs Ndyanabo to serve the local community as well as the school, and deals with family planning and AIDS. Recently they had started a primary school, and the charming teacher rounded up some of her small pupils who lined up in their pink uniforms and sang us an original song, clapping their hands in time:

Wel-o-come, wel-o-come, wel-o-come
To Kihembo Primary School.

I asked if they could do "Kabaina kabaina wakame wako, ti, ti mutiti wa" and they could and did - and it was so similar to the children in our garden thirty years ago that it brought tears to my eyes.

Chapter 7: Cakes against the Vietnam War

We returned from Uganda in December 1964. Old friends showed remarkably little interest in our African adventure.

"Where have you been all this time?"

"Well actually we've been in Uganda."

"Really? We went to Dorset for our holidays this year."

For the next seven years we lived in my mother's house in Thorncliffe Road, Summertown, North Oxford. David was teaching at the Eckersley language school at first - until one day on a CND demonstration he got into conversation with Bob Stanier, the head of Magdalen College School, who mentioned that he was looking for an English teacher. Well, David said he was an English teacher .... So for the next seven years he was a popular and successful teacher there, teaching English and German. He was also in charge of the "community service" for boys who did not want to be in the military cadets. I was teaching German at three of the Oxford colleges - St Anne's, Exeter and Jesus. Tom started going to school, Nick to a playgroup.

The Vietnam War was in full swing - one of the "proxy wars" between the USSR and USA in the Cold War. The Viet Minh, led by the Communist Ho Chi Minh, and supported by Communist China, had defeated the French Colonial power but the United States was committed to opposing Communism in Russia, Cuba and Vietnam. The "domino theory" - that if one state, say Vietnam, became Communist, then other states in the area would follow - led to more and more American "military support" being poured into South Vietnam to fight the Communist North. Images of that war, with all its horrors, haunted me – grinning GI's setting fire to peasant homes with their Zippo cigarette lighters – a child on fire with napalm on her back – the disease and deformities caused by the defoliant Agent Orange, with which the US tried to destroy the jungle through which the Vietcong moved to attack the South. I wanted to do something to help the ordinary people, caught between the ruthless Communists and the pitiless Americans. When I learned that some other women felt the same – they had heard a programme on the radio about a hospital in Qui Nhon – and were getting together, I joined them in creating "Oxford Aid for Children in Vietnam".

I got to know some excellent women – and also some unbearable ones. I urged them to have no constitution, no committee as such, and no elections – all potential sources of endless nit-picking arguments. We should have a chairperson, a treasurer and a secretary, and anyone who wanted to help should come along to a meeting and help decide what should be done. We should be non-political and send equal aid to North and South Vietnam, and we should confine our aid to children. One of the founding members, Ruth, was married to a hairdresser who had a spare room above his salon where we could have meetings. We wrote a leaflet advertising our first meeting and sent it out to 150 people. Our first meeting was attended by twelve.

Joyce became Chair, Ruth Treasurer, and I was the Secretary. Ruth was a Communist – rather slow, not very efficient, but sincere and trustworthy. She was a hopeless treasurer – quite incapable of getting a receipt book, let alone fill in and send receipts. Her sums – well – she wasn't at all clear whether she should add or subtract, whether she owed money to the funds or vice versa. She was an artist, a potter, a melancholy person with a low opinion of herself. Her two children were simultaneously spoilt and neglected – rebellious and totally dependent. But she decided to take a teacher training course, and handed the treasurership over to Nancy Rudden, my neighbour in Thorncliffe Road. Nancy was large: her shoulders were hunched as if she was trying to make herself smaller – her husband, Bernard, an Oxford law don, was unusually small. Her most obvious characteristic was conscientiousness. Her house was spotlessly clean. Her two children were fully adapted to a life in which cleanliness and order were paramount. When they came to our house they automatically took off their shoes and asked baffling questions such as: "May I walk on your floor?" Nancy was an extremely conscientious treasurer.

Joyce was very tall, with a handsome face and an extraordinary honking voice. She had been moved to join by a circular from Terre des Hommes, the Swiss child relief agency that had been founded in 1960 – so that was one of the organisations I wrote to, asking what relief work in Vietnam we might be able to support. But Joyce was a deeply disturbed person. She told me she had heard a voice coming from the gas oven saying she must kill herself or she would kill her baby – . She was admitted to the Warneford Mental Hospital in a state of deep depression for three years. ... When she told me these things, she asked if I thought she was fit to be the Chairperson of OACV. I said I thought she was, as she was warm and intelligent and committed.

I did not tell her that I too periodically fall into a mood of black despair, compounded of guilt – rage at myself, because I never did things properly – and fear of other people, whom I suspected of whispering to each other about vices or faults in me which were plain to them, but I knew nothing about. I felt there was something fundamentally wrong with me, like a bad smell – a fatal flaw, which made me incapable of success. I toyed with the idea of *asking* people why they disliked me, but never did, as I knew they would insist that they didn't. I had a great yearning to be *successful*, to write a best seller, to earn money, to be famous, to have a lover who understood me and admired me but accepted that he must love me from afar – so

I slithered from elation to despair... No doubt it went back to my childhood, when I was an *Enemy Alien*, a *Jerry*, a *dirty little German rat*; when I knew that the Germans wanted me dead because I was half Jewish, and the English wanted me dead because I was German.

We organised cake sales, every Saturday, in the Presbyterian Church Hall, which raised quite a lot of money. We also held sales of second-hand clothes and toys. David organised a fund-raising concert at Magdalen College School. And I got to know more about the horrors of the American actions in Vietnam, and also about the work of various relief organisations. But our monthly meetings were nightmarish. Different people appeared each time, some of whom knew little about our efforts and had to be put in the picture.

And then there was Elizabeth.

After two years I handed over to Thea as secretary. And she recognised that "the chief job of the secretary is to handle Elizabeth." It was Elizabeth who dominated - and ruined - the meetings. Fat, flabby and pink, flashing her false teeth, she cut across every discussion to squawk something like - "I've had the most dreadful pains in my back but not to worry, I always say, after all I've still got my two hands and so long as I can do a good turn of work I will. My husband says why don't you take it easy, let the others do a bit for a change but I say what's the use of talking like that Charles? No one else will do anything, look at those people in North Oxford, they hardly ever turn up, so what needs must I always say, so long as I've breath in my body - besides, I'm like that you know. Always have been. I always have to be doing something for others. I'm just not happy otherwise. Fifteen blankets I sewed up last week, fifteen, in the end my fingers were so stiff I couldn't hardly bend them, and I got so tired of the dark wool I was seeing blotches in front of my eyes, I was, literally -"

And so on. This would be normal. Finally we might get to read the minutes of the last meeting, punctuated by her loud whispers to the person next to her - "Did you see where that little girl - well, it's the mother's fault, I always say, some people aren't fit to be mothers. When my daughter was tiny I took her with me wherever I went, no, I'm sorry, I said, I'm not leaving her anywhere, she's my responsibility, but then I'm like that. When I worked in the Red Cross Canteen, fifteen girls I had under me by the time I was finished, she was always with me, quite a laugh it was but she was never no trouble, being properly brought up … "

I tried to raise the subject of the next cake sale.

"I do want to say something on that, dear, if I may, after all, I was there, I always am, if there's one person who's always there it's me, you can bear me out there can't you, unless I'm really ill, but I simply *cannot* bear a certain person's voice any longer, I'm sorry, I simply can't bear it, I got such a headache I thought it would split, I did really."

Joyce – "I'm sorry about my – "

Elizabeth – "Oh don't apologise, don't apologise, none of us is perfect and we can't help the way we were born. Only what I can't understand is this: Why do you talk *all* the time? There's plenty of things you could be doing – *I* don't talk, I'm far too busy, except to serve my customers of course and to my old dears – my old dears dearly love to have a chat with me, you see, I can talk to these people, I know what to say, I know old Mrs Pringle's husband's had a stroke so I ask after him, and Miss Smith's got a new hearing aid – they tell me these things because they have confidence in me – because they can see I care – ."

Joyce – "Well that's right, it's what I always thought, the cake sales give people a chance to talk."

Elizabeth: "Ah, but there's talk and talk isn't there … "

So it went on and on, with the other eight or nine people present wanting to talk but fearing that whatever they said would act like a trigger for another angry, self-righteous outpouring. Finally Nancy ventured to say – "I've forgotten where we were – oh yes, we were setting up a rota for the next sale. Well, I can come first thing and open up, if you like –"

At these words Elizabeth arose and stood quivering like a mountainous jelly.

"Oh no you will not Nancy. Oh no, there's others will have a thing or two to say about that. What - *you* open up? *You* have the key? And why should you, if I may ask? Where were you last time? It was *me* - I was there, I was dealing with those filthy Catholic women, I'm surprised you've forgotten already."

(Nancy was herself a Catholic.)

"But I only –"

"It's always the same with you people. It has been right from the start. Let Elizabeth do the work - but hide her behind the door, don't let anyone see her."

(Tears from Elizabeth, cries of "Oh no!")

But Elizabeth was in full flood. "Does it really matter if I live in a *smaller* house than the rest of you? If my husband is a chef in one of the *smaller* Colleges?

Joyce: Would someone please tell me what we're talking about?

Elizabeth: (quivering, voice throbbing) Rene. I ask you. Tell me one thing. Did you ever know that I hated you?

Me: Well, yes, I knew, because you told me.

Elizabeth: I mean, all the time, before I told you? Because I did, you know. (Chin wobble.) I did, but I didn't let it show. I worked as willingly for you as I have for Thea. I put my own feelings aside and put the Committee first.

Me: It's not the *Committee* we're working for –

Nancy: Oh can we *please* get back to the point?

Elizabeth (exploding): How dare you - how dare you speak to me like that? Why, you can't even add up! You never know what money we have or haven't got! A proper treasurer would have it all at her fingertips but you - you go fumbling in your bits of paper, you're never ready - you're useless!

Nancy: Right then, if I'm useless, I resign, most willingly.

She got up - and we all shouted "No no! Please stay!" We were all on our feet, and Elizabeth, seeing the limelight swing away from her, proclaimed, "No, *I'm* the one who's not wanted. *I'll* go" - tottered and swayed and sat down. Thea rushed over to her solicitously, and got her a glass of water ...

Nancy and I laughed at it as we cycled home, but in fact Nancy was deeply hurt, and I was angry. More and more people dropped out; in the end it was just Elizabeth and Thea, who was a Quaker, and was a willing slave to Elizabeth. I was soon absorbed in another matter - and handed all my information over to the Medical Aid Committee for Vietnam, which still exists, having expanded into Medical and Scientific Aid for Vietnam, Laos and Cambodia, and I still support it.

Chapter 8: Children

Tom and Nick both attended Bishop Kirk Church of England Primary School in Summertown, North Oxford, in the late 1960s. I used to take them to school from Beamsend, along Stratfield Road and Middle Way, past the Oliver & Gurden cake factory with its alluring aromas. Sometimes on a Friday afternoon we would stop off and buy a plastic bag of broken bits of cake at a bargain price.

The cake factory closed on the last day of 1975, and the school was closed in 1990 and demolished to make way for a block of flats. But we had left Oxford in 1972.

Tom did well at school, excelling in maths, and passing all tests and exams. Only once, when he was about nine years old, did he falter at his studies. He blamed it on the teachers at Bishop Kirk school, complaining that they were using cheap chalk that was all fuzzy on the blackboard. After several months, it finally occurred to us to get his eyes tested. He was quite badly short-sighted. The day he received his first pair of little round National Health John Lennon glasses, he was genuinely astonished at how close and clear his world had suddenly become. And he got clever again.

He was absent-minded, though. One day he accidentally came home from school at lunchtime, mistakenly thinking that school had finished for the day. Mu came home to find him sitting morosely on the steps of the house, wondering where everyone was. He didn't have a key. Mu kindly took him back to school, and his teacher, the stern but kind Mrs. Barbara Harvey, was in a forgiving mood. "He's just a little absent-minded professor," she said. And as a matter of fact, he did become a real absent-minded professor later in life.

Nick had a hard time - he seemed to have inherited my complex, feeling that he was different, unpopular, and mocked by other children. He had a horrible teacher, Mr. Hood, who took an unhealthy interest in the little girls in his class and left Nick and the other boys to sit at the back and stare out of the window. Mr. Hood never gave him a single house-point, not even for his Dinosaur Project, which was a labour of love.

And he was dyslexic. We wondered if it had something to do with the bumpy Ugandan roads on the way from Nyakasura to Fort Portal. We tried to help him at home, with all sorts of games and special books, but as time went by and the rest of the year group were given more and more interesting reading and writing materials, he felt more and more alienated. I asked the school if there was any help available, and was directed to the council's psychiatric service. This led to Nick - aged seven - being given an "EEG" electroencephalograph - with electrodes attached to his head - which terrified him, and an Intelligence Test. Finally, I was interviewed by a man called Ounstead - a big man who wore thick pebble glasses, sitting behind a desk. He told me that where he and I might be pretty intelligent, Nick's IQ was so high it was "off the chart." *I* was the cause of his difficulties - his dyslexia - because I failed to recognise that he was a genius. And I was over-protective. He did not offer any helpful suggestions. Nick *would* learn to read, he was bound to be an "intellectual high-flyer". All that was needed was to restore his self-confidence. How? I asked. Ounstead goggled at me, as if I were an idiot to ask such a question. He goggled similarly when I asked about the EEG, which had been such a nightmare for Nick. He didn't like to tell me about it. "You don't understand," he said. "You can't understand. I shall have to speak to your husband."

But then the school arranged for Nick to go to a "reading therapist" - a Mr Haines - during school time, and this unassuming little man got Nick's reading age up from age 5 to age 14 in a few weeks. I called on him and asked him what magic he had used. "I don't touch reading matters at first. These kids have developed a phobia. So I just make them welcome, chat with them, play games with them - and once they're happy coming here - then it doesn't matter which method you use." Years later Nick still remembers Mr Haines with affection.

Nick had an extraordinary musical talent - it had been apparent even as a baby, in Uganda: if I stopped in the middle of a tune, he would fit in the next note. So now he must learn to play an instrument. The obvious one was the piano, since we had one in the house, and I arranged piano lessons for him - and told him he must practice at least 20 minutes a day. However, he did not get on well with a succession of piano teachers. When I went to collect him from the first one, he was sitting on the pavement outside her house, looking cross. Didn't want to go back to her ever. What had happened? Nothing. She hadn't said anything. Later, I asked her why she hadn't said anything. "There was nothing to say. He was perfect".

Years later, Nick discovered jazz, and in his late twenties we paid for him to stay with an old friend from UCL days, Nic Cottis. Nic was as poor as a church mouse, lived on social security in a shack at the bottom of an architect's garden, kept a piano in the back of a van and played gigs at art deco bistros and hotels. In the end Nick too became a professional jazz pianist. Heavily influenced by Nic Cottis, he came to specialise in classic jazz and ragtime.

Tom also had piano lessons, and at one point both brothers were being taught by a Miss Bertrand. Tom, perhaps about ten at the time, had a crush on Miss Bertrand, but he could never please her, since she kept giving him pieces to play that were much too difficult for him. He showed no musical aptitude, and soon quit the piano, nursing wounded pride and a broken heart. Nick also struggled with Miss Bertrand, but then I found a new piano teacher for him - Jackie Cannel, daughter of my friend Pat Cannel, a fellow teacher at the Lady Verney School. Now he got on much better, and this was the start of the journey that would lead to him becoming a professional pianist.

*

One night, I heard David talking in his sleep: "*You, me and our little girl*".

We had been discussing the population explosion. Since we two had two children, we were not at present adding to this major global problem. But if we had more than two, then we *would* be guilty. Yet David obviously did want a daughter! And there was no way we could ensure a third child would be a girl - except by getting a ready-made one, by adoption! Which would also exonerate us as far as the population explosion was concerned.

So we applied to the adoption committee, and in due course a Miss Pollard appeared to see if we were suitable people to adopt a child. We showed her round the house, and the small room - the "box room" - which would be for the adopted child. Returning to the kitchen, we sat down and I offered her a cup of tea, which she graciously accepted. She kept her hat on, as she went through the set questions. She needed to know what our financial situation was - our income and expenditure - and any savings or investments. The house had been rented all those years since 1945 from Mrs Moss, who now wanted to sell it. My mother had to buy it, and had a mortgage on which we paid the interest while we were living there. So Mu was able to give up her job in Osmond House, a retirement home in London, which she was glad to do, and was living with us. She had to be interviewed as well.

Our only conditions were that we wanted a baby girl, as young as possible. Was there any race or nationality we would object to? No - but having got to know and like some children in Uganda we would be particularly pleased if she were African. Were there many children available for adoption, we asked. Oh yes, lots, and the various local adoption agencies communicated with each other, so we might end up with someone from another part of the country. How soon, we asked. "Well, we'll be *scratching around for you* ... you never know when we'll come up with something."

We thought she would now go back to the office to file her report – but she sat and sat, and in despair as we couldn't think of anything else to say I fetched a photograph album to show her. She exclaimed at a snapshot of me – "That's never you, is it?" – "Well yes, it is – a few years ago, of course." "Yes," she cried – "But some people *improve* with age, don't they!"

In due course, we were told there was a baby available in Blackpool; so there we went, to the Social Services Department. I remember sitting in a large, almost empty room with a desk, at which we were asked various questions and told to fill in and sign various documents. Did we have any more questions? Well – might we see the baby? Oh – she's over there. We hadn't noticed the carry cot by the window, and now saw her for the first time – very small, brown, with fuzzy hair ... fast asleep. So could we take her with us now? No – there were various formalities yet – legal documents concerning adoption, and the natural mother had to be given a chance to change her mind. We never met that very young woman. She was engaged to be married to a young man who had said he would treat the child as his own if it looked as if he might be the father.... I kept all these documents for years. I told Jackie if she wanted to I would help her contact her natural mother when she was 16. But she never wanted to.

So we waited. David wrote a poem about it:

ADOPTION

> These pregnant days drag by with stitch in side
> will now with no new ache be born to us.
> We labour for you, mother and father both,

With Tom, Jackie, and Nick

dark baby of my sonnet without rhyme:
these arms which held you once in that grey room
are worked into a cradle for you now,
and these white faces which your tongue-tip mocked
are still in this same world, will come again,
though they be lost as sunken stars at noon.
Among their files and three-fold documents
God's deputies dispose of you, of us –
and for your cradle rock a pending tray.

During the next weeks, months, she was cared for by a professional foster mother, who called her Jacqueline, or Jackie for short. This woman believed that "coloured babies eat more than white ones", so she doubled the quantity of powdered milk in the bottles she prepared for her, and enlarged the hole in the teat so that this thick substance could pass through it. When at last we collected her she was much bigger than when we had seen her before.

Tom and Nick remember coming home from school and being told to go upstairs to the big front room (which had been Fe's study). And there in the middle of the room lay a blue carry-cot, and a shaft of evening sunlight fell on the brown baby asleep inside it, with little specks of dust dancing in it. It was an almost mystical moment.

We wanted to call her Jenny, but Tom kicked up a huge fuss – Jenny was not her *real* name – so in the end we accepted the foster-mother's name Jackie, but officially we modified it from Jacqueline to Jacquetta, in honour of Jacquetta Hawkes, the archaeologist and peace activist who founded CND. We chose Margaret – David's sister's name – as her middle name. So as with Nick before her, it took us a while to get her name right.

Mu was thrilled with this brown baby. As she developed and grew, Jackie spent more and more time with Mu. On Wednesdays she would push the pram to the Cattle Market, where there were grocers and greengrocers' stalls, buy a week's supply of fruit and vegetables and pile it all in the pram, Jackie's head emerging above the cabbages and apples.

Mu's cooking was not refined. She would spread newspaper on the table and start cutting up vegetables and tossing them into a big saucepan - but she might get absorbed in one of the articles in the newspaper and lunch would be delayed ... or overcooked ... or burnt .... But if anyone complained, she would retort:"No-one has ever been poisoned by my cooking," or, "people are starving in China."

Nick's poem:

APPLE FRITTERS

They were my grandmother's speciality –
Cookers from the garden sliced and soused in batter,
Tipped into black encrusted medieval pan
To crackle and spit in boiling oil.
A refugee of wealthy Berlin stock
Civilisation had taught her no recipes
But no cook or servant now
For she who had survived the
Grim fairy-tale of Teutonic ovens.
She floats in memory.
Clouds of blue smoke obscuring
Her time-bent, determined form.
Broken shrapnel of burned fritters arrive,
Softened with sugar and jam.

*

In the evening, I would wash Jackie and put her to bed in her drop-side cot with toys and things to look at, and earnestly say she didn't have to sleep, but she must stay in her cot. But when I went to say goodnight to Mu, as often as not I would find Jackie sitting on her table, eating sweets and being entertained with German songs and the pictures in the great volume of *Grimms Märchen* that had come with us from Germany. At night she would go to the children's beds and put "something nice" - sweets or chocolates - next to their beds for them to find when they woke up. (Of course they generally knew she was coming and kept their eyes shut until she had gone, when they would consume the *something nice*.) Sometimes the "something nice" would be a small toy. On one occasion Tom and Nick each received a plastic aircraft carrier, complete with little plastic planes that fitted into little holes on the flight deck. They were both white on top, but Tom's had a blue hull and planes, while Nick's were red. They are vividly remembered to this day.

Mu was just as devoted to Peter and Brenda's children, who spent most of their holidays at Beam's End. (This was the name Mu had given the house - derived from the nautical term, "to be at one's beam ends" - like a ship in danger of capsizing, hence, "in a desperate situation." She got the phrase from a man who was trying to sell matches in the street, under heavy rain. He had a cardboard sign saying "I am at my beam ends." Mu thought "I don't know what that means, but whatever it means, so am I". And somehow along the way beam ends became Beamsend). She went for long walks with her grandchildren - along the rivers and the canal or through meadows and woods - no doubt remembering the hikes she had enjoyed near Berlin when she belonged to the *Wandervogel* - the German Youth Movement largely led and organised by teenagers, who would set out from the cities at weekends with rucksacks, walk through the countryside, cook over open fires - sit and talk and sing folksongs - and sleep in a barn or in the open.

One day we were shocked to find Jackie, about three years old at the time, stumbling around and bumping into walls. We called a doctor, who diagnosed her as drunk. She had somehow got hold of my bottle of sherry and drunk the lot. (In those days it was my custom to have a glass of sherry and a cigarette at 6pm while watching the TV news. I finally managed to quit smoking many years later, and these days I make do with a glass of wine and a small bowl of nuts or crisps.)

Just across the road from Beamsend was the house of old Harold Danter, a retired Catholic priest. David took us to visit him sometimes. He was rather infirm, and had his magnificent four-poster bed set up in his living-room. Sometimes we would find him in bed, wearing a lovely Victorian nightcap with a bobble. He had snow-white hair and a neat goatee. There were oil-painted, ornately-framed portraits of English kings hanging on the walls, which had become brownish in colour from decades of Mr. Danter's cigar-smoking. In the middle of the room was a hexagonal coffee table with a big brass bowl on it. In it there were thousands of postage stamps, dating back to Edwardian times. Mr. Danter didn't have a stamp album, but all his life he never threw away a stamp. Tom *did* have an album, and Mr. Danter let him help himself from the brass bowl. Tom gathered a complete set of Edwardian definitives and was most excited.

On another occasion David told Tom that Mr. Danter wanted to play chess with him. Tom was shocked. He was in the chess club in his first year at primary school, and the older kids were much better than him. Mr. Danter was *so* much older that he must be absolutely invincible. It was only when Mr. Danter tried to move his knight like a bishop that Tom realized that aging does not always work that way.

The children wanted a pet, and in the end I took Tom and Nick to a cat sanctuary, where we picked out a small black kitten whom we named Tinkle - it wasn't very original, we simply borrowed the name from a black kitten in a children's book called *Orlando the Marmalade Cat* by Kathleen Hale. (By a strange coincidence, Jackie would later, when she was about 20, have a small job cleaning Kathleen Hale's house, just outside Wheatley.) It was already dark when we cycled home with Tinkle in a button-down carrier on the back of my bicycle. At one point Tom called to me to stop - he could see Tinkle's green eyes glowing in the light of his bicycle light as he tried to push his way out of confinement. But we got him home safely in the end, and he grew up to enjoy a fat and lazy life. We also had a tortoise, who was surprisingly good at escaping and had to be retrieved from other people's gardens more than once.

My sister Maleen and her American husband Bob lived at Beamsend for extended periods, sometimes with some of their children, especially when Bob was forced to leave his post at the American Community School in Beirut when the awful civil war broke out in 1975. Bob was fiercely supportive of the Palestinian cause and hostile to the state of Israel, whereas Mu was overjoyed that the Jews had finally been able to return to their homeland, though much distressed whenever Israel committed attacks on the Palestinians and others. They would have intense arguments about Middle Eastern politics, and Bob took a malicious delight in slipping news cuttings about Israeli atrocities under Mu's bedroom door for her to see first thing in the morning. In between these political battles, however, they showed a genuine mutual affection.

*

In 1972, David moved on from classroom teaching to teacher training at Newland Park, soon to be absorbed into Buckinghamshire College of Higher Education, specialising in communication studies. It was a pretty, rural campus in the Buckinghamshire village of Chalfont Saint Giles. With his colleague Bridget Adams, he published a book, *The ABC of Communication Studies*, that for many years was a standard introductory text in the field. Years later, in 1985, he would publish another influential book, *One Potato, Two Potato: Action Poetry for Children*, this time co-authored with Dorothy 'Dot' Clancy. It is still used in classrooms today. Dot, a big blonde woman with a wild raucous laugh, became a great friend of the family. After retirement she moved to Cornwall and we visited her in the summer holidays a couple of times.

Middle-class respectability in Maidenhead

We moved to High Wycombe, living at No. 32, Melbourne Road. The other half of our semi-detached house belonged to Ray Gough, a kindly old working-class man, and his wife. On our side of the neighbouring semi lived a conservative middle-class couple, the Orchards. They also had a black cat. His name was Domino and he had a regrettable habit of cocking his hind leg like a dog and squirting a powerful jet of urine, usually at somebody's socks or trouser leg.

I got a job as a German teacher at Lady Verney High School for Girls, which I enjoyed. One of my star students, Moira Laidlaw, became a lifelong friend, and I also renewed my acquaintance with Julia Bishop and Sally Brocklehurst (née Jervis) decades after leaving the school. I was surprised to learn from Sally that I was considered a radical among the teachers there, because I was the first female teacher ever to wear trousers rather than a skirt. As for Moira, she surprised me with the following answer to an inquiry from Tom about my days teaching her at Lady Verney:

Your mother was a breath of fresh air in the classroom after years of very mundane and restrictive 'teaching' by other teachers. I was fascinated by her enthusiasm for literature, particularly Goethe and Schiller, and I remember vividly one time when Hazel, Rosemary and I (her three upper sixth A Level students) were studying Schiller's "Der Taucher" (The Diver). She made us read it aloud, and insisted we read it dramatically. With her enthusiasm, her eyes shining, she helped us to live the text. As a future teacher myself, I really learnt a huge amount from her teaching style.

She had a presence. I remember she would wax lyrical about a line of Schiller, so caught up in it, she didn't notice her wild hair, her gestures or her riffling through books to find exactly what she was looking for. She brought no ego into the classroom, she brought wonder and delight and rigour and high standards. She expected us to do our best all the time, and we did. She cared about her students. She cared about her subject, but she never allowed a concern for the subject-matter of the lesson, to overcome her concern for individuals. She was someone that students could talk to.

She cared passionately about people, and would sometimes tell us at school about her own experiences of being human because of her Jewish background. I remember listening enthralled and in awe at how anyone with such experiences could be so very human in the classroom. Whenever I talk to students about what good teaching is, I refer to her.

The children went to a friendly little primary school called Micklefield. The headmaster was a big, friendly man called Mr. Kelloway. Tom was a very militaristic little boy in those days – he had a biscuit tin full of tiny plastic toy soldiers that he enjoyed killing with matchsticks fired from a tiny metal Howitzer. He went to Summertown library and would sit there for hours copying diagrams of World War II fighters and bombers. He would spend the school playtime sitting on the little wall around the playground, reading war comics. He dreamed of becoming a Spitfire pilot, and it was a blow when he realized that the RAF no longer used Spitfires, and did not generally employ very short-sighted boys as pilots anyway. David and I let him have his way, despite our pacifist principles, and we even took him to see the film *The Battle of Britain*. It was grimly realistic, and the sight of seeing blood-drenched pilots having their innards shot out made him feel considerably less anguished about abandoning his dream of becoming one of the Few.

One day Nick took his cycling proficiency test, part of which involved a white line on the asphalt playground: the children were to cycle near it but not cross it. Nick misunderstood: he thought he had to ride ON the line, which he did, skilfully – and he was the only boy who did *not* get a proficiency certificate… He came home in deep dejection.

One other day Jackie came home from school and shocked us with the observation that she "did not like niggers." What had become of our dream of helping Britain become a tolerant multi-ethnic society?

As we questioned her, it soon became apparent that she was being bullied because of her light brown skin. Her response was to look for children with darker skin that she could in turn bully - for it is a sad but undeniable fact that most young children would rather bully than be bullied. Fortunately, this proved to be only a brief passing phase in Jackie's emotional development.

The children were generally nice to everybody... except each other. Jackie would goad Nick mercilessly, until one day he got so angry that *he* actually called her a nigger. Nowadays Jackie cheerfully blames herself for this incident. She was often naughty, and very occasionally even my mild-mannered husband David would give her a spanking. But although he seemed genuinely angry, there was no real force in his hands, and Jackie had to supress a grin as she was being chastised.

On another occasion, back in Oxford, Tom and Nick got into a tremendous fight in the bath, on the burning question of whether there were five Thunderbirds or six in the TV drama of that title. Nick insisted that the Mole was Thunderbird 6, as it appeared on the opening credits immediately after Thunderbird 5, while Tom pointed out that it did not have a number six painted on its side and that there were only five brothers in the Tracey family that operated the machines. This debate escalated into a bathtub wresting match that flooded the bathroom and damaged the ceiling of the room below.

One day we acquired a second cat. He was black and white so we called him Blotch. He got on well enough with Tinkle, although both cats were prone to ticks. These ticks would get their claws into the skin and gorge themselves with blood until they swelled up close to bursting. The children rather enjoyed popping them.

Later, after we moved to Maidenhead, Nick and Jackie rescued another black and white cat, long-haired this time, that they found hiding in our garage. It had apparently been bullied - it had a damaged tail that was smeared with blue paint, and was very thin.

We called him Scruffkin, a scruffy version of Snufkin in the Moomin stories. Sadly, both Blotch and Scruffkin were run over and killed by cars. Only Tinkle survived to a ripe old age.

While we were living in High Wycombe, Nick befriended a middle-aged man with Down's syndrome called Paul, whom he met in the park one day. Paul was a short, stooped man, with just a few strands of greasy black hair and a funny smell. He had something wrong with his lips, which were rather rubbery and somewhat twisted. That and his watery eyes, enlarged by pebble glasses, made him look permanently sad. He lived with his mother, who sat in front of the TV all day long with a lava lamp next to the sofa. One time Paul kissed Nick on the forehead and got severely scolded when he told his mother. The next time he saw Nick he made a heartfelt and tearful apology. He didn't know you could get arrested for that sort of thing. Paul had no family ties to give him emotional warmth, but he was looked after by the congregation at the Elim Pentecostal church, who took him under their wing. Sadly, though, his mother died not long after we left High Wycombe. Paul was put into a home in Milton Keynes. Nick visited him once but Paul did not know who he was.

The children's education became an increasingly pressing issue. In those days the UK still had selective education – meaning that children aged 11 and over had to take an examination called the 11+. Those who passed went to grammar schools; those who failed went to secondary modern schools ('secmods'). The government insisted that this was just a way of giving each child a suitable education – but in reality, it meant branding 80% of the nation's children as failures at the age of 11. Tom had taken the 11+ just before we left Oxford, at Bishop Kirk School in Summertown, and after we arrived in Wycombe he learned that he had passed – along with over twenty of his classmates. Among his new classmates at Micklefield, however, only two had passed. The two bunches of kids seemed pretty similar – but Bishop Kirk made its pupils take lots of practice tests, and

Micklefield did not. It was a vivid illustration of the unfairness of the selective system.

Tom duly went to Royal Grammar School High Wycombe. Founded in 1562, it affected the air of a public school, complete with teachers in gowns, Latin and Greek, and even uniformed war games. RGS also practiced corporal punishment, and Tom was smacked on the back of his calves with a gym shoe by Jock Learmonth, the fascistic Scottish gym teacher, for the offence of forgetting his P.E. kit. RGS was located at the top of a long, steep hill called Hicks Farm Rise. Symbolically enough, the local secmod, Hatters Lane, was at the bottom of Hick's Farm Rise. Every morning Tom had to push his bicycle past the entrance to Hatters Lane on his way up the hill, his ridiculous magenta school uniform making him an obvious target for the jeers of the Hatters Lane kids, and sometimes stones and spittle as well. It was almost a caricature of the British class system - a system perpetuated and strengthened by the selective education system, which we loathed.

Although Nick also passed the 11+, in 1974 we finally decided to take drastic action. That year Harold Wilson narrowly defeated Ted Heath over two elections and formed a Labour government pledged to abolishing the 11+ and changing the UK's education system from selective to comprehensive - mixing children of varying abilities and class backgrounds together in local schools to weaken class barriers and avoid humiliating the majority of the nation's children. But High Wycombe was in Buckinghamshire, one of the Conservative-controlled 'rebel counties' that defied the government and refused to switch to comprehensive education. While thousands of families were moving house into the rebel counties in hopes of gaining a privileged grammar school education for their children, we moved in the opposite direction, from High Wycombe to Maidenhead. Maidenhead was only ten miles away, but across the county border in Berkshire, which was complying with the national government.

Tom - 14 at the time - thought it was an excellent idea. He was already a keen supporter of the Labour Party, and helped us campaign for the Labour candidate in High Wycombe at the two elections of 1974. His name was Bill Back, and the posters and leaflets we handed out said BACK BILL BACK. (He had no chance – Wycombe was a Tory stronghold, as was Maidenhead.) Moving house was a major inconvenience – it meant that we had to buy a second car, for instance, since both David and I would have to drive to jobs in Buckinghamshire – and of course, we would have to sell our house and buy a new one. But to do all that for the sake of a political ideal – Tom thought it was magnificent.

Nick was three years younger and took a different view. He also supported the Labour Party and comprehensive education, but not to the point of moving house. It was only three years since we had moved from Oxford to High Wycombe, and now we were going to be uprooted again, just as he had finally managed to adjust to the previous move and make a few friends in High Wycombe. Why sacrifice one's children's happiness for the sake of an abstract bit of ideology? In a desperate bid to avert the move, he uprooted the FOR SALE sign in front of our house and buried it under the compost heap at the back of the garden. When the disappearance of the sign was noticed, he initially tried to put the blame on Jackie, who was rather obviously too small to accomplish such a deed. In the end the house *was* sold and we moved to 25 Redriff Close, in Maidenhead. It was a quiet little cul-de-sac. On one side were a deaf couple whose TV was always on maximum volume so the sound came through the wall. On the other side lived a friendly working-class family called the Palmers, from Manchester. Jackie became close friends with their daughter Gillian. An eccentric Italian teenager called Luigi roamed the streets around Redriff Close . He was always talking about his bicycle, and would sometimes ask to borrow a bicycle pump, though we never did see him actually riding a bicycle. Also nearby was a man of native American extraction who had a blue van with stickers on it saying, in red capitals on a white background,

REMEMBER WOUNDED KNEE and WANT TO LOSE WEIGHT?
MOVE TO A RESERVATION.

Tom and Nick ended up going to Desborough School, formerly
Maidenhead County Boys' School. By a tremendous coincidence,
during the War David and his mother and sister had stayed in the
headmaster's house as evacuees from Chislehurst, on the outskirts
of London, and he had fond memories of the place. It was a grammar school that was gradually going comprehensive. Tom was in
the last grammar-school year and Nick was in the second comprehensive year. It was an all-boys' school. Jackie went to Altwood
School, a mixed secondary modern that was going comprehensive.
We gradually realized that the relationship between Desborough
and Altwood was only moderately different to that between the
Royal Grammar School and Hatter's Lane. It remains a moot point
whether it was worth making the move.

Jackie developed rapidly into a very lively and cheeky girl - a
continual explosion of energy, with a strong desire to dominate.
Going for a walk with David, she would direct him to the sweet shop
- which is also where she went to spend her pocket money ... When
she started going to school, she was soon a member of a little gang
of lively girls who would flirt with boys or pretend to, and not take
their school work seriously. Her principal partner in crime was a
red-headed little girl called Georgina, or "Jaws" to her friends.

All our children got into trouble at school. When Tom was at RGS
in High Wycombe, Mu knitted him a sweater for school. It was grey
- as stipulated in the school rules - but it was polo-necked, and the
school rules demanded a vee-neck, so that the school tie would be
clearly visible. He was hauled up in front of the headmaster, deputy
headmaster and junior headmaster and accused of being a follower
of radical educationalist A.S. Neill. David and I strongly supported
Tom and wrote a letter to the headmaster, but this incident was
one more reason why Tom was glad to leave Wycombe. Once he
and Nick were at Desborough School, they both got into trouble for

using the "sixth-form entrance". It was a back entrance to the school, which happened to be the first one you came to when arriving from the direction of our house. The school rules decreed quite arbitrarily that this entrance could only be used by sixth formers. Neither Tom nor Nick could see any point in this and repeatedly broke the rule. Tom finally desisted after his third warning, but Nick was made of sterner stuff and carried on defying the rule to the point where he was given several detentions. Worse still, he received a "roasting" from Mr. Stanley, the teacher most loathed by both my sons. Nick found Desborough thoroughly unpleasant and moved to Windsor College of Further Education to do his A-levels. But there were some nice teachers there too - one of them, Joyce Kohn, who taught the remedial class at Desborough, became a good family friend. She was an Irishwoman married to a Polish man, who used her knowledge of Polish to teach Tom O-level Russian.

As for Jackie, she was in constant trouble at Altwood, as she cheerfully admits, for smoking, drinking, and not studying at all.

Tom became a schoolboy activist and spent a year on the executive committee of the National Union of School Students. He would go up to London at weekends and engage in fierce debates with teenage members of the Socialist Workers Party, the International Marxist Group, the Workers socialist League, the Spartacists, etc. After school he would stand outside the front gate selling copies of the NUSS magazine, BLOT, for 10 pence. Nowadays he tries to sell his anthropology books at conferences. An activist and an academic... but above all, a *salesman*.

When Tom went to London, he would stay at the flat of Keith Armstrong. Keith was a family friend, some ten years older than Tom, who suffered from polio all his life and needed a wheelchair to get around. We first got to know him in Oxford, where he was living with his energetic mother, Nina. Keith overcame his disability to become a prominent activist for the rights of people with disabilities, not to mention a musician and impresario. He died in 2017, just a fortnight before David. There was nobody in his family willing or able to tidy up his flat in Euston, and in the end Tom did it with his cousin Liz. They found over a hundred offbeat artworks, mostly composed with a typewriter, that they finally managed to publish in the same year I am writing this - 2022. It is entitled *RUHUMAN: The Typewriter Art of Keith Armstrong*. RUHUMAN is, of course, to be pronounced "are you human?". As for Nina, she was one of the leading members of the movement which resulted in special car-parking spaces for people with disabilities, so her legacy lives on today.

All my children suffered with the notorious British school meals. The overcooked vegetables and mountains of mashed potatoes were bad enough, but Tom and Nick especially hated the desserts - rice pudding, tapioca, semolina... so many different names for off-white goo, with soggy rice or frogs eyes floating in them as the case may be. At Bishop Kirk, Tom would sometimes be kept back after all the other children had finished lunch, struggling to eat his tapioca with such tiny mouthfuls that he wouldn't be able to taste it. Knowing of his suffering, I started making him packed lunches when he went to grammar school - and he still recalls the relief of switching to cheese sandwiches, an apple and a Penguin biscuit to this day. It can be surprisingly easy to make children happy - or miserable.

With both David and I working fulltime, we were able to afford a larger house. This time it was a very small move - a few hundred yards up the hill from Redriff Close to Boyn Hill Road. For the first time in our lives, we lived in a detached house - and, a sure marker of upper middle-class status, our house had a name, not a number. It was a thoroughly desirable residence called Wingates.

During our time in High Wycombe and Maidenhead, the family gradually became vegetarian. Nick was the first. He had a deep love of animals and could not bear to think of them being killed and eaten. I respected his decision, and for some time I would prepare special meals for him when meat or fish were on the menu. But it was not easy for him even to observe other people eating meat. One

With David, meeting the Dalai Lama on a visit to Oxford

Christmas, he refused to join us for lunch in protest at the murder of a chicken (or was it a turkey?) that we were going to eat. He left the house and, since a cold rain was falling, he spent Christmas dinner huddled in a telephone box. (Nick's idealism really shone at Christmas time. For years Fe sent the children 50 pence book tokens at Christmas. The children had to write thank-you letters, which was always a tremendous chore, and one year Nick wrote to Fe that he had sold his book token to his parents for 50 pence and given the money to Oxfam. After that none of the children ever got another Christmas present of any kind from my father.)

I myself had been vegetarian when I was a teenager, but I gave it up when I married David - he loved his sausages, and I was anxious to fit in with his ways. But one day I was driving to High Wycombe, to my job at the Lady Verney, when I got caught in a traffic jam, behind a huge lorry crammed with piglets. Those who could were poking their noses out at the sides, inquisitive, lively youngsters, obviously wondering where they were going. "I know where you're going", I thought, and a mental image of a slaughterhouse came to me. With a start I realised that I had just been thinking "must remember to get some bacon" so I thought NO! Never again! When I came home, I told David I would never buy or cook meat again - if he wanted it, he'd have to do it himself. After that he would occasionally sneak out to the local corner shop to buy some sausages for himself and our two remaining carnivorous children. But one day we watched a TV documentary that featured a chicken 'factory', with a terrifying machine with whirling blades that would behead dozens of live chickens a minute. David found it very disturbing and before long he, too, became vegetarian.

That just left Tom and Jackie. Tom was never inclined to vegetarianism. Jackie did give it a try, but did not last long. It somewhat conflicted with her career ambition, which was to work at MacDonalds. After leaving school at 16, she duly achieved that goal, but soon found it boring and quit. Finally she submitted to our insistence that she should go to college and get a qualification in catering. She went on to a successful career in catering. Tom went to Cambridge University to do English Literature and then got a job as a school teacher in Japan, later becoming a journalist and then a professor of social anthropology. Nick went to Warwick University to do Film Studies and after trying various jobs, including librarian, thatcher and assistant lock-keeper, finally became a professional pianist.

The nest was empty, and David and I were in our fifties. We decided we would both take early retirement and see something of the world, paying our way as English teachers. We started taking international students at Wingates. We thought we might get back to Uganda, or Japan, where Tom had settled, or Portugal, where we had had a family holiday. Meanwhile, there was no longer anything to keep us in Maidenhead, so we moved back to Oxford. We gave up our beautiful detached house and settled at 95 Harefields, which was a flimsy three-storey townhouse in a rather shabby outskirt of north Oxford, just outside the ring road. A few years later we moved again, to 32 Yarnells Hill, a detached house in Botley on the west side of Oxford, where we would stay for a quarter of a century, running our own little language school, Oxford Residential English, out of it for many of those years.

Early in 2011, we had an emergency at Yarnells Hill. Ever since I was a little girl I'd been used to having a real Christmas tree – not one of those fake plastic ones – with real candles, not those horrible fake electric ones. It was Twelfth Night, and we'd invited some neighbours around for mulled wine while we lit up the candles one last time before the tree would be taken down. Tom was with us, being on sabbatical that year. While we were standing there with glasses in hand, one of the candles suddenly tipped over and set fire to the tree. The pine needles were dry but full of oil. One moment there was a tiny little flame, the next, the entire tree was on fire and a black spot was rapidly spreading outward across the ceiling. The room was lined with wooden book cases full of old books. Luckily, David remembered the fire extinguisher that had been sitting unnoticed in the kitchen for a decade or two. He ran out to the kitchen, grabbed it with shaking hands, and shoved it into Tom's hands. Tom was shaking just as much, but managed to figure out how to remove the safety pin and squeeze the trigger. There was a woompf of white powder, and just like that - the fire was out. Another minute, and the whole house could have burned down, possibly taking a couple more with it.

These days I still like to have a Christmas tree, but I don't bother with the candles.

We tried to mingle with our neighbours, and David served as head of the local Neighbourhood Watch for some years, but I never felt we were truly accepted. We invited people to drinks, but they rarely invited us back. After David's death in 2017, I moved to the other side of Oxford, to Risinghurst. The people there were less wealthy than those in Botley, but somewhat more friendly.

Chapter 9: Home Helping

Our dreams of travelling the world meant that we would have to acquire qualifications in TEFL - Teaching English as a Foreign Language. While waiting for our TEFL qualifications to come through, I decided to earn a bit of money as a Home Help. This involved cycling to the Social Services, which were housed in some terrapin huts in waste land behind the Hospital. The receptionist was ensconced behind glass and a switchboard.

"Please wait over there. Miss Tinker will be along in a minute."

And she is! I've hardly had time to read the notices about Ash, Alcoholics Anonymous, and Ante-natal classes. Miss Tinker is an over-grown schoolgirl in her forties, with thick blonde hair in curls and Kirby grips on either side of her large, bespectacled face.

"How did you hear of us?" she asks, smiling. We're sitting in an empty office.

"Oh, I've always known about Home Helps. A friend of mine was one, years ago ... so..."

"I see. Now then -" She spreads some papers out on the table. She's like the Captain of a Hockey Team, or a Patrol leader in the Girl Guides, welcoming a new member, cheerily asking my name, showing me the ropes ...

"Of course you only get £1.88 an hour, you realise that. *They* pay £2.50, that's IF they can afford it. If they're on Supplementary they don't pay anything - but some of them can. The County keeps back some of it for admin - that's me, you see, I have to be paid!" She laughs mischievously, taking me into her confidence. Radiantly she says – "But it's not like charring. You can get more, charring. But as a Home Help you can be sure you're answering a real need. It's not as if you're doing housework for someone like me, when I can do it perfectly well myself. These people really need you. Many of them would have to go into a Home if it wasn't for us. So *you* have to be completely trustworthy, because you may be handling money and so on. Now let me see."

She unfolds a large computer print-out.

"Mrs Moody can be a bit of a trial. And she's getting deaf. But go there on Tuesday mornings at 9.30 and just keep banging on the door. She's sure to be in because we've always gone there on Tuesdays. Then there's Miss King. She's just come out of hospital. She's all right up top, but just a bit disorientated, so I want you to go there every day for a while. She's got a good neighbour next door, so if ever you can't get in or there's any problem it's worth trying her – Mrs Hughes her name is, and she's got a key. Oh and Mrs Moody's daughter and son-in-law live just round the corner. They're very good to her, but part of our job is to support families when they've got an elderly relative. It can be such a strain."

"Which brings us to Mrs Proctor."

She sighs. "Mrs Proctor's Russian, and she's very, *very* difficult." She sighs again. "Very. Part of the problem is her English isn't very good, and she's had a minor stroke which has made her speech a bit slurred into the bargain. So she's very difficult to understand. You may not be able to cope. The last person we sent to her left after an hour in floods of tears."

"Why?"

Well, it's hard to explain. She expects the skirting boards to be cleaned with a toothbrush – that sort of thing. I suppose it's what she was used to in the past, when she had servants. She used to be a pianist, and the first time I visited her she played the piano for me – and it was lovely. But that may have been the last time she played.

Sad, isn't it? She doesn't bother to get dressed any more - just potters around in her dressing gown. She's as thin as this" - she holds up her little finger - "but she cooks for herself. Whatever it is, it makes the place smell sort of continental. Still, you wouldn't have to cook for her. She has friends who come to see her, but she drives them away with her demands and tantrums. She always says nobody's been to see her.... Well what do you say - will you have a go? See how you get on?"

Of course I will.

I receive a pair of overalls, and a time sheet - and so now I'm a Home Help.

Mrs Proctor lives in the ground floor flat of a big Victorian house, one of the last to resist the speculators who have knocked down most of the buildings of this type and replaced them with blocks of flats. She's tall, with grey-blue eyes in a long face. The right side of her mouth and her right eye sag slightly, evidence of the partial stroke.

I decide to use one of my few fragments of Russian.

"Dos vidanya!" I say cheerfully.

She glares at me.

"Seet there!" she barks suddenly, pointing a long finger at a folding chair which keeps the kitchen door permanently open. Suddenly she clasps her cheek and bends over, groaning. "Such bain! Ees abscess!" Slowly she straightens up again, touches a dish of vegetables, a bowl, a saucepan with her long fingers, trying to remember what she was doing; then gives me a sharp, lynx-like look, her long upper lip mobile, wondering how she can use me.

She says something. I don't understand a word. She repeats it, mouthing her words, glaring at me round-eyed, tense, leaning forward.

"You go town. Ees pharmacie. You buy blaster." She holds out her thumb to show me a cut.

"Oh! You want sticking plasters from the chemist."

I get up.

"Wait! Seet!"

I sit down again. As if addressing a deaf person who has to lip-read, she mouths the words – "Health Food Shop."

I repeat the words, and she nods, closing her eyes. After a long pause, out come the words: Wholemeal bread. Then: Muesli. Biscuits.

Another long pause. Again I get up. Again she shouts furiously: "Wait! Seet!" and mumbles some incomprehensible words. At last, after hacking hand movements, she snaps: "Opposite!"

"Opposite?"

"Pap. Martell. For Mrs Proctor."

"You want Martell brandy? From the pub opposite the Health Food Shop?"

She nods.

"Will you give me the money?"

"Money."

Slowly, leaning on the table, grasping the door post, she moves into the bedroom and collapses on the bed. She hands me some of the money lying among the many things strewn on top of it, and at last I go out to buy these things.

She seems quite pleased when I return and give her the plasters, bread, biscuits, and change. But then she barks: "Martell?"

"The pub's closed at this time."

"What ees time?"

"Ten o'clock."

I take off my coat and put on my overall. "What do you want me to do?"

She's leaning against the pink silk headboard of her bed, looking very ill. After a long pause, while a counter-tenor sings an aria on the radio, she opens her eyes and speaks. After a while I recognize the word for vacuum cleaner, and look around for it. I find a little hand model with a three-inch head under the hall table, and take it into the sitting room.

It's a lovely room. The pale light from the big net-curtained window falls gently on the white linen cover of a two-seater sofa and luxuriant green plants on a low table. Next to the open piano – a Bechstein – with music and manuscript paper on the rack, there's a standard lamp, its shade draped with a white lace cloth, casting a soft and inviting light on the white piano stool on which lie five tiny glossy figures, like toy soldiers. There are photos on the piano and on the little tables, and chipped, cracked knick-knacks clumsily glued together: emblems of a refugee existence, mementos of a distant past, like this whole room, this white, light drawing room. An old Persian rug adds its glowing reds to the pale, shell-like interior.

Mrs Proctor has slowly staggered in. She starts poking around under a big mahogany chest with her walking stick.

"Why you don't help me?"

I kneel down and pull out a white cable with an adaptor.

"No! No! Black! BLACK!"

I grope under the chest again, but there is no other flex. A table lamp is plugged into the white adaptor. I pull it out.

"What you doing?" she shrieks.

I plug in the vacuum cleaner and switch it on. Her face lights up with a smile.

"Good, good! I think ees black."

I bend down and start hoovering the rug. She watches me.

"That! That!" she raps out, pointing at a scrap of paper with her stick. "Pick up! Pick up! Put in pocket! If not, apparatus will ruin. Ees expensive!"

I find rancour sitting in me as I crawl around with the stupid little machine, while she stands bossing me around. I'm only here for another half hour, I tell myself, but I can feel myself turning into a sullen servant. Everything I do is wrong. I'm ordered to pick up a mat, but she has to show me how, leaning over perilously, groaning, to hold it by its four corners. I'm to take it into the garden and shake it. I bring it back and replace it. But no, again I'm doing it wrong: this corner has to be quarter of an inch further over, that side must be pulled half an inch along: she's splenetic with rage. Then her bed is to be made: but do I smooth the sheet down properly? Angrily she pushes me aside and smooths it herself, gasping. Then we proceed to the bathroom. She cannot tell me what she wants; she has to show me. The door is tied back with an old belt. Behind it is a stack of old leather suitcases, draped in a white fur rug, and wedged between the suitcases and the door, an ironing board. Clearly she wants it out, and I take hold of it. It catches in the belt.

"Idiot!" she fumes, pushes me aside, and pulls it out herself. Silently, she points to the spot in the entrance hall where it is to stand. I set it up. "Not in my salon!" she suddenly shouts, hitting it angrily with her stick. Its legs protrude a few inches across the threshold of the drawing room. I shift it, and she nods, mollified. Then she points at the nightdress and a few rags which I'm to iron, and she totters back to bed. I find the iron in a kitchen cupboard, plug it in, and start. She lies there, watching my every move.

"Too hot!" she shouts suddenly, sitting up and stretching her hand out towards me, eyes staring in terror. "No, it isn't very hot," I say. Her face twists, she turns her head, cups her hand round her ear. "Not hot!" I shout. But she still hasn't heard, and thwacks her stick angrily on the bed. I go over and speak into her ear. "It's not very hot."

She smiles then, beautifully, pats my arm, relaxes.

My one-and-a-half hours are up. I put everything away and rouse her out of a doze to say goodbye. She glares at me.

"Where is my lunch?"

"Lunch? It's only half-past ten."

Her face expresses consternation.

"I was told you get your own lunch."

Now she mimes incomprehension. I try the sentence in German - and she understands, shakes her head resignedly, asks me just to sweep up the hearth, just to clean the kitchen, just to make coffee. I explain I have another old lady to visit.

"Where?" she asks, suspiciously. I tell her. She lets me go.

*

I knock at the door of Miss King's little terraced house, and wait. The street is quiet. Daffodils are already pushing up in the tiny front garden.

I knock again. The front room curtains are almost closed. There's a bit of privet between her garden and next door's.

I knock again. This time I hear a sound and then see a blue shape through the stained-glass panes in the door. A cooing voice, apologising. Blurred hands grope behind the glass. At last she finds the door handle and lets me in.

She has an attractive, mobile face, with brown eyes and rosy cheeks. Her sparse grey hair is parted in the middle and twirled into a loose bun at the back. Her speech and manner betray a careful upbringing; only when she's excited does she drop her aitches and say "done" for "did".

She ushers me into the back room. The walls are a dull ochre colour, the floor is covered with brown lino with a pattern of small flowers round the edges and there's a carpet, worn and threadbare, in the middle. The room is crammed with furniture: a table in the centre, another against one wall with a Thirties style wireless; a glass-fronted bookcase, four dining room chairs, a Windsor chair in a corner, a bed and a commode; and apart from the door we have entered, there is another to the kitchen. The light is dim; the window looks out onto a narrow passage and a garden beyond. There's a jagged hole in the greyish ceiling, and a new electric light hanging from it. And there's a new electric fire in the grate.

"That was done years ago," she tells me. "I had all gaslights till then, and a coal fire."

"Really?"

"Yes. They said I was the last person in the area to get electricity. I went away and stayed with my nephew while they did the work. I wish now I'd stayed here. What those men got up to I do not know. But I believe they stood on my chairs, instead of using a ladder. Look."

They're Victorian chairs, quite nicely carved; but the oil cloth seats sag, and the webbing underneath is broken and hangs down.

"They're quite old, aren't they?"

"Well dear, my mother got them when they married. And I was born in 1898, when my mother was forty-two. So I suppose they are old. But they were perfectly all right when I went away to my nephew's. But when I came home – she spreads her hands.

"Have you lived long in this house?"

"Since 1917. You see my father, he ran a dairy in North London, in Islington. Because his brother, he ran the farm, near Aylesbury, and my father, he sold the milk from the farm, you see. But the War put a stop to all that. My father, he got called up, and so were both my brothers, although my mother was blind."

"Why was she blind? Was she born blind?"

Miss King takes a breath: I have deflected her onto another of her narrations.

"My mother never saw me. I was born five years after she lost her sight. Atrophy of the optic nerve," she says, enunciating carefully. She sighs, and returns to the previous topic. "So of course, she couldn't run the business, but that made no difference to *them*. Both boys were called up, as well as my father, so of course we had to give up the dairy and we came down here, to be near my aunt, who had that shop along the road."

"The Pakistani one?"

"That's the one, dear. That was my aunt's, once. When the war was over, there seemed no point going back to London – good job too, wasn't it, we didn't have to suffer through the Blitz and all that, you see. My father was an invalid – so we stayed here. My fiancé, he was killed in the war. I'll show you his photograph, if you like."

172

She leads me into the front room. It's tiny. And an antique deal-er's dream. It's crammed with little tables and tapestry chairs, an ornate piano, two chaises longues, and the fireplace has a ceil-ing-high mantelpiece, all little shelves and mirrors. Every hori-zontal surface is covered with knick-knacks and framed photo-graphs, and there are huge framed pictures on the walls. All the vases, candlesticks, little boxes and bowls are in tip-top condition, clean and dust-free - mementoes of a settled existence. But the faded floral wallpaper has jagged circular holes either side of the overman-tel, where gaslights were ripped out; a naked bulb dangles from a white flex in the ceiling.

In the corner opposite the door, on a bamboo table, stands a doll. She's protected by a glass dome. She's at least two feet high, pink and podgy-faced, with blonde ringlets, a frilly white dress, and a fairy wand in one hand; tinsel wings on her back. She looks brand new. She reminds me of my Danish doll, Karen.

"She was given me at a Sunday School Christmas party when I was eight years old. I thought I wasn't getting anything. All the other children's names were called out, and they went up to get their presents, all except me." Her face expresses the misery of that moment. "Then they put a ladder up by the Christmas tree and they said: Florence King! So I went up, and they gave me the fairy doll from the top of the Christmas tree!" She clasps her hands. "She was too big for me to carry, and my brother Tom, he was five years older than me, he had to carry her home for me. And some of the people on the road, they laughed at him and said Look at that boy carrying a doll! And my brother Tom, he turned round and he said: Mind your own business!" She chuckles at that defiance, two World Wars ago. "Mind your own business," she repeats, turning her head in imita-tion of her brother, and scowling. "As I already had seven dolls to play with, my father, he said: 'We'll keep this one, and she can be for your little girl to play with, one day.' But, it was not to be."

She picks up a photo from the piano. "This was my fiancé, on his last leave." A sturdy young man, standing in a suburban garden. "Oh, War's so cruel!" she exclaims with sudden passion. "Cruel, wicked, pointless, war is! They all sit round a conference table afterwards - so why not before, instead of letting all those young men get killed! It's so cruel. So cruel!" She spreads out her arms with clenched fists.

I agree with her. "However," I say, "I'm not paid to listen to you. I'm supposed to be getting you lunch, because there are no Meals-on-Wheels today. What would you like?"

"Well, I don't know. What do you think, dear?"

"What have you got?"

"Well, there's a bit of cold chicken left over from yesterday...."

"Where is it?"

"Well, I expect it's in the kitchen."

She leads me through the back room to the kitchen, where a gleaming new electric cooker stands beside a Victorian grange. The walls and ceiling are yellow from smoke.

"Is this where you cook?"

"Oh no dear. We used to, when we first came here. But now I've got a gas cooker."

She leads me through to an even colder area by the door to the garden. Here is the lavatory and, on the right, the scullery, which still has a copper built into one corner, a stone sink, and a gaunt old gas cooker. The walls are flaking with damp. There's only one tap, with cold water. The small window is broken.

"They had to break that window to get in. Ten hours I lay on the floor. I couldn't get up. I was afraid to pull myself up by the table, in case it fell on top of me. I kept calling Joan, but she didn't hear me. And then next morning when she knocked and I didn't answer, she called the police, and they went round the back and broke this window to get in. They thought I'd had a - what's it called?"

"A stroke?"

"That's right. But I don't think I had. I'd just got so cold, lying there all night. They took me to hospital. Three weeks they kept me in. But there was no need to keep me in all that time. I'm perfectly all right now … "

"Now where's that chicken?"

"Well dear, I thought it was out here."

She pokes at the heap of old paper bags on top of the copper; we search the table in the kitchen, the narrow pantry; but all we find is some potatoes.

"So would you like some potato?"

"Yes, yes I would."

"Have you got a potato peeler?"

"Yes, dear, it's here somewhere," she replies, peering into the pantry, searching the table, the copper in the scullery, then we proceed to the back room and open a drawer in the table, where a few pieces of cutlery are wrapped in paper bags held in place with elastic bands.

"Well, I don't know where it's got to. Perhaps we can find a sharp knife for you. There was one here, I know."

But it's not to be found.

"Well, there was one here, I know. It had lost its handle, but it was lovely and sharp. But while I was in hospital, my nephew and his wife, they were here. They must have taken it."

So I peel the potato with a blunt knife and put it to boil on the gas cooker. There's a knock at the front door, and in comes Joan from next door: a large, energetic woman of about sixty.

"Oh Joan, where's that bit of chicken from yesterday? We can't find it anywhere."

"I'm not surprised. It's in my fridge. I'll go and get it for you. Now have you been on the commode?"

"Yes, I have, but I only - I mean, you know, I haven't been, except for -"

"You'd better have some of them prunes then."

Joan comes out into the kitchen, where I'm mashing the potato.

She pushes some old paper bags into a bin.

"Don't ever let her see a paper bag," she grumbles. "Throw them away, or she'll only go and wrap up something else."

But Miss King has sharp ears. "It keeps things nice and clean and dry if you wrap them up."

*

Mrs Moody's house is one of those detached red brick ones you sometimes see on Building Society advertisements being carried like an umbrella by a respectable couple. It's expensive. It's boring. It's dead. Even the garden is dead, with black conifers, a washing line, and a lawn as trim as a businessman's moustache. Traffic hurtles by on the dual carriageway.

I bang on the door and wait. As instructed, I keep on banging, and at last she opens it. She's a stout little woman, wearing an apron and slippers; her glasses vastly increase the size of her blue eyes, which stare out at you like fish in a glass bowl. She would be totally boring, were it not for endearing streaks of lunacy in her speech. Her windows are dirty because of *the galloping whatsits* on the road. She replaces most nouns with *whatsits* or *what you may call its* or *thing-umajig* - rather like Mrs Skewton in Dickens' *Dombey and Son* - it's like a long riddle and rouses my guessing instincts. But soon I real-ise that she's only talking about domestic things like rags torn from old towels - all these old ladies seem to be obsessed with rags: they have to be washed and dried and kept in special places, for special purposes; they are examined and discussed - and remembered. She didn't get on with her previous Home Help because she wasted her time talking. It takes Mrs Moody eight minutes by the kitchen clock to tell me this. Another twelve minutes are given up to the epic of the shoes she once bought which had a nail in one of them.

Her house is perfectly clean, apart from fluff on the spectacu-larly ugly carpets, which none of the five vacuum cleaners can suck up. The heavy furniture - all matching - is of dark, varnished wood with three fat flat fingers of wood at intervals by way of ornament.

"My hubby will be home soon for his lunch," she says. I'm puzzled. I'd been told she was a widow, and that her son-in-law and daughter live nearby, and wondered why this sturdy, well-to-do woman needs a Home Help. But if she is expecting her husband - well, all is not well and she may need help of some kind.

*

Miss King is having great difficulty opening her front door.

"I *am* sorry to keep you waiting like this. I don't know what's the matter with it. I can't seem to find the - "

Through the stained glass I watch her hands moving about like butterflies caught indoors in winter. At last they move away from the hinges and she gets hold of the Yale knob and the door handle, but still the door doesn't open and her cooing becomes more and more distressed. Perhaps her sight is failing.

"Oh dear I don't know - I'm turning both the handles at the same time but - "

At last she succeeds and greets me with a smile. She hasn't put her dentures in yet and is still in her nightdress; her sparse hair is dishevelled.

"I'm afraid I had a dreadful night, so Joan thought I'd better stay in bed a bit longer. I couldn't manage the commode, so I had to go down to the lavatory -." That would mean down the stairs and into the cold kitchen, down another step to the freezing lavatory, probably in the dark ...

She tries to dress. Her huge knickers bewilder her. She puts both legs into one knicker-leg; catches her nightdress as she hoists it up; can't get her nightdress over her head - so I abandon the broom and dress her, which transports me mentally to my childhood, dressing my big doll Karen. As this occurs to me, she chuckles and says "This reminds me of the time when I was a little girl and my mother used to dress me."

At last it's done. I comb out her hair.

"What would you like me to do now?"

"Whatever you think best, dear."

Her good manners make it impossible for her to answer directly; but her eyes stray to the table, where her pension book is lying.

"Shall I fetch your pension for you?"

"Well, that would be very kind, dear, if you could manage it."

I study the instructions. "You have to sign on the back here, look, and here." But this is enormously difficult for her. Carefully, she places her second initial an inch below the first.

"Let me find your glasses for you."

"I don't need them. I can see perfectly," she assures me, while the upright stroke of the K floats away high above the dotted line, its arm plummets way below, and its leg is almost off the paper. Then comes a crabbed *ing*, slanting sharply downwards. The dot of the i is carefully placed over the n.

However, no questions are asked at the Post Office, and when I return she counts the money and puts it into an envelope, which is put into another envelope, secured with an elastic band, and tucked into one of her handbags.

*

Whenever I enter Mrs Proctor's flat, I first look across at the lamp-lit piano stool. The five tiny figures on it aren't soldiers: they're chubby little children, in smocks. One is damaged: a portion of the left side has broken away. It's hollow.

I hang up my coat and report for duty. She's in the kitchen; I'm to help her prepare food. Very strange food. She first clutches my arm and gesticulates at the cupboard. I open it, with difficulty in the narrow space, and she points at some jars on a shelf. She appears to be speechless today. I take out one jar after the other: she screeches furiously when I take a wrong one. Finally she is satisfied with the four on the table. Then she points imperiously at a bottle of

Vermouth on the floor. I pass it to her. She rejects it, and indicates that I'm to open it and pour some into a pudding bowl. I do so. She tosses her head. I pour in more, and more; there's at least a quarter of a pint before she nods. Then I have to add three quarters of a teaspoon of ground hazel nuts; a spoonful of horseradish; a spoonful of sauerkraut; and a spoonful of blackcurrant jam. Whenever I hesitate, she hisses furiously. Next I'm to put six olives on a plate.

At this point we're interrupted by the arrival of the doctor - a large, breezy, blowsy man. Immediately she collapses on her bed, apparently dead, or at least swooning. She looks like a baroque Pieta, tragic, exhausted, limp.

"Well now Tabita, and how are we today?"

"Oh-oh-oh," she moans. She opens her eyes and sees me standing in the doorway. "Go away! Go away!"

I retreat into the drawing room. I look at the photographs. Several show a young woman in elegant thirties-style clothes, with weary Greta Garbo eyes, wide cheekbones, flared nostrils: Yes, it is she. The discipline she imposed on herself to achieve who knows what success she had in music, in society - in her life - has now shrunk to her frustrated battling with this flat, her clothes, her food; and its force is directed at anyone who enters her sphere, like myself, whom she tries to use as a tool, as an extension of her will.

The doctor comes lolloping in. He is probably not a tool.

"I shouldn't take too much notice of anything she says," he tells me, loudly enough for her to hear. "If she had her way I'd be here morning, noon and night."

"She told me she had an ulcer in her mouth."

"She hasn't. There really isn't anything much wrong with her. Nothing anyone can do anything about, anyway."

"Ought I perhaps to know your telephone number, in case - "

"Oh, I don't think so. She's forever ringing us, or getting people to ring us for her, but really, there's no need."

He isn't really callous, I suppose. He's just tired of her and her demands. I know how he feels already, after a few days – and he's probably been dealing with her for years.

He breezes out, his unbuttoned mackintosh knocking over an arrangement of dried flowers. I start picking it up.

"No! No!" she shrieks, glaring at me. "Not yet!" Summoning all her self control, to deal with an idiot like me, she rumbles: "First, you take, here – take –" she gestures at a plastic carrier bag on the floor. I pick it up.

"Wait!" she shrieks. "Why you don't wait?"

I put it down again. She clutches her head in silence. After a while, she starts rummaging in her bed.

"I can't find it," she snarls.

At last her fingers close on a small plastic box. It's empty. She points at a small heap of toothpicks on a bookcase just out of her reach. I hand them to her.

"NO!"

I turn to put them back.

"NO! Give!"

I hand them to her again. She takes three and puts them in the plastic box with unsteady hands.

"Here! In Tosh!"

I hesitate.

"In TOSH! TOSH!! TOSH!!!"

Perhaps she's saying *Tasche*, German for *bag,* so I pick up the plastic bag again and put the toothpick container into it.

"Here! Give! Show!"

I hold the carrier bag open for her. It already contains a new mouli-sieve, a packet of Ryvita, and a torn bath mat. She examines them critically, then rummages in her bed again until she finds half of an old Christmas card and a pen. She begins writing, with great difficulty, and quite illegibly, while Radio 3 booms out a sombre symphony. She asks me a question which I don't understand. Perhaps she wants to know the word for toothpicks, so I tell her, but she shakes her head. I try the German, *Zahnstocher,* but no, that isn't what she wants either. Then I write the word for her on an old envelope in big letters and hold it close to her eyes. And she smiles: a seraphic smile, a smile that belongs in the other room, with the lamplight by the open piano. Then she writes again, head bowed. She is almost bald, her scraggy neck reminds me of newly hatched bird fallen out of its nest.

At last the heterogeneous collection is complete to her satisfaction.

"Take now."

"Where to?"

"Take! Go! Take tosh!"

"But where?"

"Meeses Seemons."

"Mrs Simmons. But where does she live?"

"You know house Meeses Seemons?"

I shake my head. She closes her eyes and leans back, summoning great concentration.

"Go out my house. Over road. LEFT. Main Road. MAIN ROAD!"

She opens her eyes and looks at me expectantly.

"I'm to go to the main road," I say, dutifully.

Satisfied, she closes her eye again to aid her thinking.

"Crrross. Go straight. Ees one hotel. You go LEFT. Ees blue portals. Portals. Blue, Open. If not open, hook, hook, up, you see, eef leedle boy, then hook. Go in."

"And – then?"

"Geef. Meeses Seemons. Geef tosh."

"Er – I see … "

"Come back immediately!!"

I go. I find the blue gate, closed with a hook, and a little boy playing in the garden. Mrs Simmons turns out to be a young woman. She sighs as she looks into the carrier and shakes her head over the scribbled bits of Christmas card.

"I can't read this. I'll have to go and see her again. I can't go now

- my husband is practising." Someone is playing a piano in the next room: a Schubert Impromptu. "She used to be his teacher."

"Really?"

"Oh yes. It's very sad to see the state she's in now. But she really is very demanding. I expect you find her so. I only bought her this Ryvita yesterday. Wonder what's wrong with it."

"D'you mind me asking – but I find her so difficult to understand. What is her language? Russian? German?"

"She used to speak excellent English, but she seems to have forgotten most of it. She's from Estonia, actually, but she's lived in England since before the war. She used to do our gardening for us."

"Your gardening?"

"Yes, she's a wonderful gardener. In fact she was very remarkable all round – always so smart, even just going round to the shops she always looked a picture; and when she went up to London she was really super. She belonged to the Embassy set. We have to remember all that when she's being trying. It must be worse for you."

I return to Mrs Proctor, and give her her Vermouth soup. She opens her mouth, and again I'm reminded of a bird as I spoon it in.

*

"That's my father."

I'm dusting the ornate frame of the big picture over Miss King's piano. It's an oil painting of a thickset young man with a very low forehead and a snub nose.

"And that's my mother."

She indicates a full-length picture on the wall near the door. This one is so darkened with age it's impossible to distinguish anything.

"She was eighteen when that was done."

"What year was that, then?"

"Well, now, I'm not sure … "

"How old did you say she was when you were born?"

"Forty-two. I was the baby of the family."

"And you were born in 1898. So what's 1898 minus 24?"

"I never was any good at sums."

"Nor was I."

We laugh, and I go on dusting the crowded little museum. There's another huge picture to the left of the fireplace. The frame is made of metal, with embossed flowers – but the picture is almost completely black.

"Can you see what it is?" she asks.

I peer at it from every angle and can just distinguish a little girl in a calf-length frock and pinafore, holding an enormous doll.

"It's you, isn't it! And is that the doll you're holding?"

"Yes! That's me, when I was eight years old!"

It's like a reversal of *The Picture of Dorian Gray*: the doll, pink and podgy and perfect under the glass dome with her frilly white dress and tinsel wings; the photo – a blur. But Miss King, clasping her hands and smiling with pleasure, is still, despite her wrinkles and grey hair, the baby of the family, the nice little girl who was chosen to receive the best Sunday School Christmas present of all.

She picks up a small silver frame from one of the low tables: a snapshot of a young man in army uniform.

"My fiancé. Just after I took this photo, we went and visited one of his friends in hospital. And he'd had both his arms shot off. It was so horrible. I just didn't know what to do when he held up the stump of his right arm to, you know, shake hands. I couldn't do it. I just couldn't touch it. And why did that handsome young fellow have to be crippled like that? What good ever come of that war? None. None whatsoever." Her eyebrows curl in anger, and her hands spread out in a gesture that is becoming familiar.

Joan comes in with a cup of tea for Miss King. She brings one every morning. She has lived next door from birth. Until I started coming, Joan was doing everything for Miss King, and she still does a great deal. Miss King is very indebted to her – but there's an undercurrent of irritation. Joan is always in a hurry, Miss King complains.

And she is. She is a busy, vigorous woman. She dashes out noisily after a few words.

"You see," says Miss King. "She's spilt a little. She always does, every day. She always puts it down on the table cloth just as it is. That's why it gets stained, you see."

However, Joan also washes the table cloth, and goes shopping for her ("Oh yes, Joan loves spending money …") and cooks for her at weekends, when there are no Meals-on-Wheels. But –

"Look at this letter. It's quite clearly addressed to me, yet Joan has just ripped it open."

"Perhaps she thought you couldn't read."

"Couldn't read! Really!"

"I'm sure she means well."

"Oh yes, I'm sure she does. But I do wish she'd let me decide for myself sometimes. And there's another thing. Where's my cow?"

"Your cow?"

"We used to have this cream jug in the shape of a cow."

"Did the milk come out of her udders?"

"No dear! What an idea! The milk came out of her mouth, of course, and you poured it in through a hole in her back with a little lid. And she always stood on the mantelpiece in the front room, on the middle shelf at the top. But since I've come out of hospital I can't find her."

"Have you asked Joan?"

"Yes. And she says she's probably locked away upstairs, to keep her safe."

"Shall I go and have a look?"

"You can't dear. The door's locked, and Joan's got the key."

"Well surely you can ask her for the key."

"I have, many times. But she always *forgets* it." She gives me a dark look. "I've got quite a lot of interesting things up there. And it's my belief some of them may be missing. And Joan would prefer me not to look."

"I can't believe it!"

"Well dear, why does she always forget the key?"

"Look – I'll go and get it from her now, then we can go and have a look together."

"Oh no dear. I don't want to upset her. I should think she's quite upset already. I had the top of the milk with my Weetabix this morning. Lovely! I don't often get the top. Joan has it."

"Are you sure?"

"Well, why else has the cream always gone when I get the milk out of the pantry?"

*

Some tiny, brightly coloured objects have appeared on Tabita's piano stool by the figures. While I scrabble around with the wretched little hoover under her watchful eye, I peer at them. They are minute cotton flowers, possibly snipped out of a piece of embroidered braid.

What does she do in her *salon* all day when she's alone, with these tiny dolls and flowers? The same music manuscript paper has been on the piano all the time; the artistic arrangement of dried grasses and seed pods, too, perhaps a little dustier. Occasionally a leaf falls from an evergreen plant. Someone has brought her some geraniums; they are beginning to grow straggly. But the sitting room, the *salon*, is a sanctuary – as is Miss King's front room – and nothing mundane is allowed in it, certainly not an ironing board. Today, however, I pick up a big book lying on the floor by the white linen two-seater sofa. It's a Russian-Latin dictionary. How I wish she would talk to me about her real interests. But she sees me only as a feckless servant to be kept up to the mark by glaring looks, barked commands and a threateningly raised hand.

I realise she's been quiet for some time, and look across at her, sitting in her bed, fiddling with something small. She looks up, and quite politely asks me to open a small gold wrist watch. But the actual watch has been replaced with one of the little cotton flowers.

She indicates a small gold medallion, engraved with a star of David. I put this into the watch case and close it. She holds out her wrist, and I put it on for her. Then she actually thanks me with a deep rumbling voice, and gives me one of her rare beatific smiles, glancing down happily at her timeless watch.

*

Mrs Moody opens the door for me with the words – "Oh there you are, I thought so. I said to my hubby what day was it she come last week – you know – was it Thursday – but he didn't answer".

She stares at me, her huge blue eyes unblinking behind the convex glasses.

"Didn't say a word. I keep thinking this what-you-may-call it here, it just seems like there's someone there, just behind me. Do you get that feeling? Just there, behind me. Don't know who it is, but he disappears when I turn round."

"I expect it's your glasses, some sort of reflection," I say as cheerfully as I can, and hurry upstairs to run the noisy Hoover ineffectually over her hideous carpets. She sleeps, evidently, in the marital bed: Neville Shute, in paperback, open, face down, on the bedside table one side; Dorothy Cookson on the other. For how long has the Neville Shute lain there, where Mr Moody put it down for the last time?

She is haunted, not only by the figure out of sight behind her right shoulder. When I come down backwards, sweeping the beetroot red stair carpet, she says –

"Did you hear someone?"

"No. I can't hear anyone when the vacuum cleaner's on."

"Oh."

I try to divert her attention by asking about the table in the entrance hall. It's encrusted with carvings; the legs are elongated elephants, with tusks.

"This is a very unusual table."

"Yes. It's from – wherever it is –"

"India?"

"That's it, India. I went with him."

"Really? You've been to India?"

"Yes, well, I said, if you're going, well, why not me?"

"Quite."

"I told him it was pointless. I mean, they don't eat them things over there. They has other things. But he would have it, so, well –"

"What things?"

"You know, little, what d'you call them?"

"Nuts?"

"No no, not nuts. My hubby was in the trade, oh, you know the things, for kiddies, like."

"Sweets?"

"Well, you could call it that, only, what's the word?"

"Confectionary?"

"That's it, confectionary. So he, well, he thought he could start it up in thingummy."

"India?"

"Yes. Only, I said, I told him from the start, it's stupid. The cost – oh!" She laughs. "But he – he would have it. So I said, well, if you're going, well, why should I, sort of, nothing to do, so – "

"Quite. I don't blame you. I'd love to go to India!"

"Ye-es, well –" She's staring over my shoulder. I look round at the lavatory door.

"See?"

"What?"

"The door. It sort of moved. And I thought I heard a sort of, sort of click."

"You think there's someone in there?"

"I don't know…"

"Shall I look?"

"Well, but, if he is in there – "

I go to the door, and find it is bolted on the outside. I show her.

"So there can't possibly be anyone in there, can there?"

She clearly isn't convinced, her magnified blue eyes gaze at the door. So I open it.

"See?"

"It's these glasses," she says, tapping the rim.

"I'll do the dining room now, shall I?"

She shuffles into the room ahead of me. It's very big, with heavy black furniture. Spuriously leaded windows overlook the bleak garden.

"I've been trying to get him to sort out these," she says, showing me a pile of brochures, bills, invoices: the top one, for a lawn mower, bears a date more than five years ago.

"That's no use to you," I say. "It's years out of date. Why don't you throw it away?"

"That's what I said. "Throw it away, I said. Throw them all away, they're no use. But he won't. Won't even answer me." Her big eyes swim to me. "Sits there by the hour, going through them - what's-its. Throw them away, I say, they're no good; put them in the bin." She gives me another baffled stare. "Why won't he speak to me? He doesn't. Not one word."

She shrugs her shoulders and starts going through the documents again herself, muttering.

*

I'm sitting on a low stool, or maybe the floor, hugging my knees, in Miss King's kitchen, and looking at the fireplace which has replaced the old black range: a brick fireplace, open to the ceiling; a bright fire burning. A young man has been hanged in the open space above the fire. His curly head lolls on his left shoulder. He dangles to and fro slightly on the rope round his neck. His khaki clothes catch a rosy glow from the flames where they're crumpled.

A stout woman is kneeling on the right side of the fireplace, brushing the hearth with a shiny brass brush. And she's talking to the young man. She seems to think he's sitting in the chair on the other side of the hearth.

I'm only a child. I want to draw the woman's attention to the fact that he isn't sitting in the chair, but hanging above the fire, dead. But I can't speak out to correct my elders and betters, so I whisper: *where is he?*

At the same moment I realise he's no longer there. The flue is clean and empty. I begin rocking backwards and forwards.

Where is he? Where is he? Where is he? I whisper through clenched teeth. Other voices join in, more and more, hissing *Where is he? Where is he? Where is he?* Louder and louder.

But the woman kneeling by the hearth, brushing and brushing with her brass-bound brush, doesn't notice.

Now a deep-throated voice joins in, like a big bell tolling through the jangle of whispers: Where? Where? Where?

Then I realize that the deep voice is coming out of my own throat, and I wake up sobbing.

*

"This was the last present I ever had from my fiancé. Go on, open it," says Miss King. Inside the little box is a gold wrist watch. "And it's always kept perfect time."

"But it's stopped. Shall I wind it up for you?"

"Oh no dear. What time does it say?"

"It says ten past four."

"Then I'll wait till it's ten past four and then I'll wind it up."

"But why? Why not set it?"

"I never change the setting of a watch or a clock."

"Why ever not?"

"I don't know why. I just never do. My mother was the same."

I notice that the mantelpiece clock is ten minutes fast.

"I know it is. I go by Big Ben on the radio."

"And you won't set that either?"

"No dear. I'll wait till it stops. Then I'll try to catch it at the right moment and wind it up again."

I start cleaning the lino round the edges of the room. Suddenly, as I pick up a box full of empty paper bags in the dark corner by the kitchen door, Miss King is at my side.

"He's still there, then."

"Who?"

"Why, the cat of course."

"What cat?"

"There, on the floor. Can't you see him? He's looking straight at you."

"You're joking. There's no cat there."

I put the box back, and she chuckles.

"You've just put the box on top of him. He won't like that!"

I lift it up again. "Look. There's nothing there. Feel with your hand."

"No thank you. He might scratch me."

I run my hand over the floor where her gaze is fixed.

"Why can't I feel him, or see him, or anything, if he's there."

"He's probably gone under my bed now."

I look into her eyes, and she smiles with superior knowledge.

*

Tabita's sitting up in bed, telephoning, her glasses askew on her nose.

"I vish to speak with Meester Hamilton, please," she shouts, with a guttural H. Meester Hamilton! Is dental surgery, yes? Please, you tell me, what ees number dental surgery Meester Hamilton? You in phone box? You look in book, you tell me number dental surgery? Thangyou. Thangyou very much. You phone back soon yes, please."

She puts the phone down on, presumably, a bewildered passer-by who heard a phone ring in a kiosk.

There are three little cotton flowers on the bed. She appears to be quite exhausted and leans back with her eyes shut. The radio is tuned to a Brandenburg Concerto.

Suddenly, she seizes my arm.

"In kitchen."

I nod.

"On floor."

I nod again.

On kitchen floor. Ees ball."

I look into the kitchen, and see a plastic bowl full of wet washing on the floor.

"Heavy," she says, with her guttural H. "Poot - whole - in - in -"

"In the sink?"

She nods, eye shut. Then, in sepulchral tones, she cries "Press!"

Slowly the simple instructions emerge. The washing is to be wrung out, then hung on the line. And the kitchen floor is to be cleaned with the soapy water - and *cotton wool* from the bathroom.

When I return from the garden, she's on the phone again.

"Meester Hamilton!"

She starts tugging at the mat on the floor beside her bed with one hand. Trying to tell me to pick up the mat while summoning the dentist causes a mental short circuit, with meaningless yelps at me and into the phone. I disengage and go into the bathroom to gather up the torn bath mat and the toilet seat cover, and into the kitchen to pick up the small rug and carpet remnants. Meanwhile she's got into her stride on the phone.

"I am in great bain! Please you say Meester Hamilton come soon! But soon! Soon!"

She starts tugging at the mat on the floor beside her bed with one hand. With my assortment of rugs I head for the garden, but am held back as I pass her bed. In relatively mellow and coherent terms, she describes how I am to take the bedside mat as well, brush them all in the garden, sweep up the leaves on the patio with the broom outside the back door, and bring in a jug of rainwater.

The only brush I can find is a nail brush. Still, I go, and brush the wretched little mats with the wretched little nail brush, sweep up the leaves, and find the tub of rain water and the jug. I do everything exactly as instructed. I don't want to be shouted at. But I take my time. Rehearsing in my mind my self-justification, I enjoy the mild November weather, the sunshine, my momentary freedom - and feel at one with slaves and servants down the ages. Reluctantly, I return.

She's got the TV on. The muzak accompanying the programme assorts ill with the Wagnerian singing now on the radio, but she seems to be oblivious to this. I tell her that there's now just half an hour of my time left. Perhaps this is the cause of the mounting hysteria that now sets in.

"Potch!" she shouts.

I don't understand.

"Potch! POTCH! MY POTCH!!"

I look round helplessly for a clue to her meaning. "Vot you don't vont?" She heaves herself out of her bed. Leaning on me and her stick, she totters slowly out of the flat to the front door. At last I understand: I'm to sweep the *porch* with - ah! - with the broom I was using behind the house earlier. Fine. I do so, and return with seven minutes left.

"My floor! Kitchen! In my kitchen!"

"I have cleaned the kitchen floor." She looks at me suspiciously. I have replaced the rug and the carpet remnant - and the lavatory seat cover - exactly where I found them.

"Valise! Koffer!" she gasps, leaning over precariously and prodding at a battered Gladstone bag under the table with her stick. I shift it.

"You not clean there!"

"I did."

"With?"

"With cotton wool from the bath room."

"But look! Ees not clean!"

And there indeed where her walking stick points accusingly is a fragment of cotton wool. I pick it up. I note a new bottle of Vermouth in the corner, three quarters full. And now it's precisely twelve thirty, and I tell her so. I fetch my time sheet for her to sign.

"And vile I sign," she quavers, "you - here, here -" and she indicates the chaos of medicine bottles, brush and comb, papers, crammed onto the tiny bedside table with the ballerina lamp and the phone book.

"No," I say.

"Vile I sign."

"No. My time's up."

"Then if not for job, then for the" - she rolls her eyes up to the ceiling, like St John on Patmos - "then for love" - she points up with my biro - "love of God!"

I laugh, and shake my head. She flings my pen across the room, screws up my time sheet. I retrieve them hastily, while she booms - "Then Take your things! Go! Go! You - *SLUT*! And never return!"

I find I'm shaking as I leave.

*

Miss King is being dressed by Joan when I arrive. Today is wash-day, so Joan has fetched clean clothes - from the room upstairs, that is always locked?

After Joan has gone, Miss King bashfully indicates that she wants to use the commode, so I leave her. Perhaps the room has been left unlocked? I go up the steep stairs, the wallpaper beside it represents cracked blocks of stone. The front bedroom is locked, but the back room is open. It contains a wrought iron bedstead adorned with brass flowers, and a Victorian wash stand, complete with bowl and ewer. There is a third bedroom. Part of the ceiling has come down; plaster dust covers innumerable sacks and boxes.

I go back down, and find Miss King deeply troubled. She can't

Home helper

get her skirt up; and she can't get her knickers down from her vest. I help her, and she approaches the commode.

"I can't remember what to do next," she laments. She's holding the two arms of the commode, looking down at the cover over the seat.

"Well, first I think you'd better take this off," I suggest

"Oh yes, of course." She takes hold of the edges, but can't lift it. I show her how to tilt it. Then there's a lid on the chamber pot. She manages that after a while. Still she stands, leaning over it, muttering unhappily to herself.

"Now you'll have to turn round."

"That's it!"

She turns, cautiously. I place her hands on the arms of the commode.

"Now you sit down."

"What, like this?"

"Yes, that's right."

This is disorientation, not knowing which way to face. At last she's seated.

"Look out of the window," I suggest. "Remember you've got to be looking out of the window before you sit down."

"I'll try to remember, dear."

After I've helped her off the commode, and emptied the pot in the lavatory outside, I tell her of my discoveries upstairs.

"Two of the bedrooms are open."

"I know they are. The one above here is where my dear mother lay during her last illness. Eight years I nursed her, till she died. She couldn't get out of bed. It wasn't easy. And then, after she'd died, I started getting letters from people - old so-and-so needs looking after, will you come as you know how to - so I thought to myself, aha, so that's how it's going to be, is it? But I thought - I don't want to spend the rest of my life like that. So that's when I went and got myself the job in the sweet shop. Best thing I ever done." She gives me a small triumphant look. "But the front bedroom, that's still locked, isn't it? That's where all my treasures are. There's a fur coat in there. Or there *was.*" Her eyes are black with suspicion.

"Oh Miss King, I'm sure Joan wouldn't –"

"I don't know what to think. I'd like to go and have a look. But Joan won't let me have the key. She says I couldn't manage the stairs." She spreads her hands, stiff fingered, doll-like. "Lots of things I don't know where they are. Where are my wine glasses? Where's my cow? I'd like to know!"

"Well, have you asked Joan?"

"She's always in such a hurry … "

I brush her carpet and shake the hearth rug out in the back garden. I return to find her staring out of the window.

"See them?"

"Who?"

"Why, the men. Over there, look."

She points to the tree tops above the roofs of the houses.

"I can't see any men."

"Well, they're there. With their horses."

"You mean in those trees?"

"By them."

"What are they doing?"

"They're just standing there, looking at us."

"I can't see them."

She gives me a pitying look.

"I always did have exceptionally good eyesight," she says, primly.

*

Scrabbling around on the floor beside my bed in the morning twilight among books and boxes of tissues I am reminded of Tabita scrabbling despairingly among the bits and pieces accumulated in and around her bed. Will someone watch me one day, as I watch her, rather coldly, rather impatiently, trying to guess my purpose, which

I keep forgetting? And will I throw up defences for my crumbling
self-respect, as she does, by hurling imprecations at some would-be
helper who fails to answer my needs?

Chapter 10: Japan

When my son Tom, after getting his degree in Cambridge, went to Japan to teach English, I was less than enthusiastic. The horrors of banzai charges, kamikaze and mass suicides at the end of the war had filled me with horror. Otherwise, what did I know about the Japanese? Very little - nothing very enticing. Short in stature, rather like Chinese - humble - self-denying, toiling - a bit ant-like in their obedience, willing to die for their emperor - or their country - or the dream of an empire - scornful of other nations - with a terrible writing which it would take years to learn - artists and musicians equally esoteric. I had heard - with horror - of hara-kiri, when a samurai would *disembowel* himself in public.

In due course Tom met and married Kazuko - with a celebration in Oxford at which she and Liz and Jackie wore traditional Japanese garments which struck me as being impractical and stiff and complicated and not very beautiful. When we went to visit Tom and Kazuko, I got to know more about the Japanese way of life - the absence of chairs, everything happening at floor level - getting *down* to go to bed, *kneeling* at little tables which after the meal were stowed away in big wall cupboards along with the futons and everything else ... People's short bent legs were surely caused by this lifelong kneeling ... And the insistence on removing your shoes and putting on slippers when you came in to a house - I soon got into the habit of doing this and introduced the custom back in Britain - I still observe it now.

A couple of years later, in 1989, Kazuko was having a difficult pregnancy, and Tom asked us to go and stay with them for a while - she had no available relatives. They lived in a huge block of flats - a "mansion" - called "Gyotoku New Grand Heights". Their flat had a narrow balcony which was also the way to the staircase. Occasionally we could see Mount Fuji in the distance - it was usually veiled in mist and clouds. But one evening when we came home from an outing at twilight, we turned at the front door to see that sacred mountain looming enormously before us. A trick of the light?

Lying on my futon one morning I was startled to see my kimono, that had been hanging on the door, tilt sideways for a time before returning to the vertical. When I told Tom and Kazuko about it, they said it was *just a minor earthquake*! Nothing to worry about! Happens all the time! And indeed, we did gradually get used to them.

One morning there was some shouting outside. The whole huge building - 12 storeys high - was to be repainted, and the foreman was telling us that today, scaffolding was being put up. All day long mammoth cranes hoisted the components up, to be slotted together by helmeted workmen wearing baggy plus-fours with belts crammed with tools and special boots with a split between the big toe and the rest of the foot. Then some sort of green plastic was draped over the scaffolding.

David wrote this poem:

FACE-LIFT

It is the day of the spidermen.
They are legging it all over the grey façade
of our battle-cruiser apartment block
wearing a light Meccano shroud ...
their intentions are thought to be friendly.
They trot outside our third-floor windows
like feudal pikemen in some lord's livery.
It's as if they'd been drummed from their fields

by some daimyo to storm a castle.
Their breeches hint at horses
left to graze in the car park. Business-like
their cummerbunds bristle with wrenches ...
It's as well their intentions are friendly.

In the midst of all this drama, Jake was born – on October 5th. Now Kazuko started shovelling food into him, convinced he was starving. If he showed signs of unwillingness she would immediately switch to another dish; she had a dozen prepared in readiness. Soon he was extremely fat, but that did not deter her.

The other drama in Tokyo at that time was the slow death of Emperor Hirohito, whose effigy Anne and I had watched being burned. Tom was then a "stringer" for the Daily Mail, and this is what he wrote:

"Who would have thought the old man had so much blood in him?"
(Shakespeare)

It was late September when I took a stroll in the Imperial Palace Gardens, thinking of Emperor Hirohito who lay dying nearby. Here and there people came and went between the manicured lawns and well-groomed shrubs, talking in low tones. There was peace in the air; the last cicadas of summer were sawing in the trees.

It would have been a good time to die, with the old mourners bowing by the imperial gates, with the government bringing the life of the nation to a standstill, with those who loved him and those who hated him holding their breath.

But Hirohito didn't die. The old man hung on, while the days stretched slowly into weeks, a month ... forty days ...

Quite simply, Hirohito has overstayed his welcome. The crowds outside the palace dwindle daily; the local governments close their well-wishers registers as the number of those signing approach zero. It's simply beyond Japanese to keep worrying for so long. Life goes on. Even the public and private organs, which dutifully cancelled anything smacking of fun in the early days of the illness, are quietly resuming business now. At Nakayama the Emperor's Cup, Japan's premier horse race, will run as scheduled tomorrow.

The unexpected length of Hirohito's illness has proved what many of us had long suspected - that feeling for the emperor is not as deeply ingrained in the Japanese consciousness as the domestic and foreign media would have us believe.

*

One sunny October Sunday we took the train out into the country and got off at a small station - it was good to be away from the high-density housing and industry. Two peasants were at work - the man dropping seeds into shallow furrows, and the woman pushing earth over them with her feet. This was typical of the work done by elderly women, often crouching on the ground all bundled up and tending each lettuce, or ginger plant, or *sato-imo* (taro; big leaves and edible tubers). The tangerines are called *mikan* and are very cheap, plentiful and delicious - and so cheap that many orchards are being abandoned. In fact Japanese agriculture is in a parlous state. The victorious Americans broke up the big estates after the war and distributed the land to the peasants. Very laudable. But the produce is expensive, and now Japan is under pressure to import from the USA and other Asian countries. Their rice is the most expensive in the world. Once import restrictions are lifted, the rice farms will probably be abandoned, and most other farms too, and everyone will migrate to the cities.

We visited the Dobashis out in Yamanashi. Mr. Dobashi's first task every morning is to water his bonsais. He has about a hundred of these, each quite different in form and feeling. Some he inherited from his father. He judges and tends them as works of art, intent on a true balance, but not symmetry. It takes at least twenty years to produce a bonsai, and they sell for as much as a million yen. I have mixed feelings about these miniature forest trees - admiration for the skill and patience that produce these emotive and aesthetic plants – but some qualms when I think how this tree has been denied the right to grow and develop naturally. It reminds me of those Chinese women's feet: from an early age little girls suffered agonizing pain as their feet were tightly bound – because large feet were considered ugly... Mr Dobashi also has normal sized trees which are severely pruned to look ornamental. And he showed us an enormous ancient tree at a nearby Shinto shrine, which he measured with a pink string – much to the distraction of some children who were attending a "shichi-go-san" (7-5-3) service. There was a huge stone with a carved inscription dedicated to the earth god, and a ferocious-looking stone guard dog: both had offerings of fruit and rice set out before them.

David and I both got work, and earned a little money, teaching English – while making some unsuccessful attempts to learn Japanese and to understand what was going on. David was a language adviser at Marubeni, a big and powerful trading organization. He got this rather interesting job through a lucky introduction from our next-door neighbour at Gyotoku New Grand Heights. David was fascinated by the calm, courteous atmosphere in the office, and wrote this poem about it:

THE GENTLE MACHINE

Smooth the seconds, smooth the minutes...
the long linctus hours, the soothing days...
The cockcrow commuters march in silence
along the cement-grey station approaches.
Soberly they stand compacted together
in countless trains that rock them softly
into metropolitan darkness,
cotton-gloved drivers crooning the stations,
masseurs of the morning, mothering the movement,

to the high-rise where tender lifts bring Taro and Yuki
to their polished computers. And smooth, smooth
is Yuki's black hair. She's a turned wooden doll.
And smooth, smooth is Taro's chin,
and his grey suit blends with all the rest.
Smooth the seconds, smooth the hours,
The office murmurs, the voices sharpen.
Yuki brings tea which is almost tasteless,
while Taro types letters that bow, bow, bow
before they are folded, and then piped music
when all with lifted arms begin
to sway like pine-trees in a storm.
They're the moving parts of the gentle machine,
that huge smooth gentle machine called Japan
that runs, runs, runs without friction.
A faultless machine where no-one's at fault.
And money's a lubricant (bribes a mere courtesy)
where politicians as twisted as noodles
slip through life lightly, tastelessly, smoothly,
the red-handed bowing, shamed yet comprehended.
And whisky, golf and bargirls attend to
the gentle meshing of a million cogs,
and smoothly, smoothly the subway trains
warm in the womb of the somnolent city
carry their soft-smiling drunkards toppling
home to their wives marooned in their mansions.

Yet anger there must be, and sometimes despair
that turns the workaday dream to horror,
the fear of mayhem in the rebellious earth,
of typhoons thrashing among the power lines,
of Shinto rigour and violence revived.
But all for the moment must bow to the massage,

to the peace of the soft cybernetic machine
that smoothly, smoothly caresses itself
daylong into the diligent night.

(mansions = blocks of flats)

One story that David told us about life at Marubeni must, I feel,
be preserved here. Marubeni was a big, powerful trading house
with branches all over the world. They had close relations with
the governments of various third-world countries, sometimes
of a rather scandalous nature. One of David's jobs was to handle
English-language correspondence with these VIPs. One day a letter
arrived from the king of a small African country, asking whether the
chairman of Marubeni had received the vase he had recently sent
him as a token of his esteem, it being a fine example of his nation's
arts and crafts.

No such vase had been received.

The Marubeni bigwigs were nonplussed. Perhaps they should
tell the king that the vase had sadly not arrived. But would he believe
them? He might think they had lost it, or broken it, and were covering up. He might be mortally offended. In the end they asked David
to write a letter to the king, untruthfully stating that the vase had
indeed arrived and was being displayed prominently at the corpo-
rate headquarters right opposite the Imperial Palace in Tokyo.

David quite enjoyed concocting this confection – but we often
wondered if the king ever visited Tokyo, and if so whether the firm
would try and acquire a convincing vase to stand in for the myste-
riously missing one.

My job was more mundane – teaching English at a drainpipe
factory some way out of town. It involved a long train ride on the
metro, when I watched my fellow passengers without ever feeling
that anyone was watching me. They sat or stood with their eyes on
their mobile phones, or staring blankly into space. Just occasionally

two might be travelling together and might exchange a few words; but generally there was no communication. I had to change trains at one station – so did many others – and they would silently steer their way through the crowds to their next platform. Fortunately most notices were in Japanese and English, so I usually ended up in the right place. But if I caught someone's eye and smiled they would turn away and not return the smile. A bit like the people – the "numbers" – in Zamyatin's novel *WE*, whose lives are planned and controlled in every detail by The One State.

I wonder if this "smoothness" is partly responsible for Tom's decision to make friends with people outside the main stream – "day labourers" – who lived in certain districts in the big cities, where there were cheap lodging houses – *doya* – and where big employers recruited men for a day's work. These men were entirely irregular, not at all *smooth*. They lived largely in the streets and drank and talked. Tom moved on from journalism to social anthropology and got close to one astonishingly intelligent and well-read layabout, Kimitsu Nishikawa (as described by Tom in his book (*Yokohama Street Life: The Precarious Career of a Japanese Day Laborer*, Lexington: 2015.)

*

You should not go to Japan in August – that's when the heat is most intense and humid. I had experienced it before – in 1985, when David and I stayed at Tom's little wooden house in a widow's back garden in Tokyo, and resorted to taking it in turns to stick our heads in the fridge. And there are vicious mosquitoes. But I experienced another Japanese summer when David and I lived with Tom for a year when Jake was born (1988-89). Thirty years later, in 2019, I did it again. By this time poor David was no longer with us, and Tom was divorced and remarried, to Manami. August was the only time Tom could escape from his university duties, and Jackie from hers at the school, so that's when we went. We flew – eleven hours in the air once we'd got to the airport and been duly vetted, weighed and measured and had waited for our plane to be announced: so that was a very long day.

Tom and Manami - Tomanami - met us - Jackie, her three sons Ben, Mickey and Harry, Ben's girlfriend Robyn, and me - at Tokyo's Haneda airport, and we were duly transported by train and finally taxi to Tomanami's house in Oiso. It's halfway up a hill, and you have to climb quite a few steep steps to get to the front door. There's a bit of a garden round the house, with grass and roses and nasturtiums and strange outlandish plants - and geraniums, in pots and hanging baskets. The house is made of wood, with a steep curving staircase and a big open-plan sitting room cum dining room and kitchen downstairs. I was lucky - there was air conditioning in the room I slept in (normally Tom's study) - and in most of the other rooms in fact.

Oiso is very close to the Pacific Ocean, and soon I was on a shingly beach, with Tom and Harry flopping around in the water with a giant rubber ring. And later we strolled through a steep park and moved on to Rokusho Shrine, with its two pools *boiling* with large, colourful carp frantically hoping for something to eat - you can get a packet of titbits for them at the shrine for a few yen. The steep, curving roofs of such older buildings, wooden, with touches of red and gold colour, are very pleasing. My mother believed the curves ended in an upward twist so that any malevolent spirits descending would be shot back up again.

Tomanami are blessed with extremely nice neighbours. A Canadian / Japanese couple, aptly called Goodman, invited all of us to a lavish supper. Next day we travelled to Yokohama, and got a taste of Chinese food and goods at shops in Chinatown. In the evening, we watched a baseball game - actually *I* watched the crowds sitting around me, who were watching the game on a giant TV screen. The people reacted so emotionally to every move - leaping to their feet, shouting, waving their fists in the air, hugging each other - a joy to behold. Mostly I was struck by the seriousness of people. If on public transport I caught someone's eye and smiled, he or she would look away as if embarrassed - just like thirty years before. Perhaps they were anxious - am I on the right train? Will I get there on time? The uniformed staff at the elaborate tourist attractions we visited all seemed earnest and dutiful and rather tense - and I remembered how David and I had felt people were rather too intent on their duties, and how we thought Tom's predilection for the drunkards and layabouts in Kotobuki was understandable.

We often needed taxis, and these were not booked by phone: Tom would stand on one of the big roads and soon he could stop a taxi - very different from here, where "no booking, no ride" is the motto. There, the taxis cruise continually. The drivers - in uniform, with cap and snow-white gloves - work 17-hour shifts, with an allowance of three hours rest. They were often happy to chat with Manami, who sympathised with their obvious tiredness.

Tom had signed up with Airbnb, an organisation that helps people let empty properties to tourists, so we stayed in family houses rather than hotels. These houses were like ingenious packing cases, mostly made of wood, with thin wooden walls between rooms, doors which slide rather than swing open, stairs like ladders - not an inch of space wasted, but complete with TV and baths and showers and washing machines and wifi - its complex number displayed. No space outside: a square yard of gravel and grass was the "garden", and the "road" outside barely a yard wide. Houses are crammed in the space beyond the highways; they open directly onto the road - not so much as a doorstep. Overhead, everywhere, a confusion of electric cables going in all directions.

We travelled to Kyoto on the Shinkansen - the brilliant bullet train - in which the sets of three seats can be swung round to face the other way, producing little six seater open rooms. Their phenomenal efficiency and punctuality are a stark contrast to British Rail. If your ticket says "4", then you must wait on the platform where it says 4, and when the train stops, the door to wagon four will swing open exactly there, and the barrier between platform and rails will be opened there by an official so that you can squeeze in with the crowd, quickly - the train only stops for a few minutes. But Tom told me about one rare train accident that happened in 2005: A young train driver realised he was a few feet beyond the correct stopping place, so he backed. This meant he had used an unscheduled minute or two, so he accelerated to make up the time - on a bend - and the train shot off the rails and plunged into an apartment building. 107 people were killed, including the young driver, and 562 injured. If only the standards of precision and punctuality were not so rigid!

I wonder whether the super efficiency of so many Japanese people, the rigid adherence to rules, might go back to a childhood devoted to a considerable extent to learning to read and write. How many hours a day must be spent memorising the intricacies of the kanjis! What discipline! And there's *hiragana* and *katakana* as well! And our alphabet! They are all in use, wherever you look you see them on notices, posters, etc.

Our stay in Kyoto happened to coincide with the end of Obon, the period when the dead are believed to revisit our world. Fires are lit on five forested mountains in the shape of five kanjis to celebrate the return of the dead to "the other side". We joined the crowds on the river bank in the slightly cooler evening, and punctually at eight we saw the fiery shape appear on the mountain opposite. Some of us joined in a very slow dance, singing a simple phrase of music, and afterwards a woman held a speech, which Tom interpreted for me: she was regretting the fact that many of the dancers were foreign tourists, that old customs were dying out, that young people are more interested in American culture.

We used another bullet train past town after town, massed blocks of buildings, 20, 30 storeys high, of whitish concrete, very square and solid and regular with identical windows spaced in straight lines. People live in them like goods on the shelves of supermarkets

Surrounded by family at Kinkakuji Temple in Kyoto.

or convenience stores. "Crowd Management" is efficient and smooth - tremendous efforts to keep the masses not just in order but amused. What ingenuity! The "Sky Tree" in Tokyo, tremendously tall, a huge construction, has no reason to exist apart from getting people to climb or be carried up, level after level, and look across Tokyo spread out below. Wherever you may have to wait for a connection there are slot machines where for a few yen you can get a fizzy drink or packet of something edible - or a small plastic toy, cleverly designed, mass produced, perhaps computer generated. Excellent railways transport thousands swiftly and cleanly to designated tourist centres - such as ancient shrines on the slopes of sacred mountains. The crowds are very disciplined, listen attentively to instructions being broadcast and hurry to act accordingly. We saw no homeless people, no beggars anywhere.

Since 1945, when I was twelve, the word Hiroshima has meant just one thing to me. As my grandmother wrote - "So now the human race can destroy itself. And good riddance, I'd say!"

And I would add - not just the human race - all life on earth.

Human brutality, as witnessed in the fire-bombing of Dresden and Tokyo, and at Auschwitz ... has no bounds. Instead of starting back in horror at what had been done in Hiroshima and Nagasaki and swearing "Never Again!" - more monstrous engines of destruction continue to be developed. They are stockpiled, those in authority threaten each other each other with them, there's a "policy" called "Mutual Assured Destruction" (*M.A.D.*) as a means of averting nuclear war - instead of disarmament. CND - which wasn't launched till 1958 - presented the obvious, sane arguments for nuclear disarmament and was supported by thousands. But what has happened to it? People seem to regard it as a quaint anachronism - as they do me. It was the hope that my grandsons might come round to supporting CND that led me to include Hiroshima in our Japanese holiday.

The centre of the town is a "Memorial Peace Park". It lies between two rivers which merge here. The park is dominated by the skeletal dome of the one building that survived the pulverisation and burning of most of the city. In front is a pool of water – "the pond of peace" – and a curved stone cenotaph overarching a chest containing the names of the 297,684 killed by that one bomb. On a plinth in the pool is a "Flame of Peace" which is to burn night and day while there are nuclear weapons in the world – it will not be extinguished until the last one has been dismantled. The ashes of the thousands of corpses that were cremated are gathered under a grassy memorial mound.

There is a Children's Peace monument with the figure of a child with a bird in memory of Sadako Sasaki, who hoped that if she could make one thousand origami paper cranes she might recover from the radiation sickness which did, however, kill her, and so many like her that had survived the initial explosion. Children send or bring their own paper cranes – there are thousands of them festooning the surroundings of the memorial.

In the museum, with the motto *Never Again!*, photographs show the hideous burns suffered by victims before they died, and the victims of the daylong radioactive "black rain". The tattered remnants of clothes are displayed, and library images and records and spine-chilling descriptions are available. I couldn't bear to stay there long.

In the cooler evening, we sat by the pool – paddled in it – watched the flame flickering.

But modern Hiroshima with its shops and traffic is lively and efficient. A short boat ride took us to the island of Miyajima, where amazingly tame deer nuzzled in our bags and gazed longingly – they really were "doe eyed" – at our packets of crisps. In the water stood a *torii*, a great red gateway leading from nowhere to nowhere, as so many torii do. They are fascinating and beautiful. Perhaps, to some, they have profound meaning, a religious or mystical gateway. They are included in the lists of "tourist attractions" to be photographed, "scenic spots", like the magnificent old castle at Takamatsu – a "world heritage monument" - which we approached via a sort of funicular called a "ropeway". In one room you can try on a samurai costume, and be photographed, which Harry and Mickey did.

Everywhere we went there were shopping arcades where mass-produced, cunningly devised "souvenirs" can be bought, or burgers, or clothes; we were never far from slot machines where a coin will cause one of dozens of small plastic toys or ornaments to tumble down to a drawer - and there was karaoke, where, in one of dozens of small rooms, you can hear any popular song, one after the other, - and sing and jig about to it, and you can order drinks, alcoholic or sweet, and other refreshments by phone and they will be brought to you by a member of staff.

Such entertainments made me feel uncomfortable. I was a member of the public, the *hoi poloi,* like the crowds in that terrifying film, *Soylent Green.* We were being kept reasonably contented by ingenious amusements while in the background the preparations for the end are being quietly put in place, the weapons of mass destruction, the carbon in the atmosphere, "global warming" - all preparing for mass extinction.

The last evening was the best. Quite near the hotel where we were staying was the magnificent Kawasaki Daishi, a sprawling complex of Buddhist temples with a tall pagoda. We wandered around there in the cool of the evening - sat on some steps and saw the moon rise - and stroked a cat. Then we saw another cat. And an old man was feeding it. Further along, a woman was feeding another cat. "No, they don't belong to anyone - they just live here, we feed them every night. There are about 14 of them." We wandered on. It was so calm, so quiet, so peaceful. We came to a beautiful pool with lotus and other plants and behind and above it a beautiful golden statue of the Buddha.

Chapter 11: Vietnam

One day in 1989, during the year David and I spent living with Tom in Tokyo, I saw an advertisement for tourism in Vietnam, and I decided to sign up for it. I was never going to be this close to Vietnam again. And for years and years, during the Vietnam War, that country had been at the centre of my consciousness. It has been called the first televised war, and it worked for me, and millions like me, protesting and demonstrating at U.S. Embassies throughout the world. Night after night, we sat frozen with horror in front of the TV as we saw villages of straw huts invaded by sweating G.I.s, cursing because no-one was there except some skinny old woman staring as they tipped out stores of rice and casually set fire to the thatched roofs with their cigarette lighters. The ditch full of corpses at My Lai. Hideous images of the sadism of the authorities in Saigon, torturing prisoners, cramming them into Tiger Cage prisons... An abiding image is the one filmed inside a helicopter across the shoulder of a G.I. sitting casually by the open door, one leg dangling outside, chewing gum and exchanging banter with the pilot, when suddenly the green fields below are speckled with black-clad peasants running for their lives. The G.I., still chewing, raises the machine gun and pins the distant figures to the ground. And the little naked girl running and screaming as the napalm clinging to her back blazes. It was seeing such sights that inspired us to start *Oxford Aid for Children in Vietnam.*

Finally, in 1973, the Americans withdrew. Saigon was renamed

Ho Chi Minh city. It was the only time the USA had been defeated. And now, on May 14th 1989, I got a flight - to Hanoi, stopover at Bangkok.

There were half a dozen Vietnamese planes at Hanoi airport, and a couple from other airlines. The airport building looked like a battered school from the thirties, though I was told it was only 15 years old. There was one toilet for women, its lid off and a Heath-Robinsonian arrangement of strings and bits of rubber to flush it. I had to show my passport at one of four sentry boxes, and fill in customs declarations at a Bob Cratchit style standing desk. Military-looking men took turns looking at what I'd written - and they were *lounging*. I saw a lot of lounging in Vietnam, people stretching, or cradling their heads in their arms, or leaning against walls with lolling heads. Outside, I was greeted by my guide, Hoa, and driven in a "sedan" (a grey, air-conditioned Nissan) through the lush, flat, green country for some 45 minutes to Hanoi. Here and there in the vast rice fields was a bent figure with a coolie hat; and we came past small houses, some with two storeys, open on the ground floor, with cane awnings under which groups of people were sitting and talking or eating and drinking. The hotel where I stayed, the Thang Loi, was outside Hanoi. It was built by Cubans, and though my part of it - very picturesque, on stilts in a muddy lake - was only finished the year before, there was a 1930s feel about it, a certain shabbiness, shadowiness. I realized later that it was the absence of plastic, thermo plastic tiles, etc. There was rattan furniture, plain unvarnished wood, simple designs.

The other guests were mainly Westerners, or from the Communist bloc. There was a group of corpulent Czech engineers, a large party of Russian tourists, and various entrepreneurs from the West hoping to take advantage of the new policy encouraging investment. I had a long talk with an Australian mining engineer, Les Wilcox, who hoped to re-start a gold mine near Danang, which the French worked profitably until the war put an end to it. Apparently

Vietnam would be happy with the taxes he paid and the employment he would give Vietnamese miners in return for his investment and expertise; he would have a 100% claim on the gold. A likeable man, a conscientious objector. He told me there was a high incidence of deformed births ascribed to Agent Orange, notably Siamese twins: the two that had hit the headlines when they were separated, Viet and Duc Nguyen, were two of many - and probably there were more than the authorities knew about, as it was believed they were killed at birth in the villages - and who can say that's a crime?

Hoa drove me - in my "Sedan" - into central Hanoi and we walked through the market. It was amazing. The first thing that hit you was the combination of hubbub and smell - dried fish and stagnant puddles. And there sat - *lounged* - people who had probably been there all day, not selling much, jammed up against each other. Old, old people in black peasant trousers, crouching on the ground, chewing betel nut, the red juice trickling down their chins, and totally black teeth. Rather weedy vegetables for sale, and heaps of home-made vermicelli - great bundles of it tied together; rice, flour, millet in heaps; bales of material and cheap clothes - Hoa told me that now the frontier with China had been opened, Chinese clothes were putting Vietnamese makers out of business. A few beggars, especially a group of three children, very dirty, probably suffering malnutrition. Hoa said the usual harsh things people say about beggars, in this case about the children's parents - but she had told me herself that there is high unemployment and no government assistance... .

The houses in central Hanoi were fantastically decayed and in French provincial style. They had a sordid glamour, they had style. Their façades, with balconies overhung with plants, were actually crumbling. The ground floors were mostly shops or cafés, and there were traders sitting on the pavement selling, or trying to sell, just about everything, including watches and cigarettes. Some people crouched over tiny stoves on the pavements, cooking food and selling it to passers-by. The road itself was a continuous mass of bicycles and *cyclos* – gaunt and battered old bicycles with a seat in front for passengers or goods and a muscular man pedalling it along; mopeds with families aboard – and there were apparently no traffic rules. The driver kept his thumb on his hooter pretty permanently but even so there were frequent near misses. Bullock carts, drawn by these gentle giants who have a hump on the back of the neck as if they had been designed to take a yoke, sleek and well fed. And there were caged birds, cats and dogs and monkeys for sale in wickerwork cages.

There was a floating plant with blue water hyacinths in some parts of the lake at the hotel which people gathered for cattle food. I watched a man and his young son, each paddling a boat which looked like a box, piled high with the plant. When they got to the shore, they flung the plants onto the land, lifted the boats out of the water, when I saw they were made of corrugated iron, beaten flat and bent into a shape rather like a punt. Then they piled the plants back into the "boats" and dragged them up the steep slope and across the road on the far side.

In the evening, the lights wouldn't work in my room, so I went across to the reception and was told they would work now, as a power cut had just ended. But when I returned, they still weren't working, so I went back, and the receptionist said she would tell "him" to come and fix them. Sure enough, after some time a man appeared and showed me that I should have hung the key on a certain hook, which acted as a mains switch. So now the lights came on – but not the Toshiba air conditioner, as he quickly noticed. He fetched a small home-made ladder with which he climbed up into the attic, where he hit something hard several times. Immediately, the air conditioner sent out a roaring arctic gale which practically tore the sheets off the bed – and then stopped again. Up he went again, and the whole performance was repeated. Six or seven times. In the end, he won, and I spent a cool night with a fair amount of rattling and humming. In fact the weather was not very hot - warm and muggy, overcast.

Hoa took me to three Buddhist temples in the morning. They were smaller, a bit shabbier and more cramped than the great establishments in Japan, the figures often ranged in threes to symbolize the past, present and future. Hoa - herself an atheist - explained the Vietnamese version of Buddhism to me: when you die, you go to Nirvana, whence you watch over the members of your family... While we were in one temple, a wizened little woman came and humbly placed a potato in front of each altar and prayed devoutly. Outside, in front, some beggars held out their hands; at the back some women were polishing brass figures with sand and bare hands (no rags, no Brasso) and then dipped them in water to clean them - this in preparation for the Buddha's birthday on May 19th. In the garden there were some bonsais trained into the shape of deer.

I felt three temples were enough, so instead of taking me to yet more, Hoa readily agreed to take me out into the country, and this was perhaps the best part of the tour.

We got out of the car and walked along a lane with huge rice fields, stretching to the horizon on one side. There were little eucalyptus trees beside the road casting shade. We were closely watched and followed by numerous children. They stared at me with friendly curiosity. They weren't particularly clean, especially as to the teeth, but they were healthy, bright and confident. There was a constant coming and going along the lane, mostly on foot, but there was one horse-drawn cart. People were carrying loads - fish traps, or baskets full of vegetables. Everyone was purposeful but they had time to stop and talk; the atmosphere was of a true self-supporting community. We came past a brick kiln, and further along people were building a house. Progress was slow - no cranes - hod-bearers trotted up and down wooden ladders - and no cement mixer - the cement was being mixed in a heap on the ground. A small field was being ploughed by a man with a bullock. Other bullocks were grazing in a recently harvested field. We crossed a small river where there was an elaborate structure for lowering and raising fish nets; further along a man was watching over a flock of ducks. Another large family of ducks was being noisy in the ditch beside the lane, and the children laughed when they saw the ducks stretched out on a branch of a tree, fast asleep, and in imminent danger of falling into the ditch. We came past a school, which works on a shift system: one shift was just coming out and joined my retinue. And the Community Centre, a plain, low-slung building with the figure of a serpent on the roof; I saw such sculptures on many buildings in Vietnam. People were getting ready for some kind of gathering there, carrying benches and shouting to each other on the spacious forecourt.

After all one had read about Vietnam, it was wonderful to observe these busy, cheerful people, hard at work in tranquillity.

In the afternoon we went back into Hanoi and had a drink in a café of Hoa's choice. It was the size of a small sitting room, with bare walls and two tables, with minuscule stools. An ear-splitting ghetto-blaster. You could have fizzy pop, mineral water, Coke, domestic beer, Heineken, or coconut milk - cooled with a rough chunk of ice hacked from a block. Although there are so many fruit trees in Vietnam - mangos, oranges, lemons, papayas, pineapples, bananas - fruit juice was not available. When I asked for orange squash, an orange was cut into quarters and pushed into a glass of sugar water - peel, pips and all - plus some hunks of ice. The proprietress watched me solicitously as I tried to drink this, and showed me how to take the ice out with a spoon, like a mother with a slow child. (No drinking straws, no ice cubes.) Sugar water was produced from sugar cane, passed through a metal mill with a wheel. Every house seemed to have its escort of lofty palm trees with thick clusters of coconuts among the fronds high above.

Outside I saw the same beggar children as the day before, being jostled and pushed aside; when a girl approached me the proprietress shooed her aside angrily. When an old man approached me, I was "defended" from him.

There are many lakes in Hanoi; the Red River's meanders have been cut into six or seven -and since most families live in one room there are always people by the lakesides - especially lovers of course, but groups and individuals also spend a long time in the shade of the flowering trees, as I did.

In the evening I spoke with two Vietnamese from abroad. One, a Catholic, had moved South when the country was "temporarily" divided by the Geneva agreement in 1954, after the French defeat at Dien Bien Phu and then, after Liberation in 1975, had become a Boat Person and got to Australia. Now he worked for Shell. The other had always worked for the U.N. Technical Assistance Programme, and had the enviable task of visiting numerous countries to assess their needs. Both were highly delighted with present developments - as a result of Perestroika the Boat People and the like were no longer labelled traitors and imprisoned if they returned but invited to come as visitors: the government knew they wouldn't come empty handed. Earlier, I had spoken with Jean, a very charming French-Vietnamese *consultant* who would put any would-be hotel developer, for instance, in touch with the appropriate Government official, here or in several other countries - "In 48 hours all the documents can be ready", she said, to develop a hotel on a prime site with plenty of land around for tennis courts and the like. People spoke of tourism as the great white hope for Vietnam.

Next day I said goodbye to Hoa and flew to Danang.

The airport there was huge - acres and acres of asphalt and concrete, with hundreds and hundreds of arched concrete hangars at the edges, each big enough to take one plane, all completely empty now - it was in fact the American base we had read and heard so much about. The narrow, rather shabby plane I had arrived in looked quite incongruous in all this empty space. An Oxfam representative had been on the same plane: most of his work was in

Cambodia, but there were some irrigation projects in Vietnam. He was met by two vans with OXFAM written on them. I also spoke with an American professor, Arnold Schecter, who was investigating the effects of Agent Orange. He had been coming to Vietnam for seven or eight years. A dour and dead-pan man: "It is extremely difficult to distinguish the effects of Agent Orange when it has been administered to people who are already suffering from debility caused by malnutrition, intestinal infections and the like". He was an expert on dioxins, unwanted contaminants. No-one dreamed that Agent Orange contained these - people were using it in their gardens as a weed killer without any precautions. "It cleared the jungle all right, that is not in question; the question is what effect if any did it have on the people here. The real problem in this country is the poverty, caused in part by the United States' embargo; I have never been able to understand why your country also imposed that embargo on Vietnam."

He meant Britain, of course.

I was met by two guides, Lieng and Tien, who now drove me to my hotel - Huong Giang - Pacific Hotel. It was old - the writing in the lift was in French - and rather shabby, the plumbing and electricity extremely defective. The best thing about it was the breezy restaurant on the seventh floor, with views across the city to the sea and to the mountains. In the afternoon we went to a small museum, containing a collection of Cham sculpture. Cham was the name of an ancient civilization in the South which has been excavated. Then we drove to the Marble Mountains: five great jagged sugar loaf formations which are supposed to represent the five Buddhist elements: air, fire, water, stone, and wood.

The village where we stopped was loud with hammering, filing, chiselling; everyone was making things of marble: Buddhas, Virgin Marys, bracelets and ornaments of many kinds, while children carried trays full of them for sale. Three girls, barefoot and smiling and giggling, followed us up a rather breath-taking staircase cut in the marble to an idyllic little temple where some king used to come to visit his sister, who was a nun. Catching my breath on a slab of marble, I heard a shout from higher up and everyone rushed to the other side of the path. It was a snake, a large, yellowish one with black markings, and it slithered at lightning speed across the stone on which I'd been sitting.

There were tremendous caves and tunnels, now empty except for Buddhist statues, but once full of Vietcong, who had a hospital there - so the area was bombed by the Americans, and the grottos and small temples had to be reconstructed. It was wildly romantic, with the roots of trees twisting in and out of the rock, and glimpses of the blue ocean through natural archways. Later I bathed in the shallow warm seawater - the breakers were very powerful, and the undertow sucked the sand out from under my feet. Meanwhile, Lieng the guide and Tien the driver drank Coca-Cola in a small café; next door, fenced in, was a hotel, formerly an American rest home; now it was full of vast Russian men and women who went panting up and down the beach and in and out of the hotel.

Nobody liked the Russians; everybody liked the Americans. I thought this was extraordinary, and never heard a rational explanation. After all, the Russians had stood by Vietnam both during and after the war. On top of the horrors they perpetrated during the war, the Americans slapped an embargo on Vietnam afterwards. It makes no difference. People will say they don't like the U.S. government, but they like the people - they're friendly and generous, whereas the Russians are considered surly and uncouth. The GIs were mostly drafted - as if that excused what they did - and the small individual acts of kindness from veterans who have revisited the country and done voluntary work - doctors have performed operations on children - some group has built a hospital - seem to outweigh the barbarisms of the war in people's minds. Later I learned that the Russians exacted quite a price for their aid. They had taken over the US Naval Base at Cam Ranh Bay as payment for their military aid; and the goods they supplied, buses and lorries and whatever else it is, were bartered for Vietnamese goods; but while the Russian goods were priced at world market rates, the Vietnamese were priced at internal, Vietnamese rates ... that may be why so much Vietnamese rice went to the Communist bloc that Vietnam was having to import rice for its own use.

I did not like Danang. The streets and pavements were so defective you could easily break an ankle; there was no cover over the deep drains under the pavements for long stretches and little children were playing round these three- or four-foot drops with stinking foulness at the bottom. I saw a dead rat lying on a heap of rubble. Only the splendid flowering trees cast their blossom across the rusty corrugated iron roofs and the people crouching on the pavements at their work: cutting out spare parts for vehicles from bits of rusty metal using hammer and chisel; punctures being mended. The ceaseless traffic consisted mostly of bicycles, and some scooters with miniature buses built around them – as many as 10 or 12 people crammed into them, and the driver astride of the scooter in front, puttering along in blue smoke. It was very hot, and the people squatting on the pavements by their small stock of cigarettes or bananas looked extremely languid. In the evenings people watched TV, for instance in the lounge of my hotel, a rather bare area on the ground floor. I'm sure I'd seen this hotel before from outside: surely with GIs and Vietnamese girls hanging out of the windows and waving at the cameras.... Whenever I saw TV here it always showed a woman in close-up singing very soulfully, long slow phrases with huge intervals, plunging from high notes to low ones and back again; occasionally the camera moved back and you discovered two other women behind her in long night gowns moving about to the music with sad, slow gestures. The volume was always high. There was some live music, with similarly doleful melodies sung by a male voice accompanied by synthesizer and guitar and percussion. The hotel stood at a junction of five roads, and an endless stream of bicycles passed along the main road. There were no street lights; a few mopeds had headlights, and a few of the shops had a light bulb or a strip light where a man sat mending a sewing machine or a woman lounged by her small case of buns and fizzy drinks. I watched the melee of bicycles for a while - most with two people on the bike, talking and laughing - when two little boys came and asked me for money - a six-year-old and his very cheerful, cheeky toddler brother. At first they thought I hadn't understood, and pointed at my bag, their mouths, and held out a 200 dong note, but when I refused, they went on smiling, and we pulled faces and made funny noises to make each other laugh.

*

Highway One runs along the coast all the way from Ho Chi Minh City - aka Saigon - to Hanoi; the stretch from Danang to Hue took about three hours in the car. All the way, the blue sea with its rocky islets and distant hazy islands was on our right, the steep, green mountains on our left. We serpentined across their spurs, dropped down to the edges of coves, and climbed up again on the grassy flanks of the mountains. It would be easy for guerrillas to block this road by pushing down some of the boulders up there; indeed, there were numerous rocks lying on the road which no-one had bothered to clear away. We passed two lorries that had broken down and were being mended by men lying on their backs underneath. This is the only road connecting Laos to the sea and many of the battered lorries were going to or coming from that land-locked country. Buses were packed, luggage piled high on the roof, and as they negotiated the sharp bends they teetered perilously. In fact there was a high accident rate, and last year a doctor friend of Lieng's died when a bus overbalanced and rolled down hundreds of feet into the sea. The spot was marked by small shrines and incense stuck in the roadside mud. Lieng added his incense and prayed.

Far below, a silvery spit of sand ran parallel to the coast, with a village of small thatched houses nestling among coconut palms. We drove across a bridge to reach it. Next to it was a broken down bridge, bombed by the Americans as the village was believed to harbour Vietcong. The shade under the coconut trees and the thatched awnings was very pleasant. Here we sat and drank coconut milk cooled by the usual jagged chunk of ice. The village had no electricity - the ice was delivered from elsewhere. An old man came up and addressed me with great dignity. The last word was "dong" so I gave him some money and he thanked me gravely and moved away. The usual group of children gathered and stared. There was a village school, but for secondary education they had to make a 15 kilometre journey on foot or by bike: there were no school buses. Lieng thought nothing of this: he had had to cycle 25 km each way for school. Twice, once at school and once at university, he came top of his class and was entitled to a spell of study abroad; each time he was prevented by developments in the war - he was not a happy man. His English was excellent, and he was really obsessed with improving it. Once I used the word "well-worn" and he repeated it and muttered "past participle preceded by adverb, yes, I see." He was often imparting knowledge like this, and details of phonetics, to other Vietnamese. There had been no new English books since Liberation in 1975, whereas Russian publications were widely available. He lusted after my Raymond Chandler so I posted it to him from Ho Chi Minh City - I hope he got it (and was more successful than me at unravelling the plot ...).

There was a well opposite our restaurant, and an American helmet hanging from a post. It was used to draw water. I saw a similar arrangement in Ho Chi Minh city: a helmet full of water being used by a roadside bicycle mender to detect punctures.

After this the road climbed steeply to a narrow pass across a spur of the mountains that extended all the way to the sea. This pass had been the scene of many battles, being a bottleneck between the North and the South of the country. The French had built a grim looking fortress here. Nearby there was a machine gun emplacement, and underground bunkers now inhabited by a family of pigs. A desolate place, with magnificent views across the sea in both directions.

We came to an area of flat farmland, with a railway running parallel to the road. In the vast green rice fields, bent figures with conical hats were cutting rice using small sickles - what terrible work in that heat! - tying it up in bundles which were attached to the ends of bamboo shoulder yokes and carried long distances at a rapid jog trot to the road, where they were untied and flung down so that vehicles would drive over them. These canny farmers were using the traffic to thresh their rice. Afterwards they would stack up the stalks for cattle feed and spread the golden grain on the warm tarmac to dry out.

*

The hotel in Hue was built by the Americans in the sixties for their officers, and a very nice place it was, too, with high ceilings and big rooms and shady terraces and verandas. From my room I overlooked palm trees standing on the banks of the Perfume River - it isn't really perfumed, but has the faint sweet smell of clean water. There were numerous sampans on it, not much bigger than punts, the prow curved up and a big fixed oar at the back which was pushed by men and women - though a few had puttering outboard motors. The centre of each sampan was covered with palm matting slung over a hoop, and whole families lived there. Some of the boats were clustered together. Tiny boats were paddled to and fro, bringing in the shopping or just visiting, and children were having fun in them. Life in these boats was lively. Some of them were moored against the opposite shore, where corrugated iron shacks were linked to sampans by washing lines. The river was very shallow - people could stand in it, and a couple of platforms had been set up on which they could keep some of their belongings.

Next day I was the sole passenger on a "Dragon Boat"- a large boat with a carving of a grotesque open-mouthed monster on the prow and seating for some thirty passengers, its emptiness in sharp contrast to the crowded sampans I looked down at from my lofty seat on the deck, behind the monstrous dragon's head. We - the captain, the tour guide and myself - sailed past an ancient "Royal Mausoleum" with a serpent of clay on the roof ridge, where in the past kings went to meditate - and were worshipped after death. The king who is buried here had 103 wives and concubines but no chil-dren, being impotent after mumps. The exact position of his corpse is not known, as the 30 men who buried him were all beheaded before they could tell. Has life always been so cheap in this coun-try? There was a collection of rusty American weapons near the mausoleum.

The journey back to Danang from Hue was delayed by a puncture. While Tien changed the wheel, I looked around, and was thoroughly looked at by children who - as usual - appeared when I was station-ary. There was a roadside workshop - rather like the ones we saw in Uganda - where hammers and chisels and scraps of metal were being used to repair mopeds. Crossing the pass this time we got into thick fog. Emerging from it as we descended on the far side was like coming out from under a dark grey curtain, and there was the bril-liant blue Pacific again, with its odd little rocky islets. It was very shallow in the bay - people doing things to their boats were hardly up to their thighs in water.

In the evening I went to the theatre with Lieng. I suppose the most extraordinary thing about the altogether extraordinary perfor-mance was the microphones. There were about six of them, hang-ing from their cables above the stage, with strings looped round the cables being manipulated by people up in the flies. At the beginning of the play, there was one hanging by the lips of a girl who talked and sang into it, ear-splittingly. Then a young man entered and applied his lips to another microphone. After the lovers had talked for a while, suddenly two other microphones swooped down and came to a quivering halt above two chairs on which, a few seconds later, the two sat down with microphones conveniently at mouth level. They were like Actors themselves, these microphones, very conspicuous, hurtling hither and thither. In the middle of a poignant scene, one of them flew to an entrance, and sure enough, in came the father. The actors studiously pretended they weren't there at all, though they were often threatened with concussion by one, and remained unperturbed when a loose connection sent ferocious crackles through the loudspeakers.

*

Next day I flew from Danang to Ho Chi Minh City, where I was met by my next guide, Duy, who took me to my hotel, Thang Long, formerly The Oscar, built for G.I.s in the sixties. It was fairly smelly and noisy. The strip light in my *en suite* made a noise like a pneumatic drill, though it was a Japanese NEC. The lift was fairly erratic, given to carrying me up and down past my fifth floor several times before depositing me. I was shown my room by a chamber-maid, a woman about my own age, friendly and tired, barefoot – she had a tiny cubby hole and a couple of chairs on the landing where all the air conditioners blast out their hot used air. I invited her to rest in my room, but she seemed horrified at the idea.

There was a modest art shop next door. I saw a fine pastel of a Buddhist monk at prayer, about to strike a sounding bowl; there were several sentimental girls drooping at riversides, and blissful babies with their heads wedged between their mothers' bulging breasts. A water colour had this note:

Painter's biography. Lan Tuen, painter, was a Chinese monk coming to Vietnam as a hidden modest monk and an instructor. His specialization is flowers and birds, characters and landscapes. He died in the Tan Ti year 1881, not precisely at Hoy Am (Fly Fu).

In the afternoon I was shown round the Presidential palace built in 1962 – but Dien was assassinated before it was finished. It was palatial. On the ground, first and second floors there were vast reception rooms and banquet rooms, with red plush carpets and highly polished tables with umpteen identical chairs ranged round them. There was a helicopter landing pad used by South Vietnamese president Nguyen Cao Ky – who famously once told a journalist: "People ask me who my heroes are. I have only one: Hitler." Inside we saw the president's great bedroom and the president's wife's great bedroom, and on the very top floor their games room, with a glassy dance floor and snazzy colourful furnishings. I was shown all this in the company of three West Germans, who kept making helpful suggestions such as: You could use this for dances – it would make a lot of money. The guide, whose rage at this all this ostentation and waste came through in all kinds of finely ironic remarks, said: "No, we want to keep this as a museum. If one compares this with Ho Chi Minh's headquarters, one understands why that side won the war."

In the evening I went to a performance of traditional music at the Rex hotel, which had a nice little air-conditioned theatre. There were two or three large groups of large East Germans, about a hundred of them in all, and the three West Germans, three French people, and me. It was a polished performance by half a dozen members of one talented family. There was a one-string fiddle, with a beautifully decorated sounding box, the single string attached to a metal spike. The player could produce any note by moving his left hand along the string and plucking it with his right. A special trick was bending the spike while a note was still sounding, so raising or lowering the note. There was a type of zither, various flutes, a large frame supporting four gongs of various pitch, and a row of drums played with great verve and fire. And there was some acrobatic dancing, too. All most enjoyable.

The road was thick with bicycles as I walked back; many cyclo drivers smiled at me encouragingly, and must have thought me a bitch for not taking a ride. Crossing the millstream of bicycles requires some skill. It must be fun, once you know how, to be part of that mass of whirling, laughing cyclists. On a traffic island, a family was settling down for the night. In the middle of all that hubbub, a child about Jake's age was already asleep.

I saw a lot of beggars next day at the big Buddhist temple built by migrants from the North after the Geneva Accord of 1954 divided the country at the 17th parallel - temporarily, until the elections which were to be held the following year, but weren't, for the cogent reason that Dien knew he would lose. This led to the Vietnam-U.S.A. war. In 1954, most Catholics moved South, many Buddhists too. The temple was celebrating Buddha's birthday and there were thousands of people making merry outside - and beggars: lepers, writhing helplessly on the ground, stretching out the knobbly remains of their hands, old people, mothers with babies, children. The "Boat People" who risked so much to get to Hong Kong and other capitalist countries - many of them perishing on the way - felt oppressed, endangered by the Communism of Ho Chi Minh.

Chapter 12: Four Days on a Kibbutz

In October 1999, I decided to visit Israel. I had not wanted to, because of Israel's fascist treatment of the Palestinians, and possession of nuclear weapons. I was - I'd been told - able to claim citizenship as a female descendant of female Jews. In fact I was connected to the country, I had relatives there. I had learned that one, Jehuda Zuntz, was compiling a history of the Zuntz family, so I wanted to see him; also some dear friends of my mother, founding members of a kibbutz: Rafael and Devora Tabor. They had been Zionists in the early years of the century, keen to reclaim what they believed was a desert country and restore it to the "land flowing with milk and honey" *given to them* by God ... But - as we learn from the Bible, there were people there - who had to be fought ...Rafael and Devora changed their name from *Berg* to *Tabor* **and** prepared themselves for immigration by learning farming ...

I flew to Haifa from Gatwick. I assumed that the man holding a piece of paper inscribed **GIL Irene** was Rafael's son, who was to meet me. He was fat, in jeans, shirt and trousers, with slightly bulging blue eyes. We shook hands; he clearly didn't understand my English, or my German – "Hebrew?" I asked. He nodded. "Yiddish?" I asked. He nodded again. He was in fact a taxi driver. Rafael's son had been unable to meet me and had arranged this taxi instead. Somehow we managed to communicate on the long drive North. He was born in the Ukraine, and in his community there everyone spoke Yiddish. (I was very surprised to learn this.) He had moved to Moscow,

My mother Leonore, known to me as "Mu", to my children as "Oma" (grandma), to her friends as "Lore" or "Lorschen". She loved Israel, but wept at the cruel treatment of Palestinians

where he had lived for nine years, and got married, before coming to Haifa, six years ago, with his wife and now fourteen-year-old daughter. We crawled along in the evening rush-hour out of Tel Aviv and then bowled along a new motorway through mainly flat country with big ugly modern businesses-like furniture shops and car show rooms on our left, and slightly hilly country on the right. Some of these hills had clearly defined skeins of lights outlining what the driver told me were Arab towns. On my map of Israel there are a large number of areas coloured brown which indicates "Palestinian responsibility for civil affairs, internal security and public order", and larger patches of yellow: "Palestinian responsibility for civil affairs and public order of the Palestinians, Israeli responsibility for security of Israelis". Some of these have names that are only too familiar, and not only from the Bible: Jericho (Yeriho); Ramallah; Bethlehem; Hebron; Gaza ... Then there are blue lines with various kinds of subtly different shading to show "Line of disengagement" and "Israeli Settlement Area". One is in a "war zone".

Finally we reached Kibbutz Hazorea, drove in past a sentry box, and there stood a funny little electric vehicle with a twig of a man in it: Rafael Tabor. He gave me a lift to a guest house where I was mistress of a large room divided in two, with a fridge, sink, table and shower room in the part nearest the entrance, two beds and three armchairs in the other. Then over a little bridge to his own house, with a similar arrangement: a large room divided into an entrance lobby with a shower-room, a sitting room, and a kitchen area with a dining table. It's all very attractively arranged with plants and pictures and bookcases, comfortable chairs and a carpet on the tiled floor. Here he and Devora have lived for forty odd years. Two small bedrooms have been added fairly recently, and there is a little garden behind, with a dried-up stream or Wadi running alongside it. These two, my very distant cousins (Rafael's mother's father, Nathan Zuntz, was my father's grandfather), founder members of this kibbutz, are a lively old couple, alert and quick on the uptake.

Devora is very perceptive and with a nice line in tactful irony, where Rafael tends to see the flaws in things and people. She tries to brush his pessimism aside. Both take a lively interest in the present and the future as well as the past.

The kibbutz kept reminding me of Nyakasura School, in Uganda: numerous single-storey buildings dotted around a spacious terrain, coarse grass cut short (not in the same category as an Oxford lawn), splendid huge trees, including palms, cedars and cypresses, and many flowering plants which also grow in Uganda. Plenty of birds, some raucous, most twittering. Also a certain shabbiness, peeling paint, plaster falling off walls, cracked paving, replacement locks not fitting the holes in the door. Here and there a determined stab at ART – there is a fine modern sculpture by the entrance, and there are more almost two-dimensional sculptures outside the small Museum, which has a collection of East Asian Buddhas, an archaeological section with local finds going back thousands of years – and a contemporary exhibition of holographics by Shimon Hameiri. And the two-storey central block has concrete reliefs on one wall and a wall-hanging inside the refectory made of squares embroidered by many hands, rather like the hassocks in an English church. Here we had virtually all our meals. Devora has never had to cook; the food is available three times a day, free, like everything else in this money-less experiment in true socialism; and it is healthy, with quantities of vegetables, both raw and cooked, and meat/fish/egg/sosmix dishes; but all a little insipid and lukewarm. Efficient self-service, and a clever washing-up system involving a conveyor belt. This unfortunately broke down on my last day and we used disposable plastic cutlery and crockery.

"From each according to his ability; to each according to his need." The Socialist principles in action here also mean: equality and rotation. No-one has any money, but there is a theoretical Budget for each member, and expenses are deducted from it – mains services, use of a Kibbutz car, or the computer, or actual money for travel, and so on. Young people, when they finish school, are given the means to travel all over the world before they have to do their military service. Rotation means that you might work one week in the kitchen, the next in the plastics factory; or you might be running the garden centre for a while, and then arranging the books in the library. It must be wonderful for these octogenarians to see this land, which was "all stones" when they came half a century ago, with about a hundred other Socialist *Werkleute* from Germany - now with a forest - some of which they planted with their own hands - clothing the hillside, and about 1000 inhabitants. There are plenty of children, for whom there are a Children's House (where they used to spend almost all their time - now they sleep in their parents' houses), schools, a little farm-zoo where they come in the afternoons to tend the goats, rabbits, hens, birds, etc., and an adventure playground. The Tabors' youngest daughter, having grown up here, lives here with her three daughters and teaches in the school. Her partner is a fish farming expert, at present acting as a consultant in Mexico.

However, the Socialist Paradise is not an unqualified success. Rafael laments the fact that many fail to attend the General Assembly, or to volunteer for responsible positions, since they don't want to be exposed to criticism and hostility; even to vote - only about 50% do. While I was there they were voting on accepting certain new arrivals as members.

In this - its failure to live up to its own lofty ideals - it reminds me of the École d'Humanité in Switzerland with its *Schulgemeinden* which were supposed to be perfect democracy, with every member of the school, from the smallest child to the catering staff to the teachers and the owner-directors, equally entitled to discuss problems until the best solution was found (voting, with majorities suppressing minorities, were abhorred there); but in practice the Schulgemeinden consisted of Edith and Paulus taking turns to harangue us for our wrong-doings. At Hazorea, all sorts of changes are underway. Some who have the capacity to do good work as managers or bursars etc, prefer to work outside. They hand over all their earnings to the kibbutz, keeping just a few perks like company cars for themselves. But they prefer to live on the kibbutz, because life here is so tranquil and pleasant, with beautiful surroundings, and safe for the children. Some people even pay rent to live there while working elsewhere without being kibbutz members.

And it is idyllic – lots of birds; dogs and cats lazing in the sun, virtually no traffic apart from bikes and the little electric vehicles for the old people, plugged in to be recharged when not in use, whining slowly along the narrow asphalt or concrete paths that criss-cross the terrain. This kibbutz, unlike others, is expanding; houses are being built on the other side of what used to be a highway, now cut off and replaced by the new motorway further away. So now a new fence will have to be put up to enclose these new houses.

The whole kibbutz is surrounded by a ten-foot-high metal fence-with numerous gates, all open and unguarded now; but: "It's easier to defend the place when it's fenced in". And the grim little concrete blocks that are entrances to underground shelters have not been used for years,and have been painted in bright colours. One effect of the Gulf War, when Saddam Hussein attacked Israel,was that the carers felt unable to guarantee the safety of the children; so their parents' houses had rooms added so that they could sleep at home.

An example of something that Devora, the optimist, likes to observe: that something good often results from evil. She was always against the system that kept the children away from their families so much, and she and Rafael actually lived outside the kibbutz for a short time so as to be able to keep their children at home. They have three – Joel, another daughter whom I didn't meet, and Naamit - who is seventeen years younger than Joel. This kibbutz has a herd of cattle, some being raised for meat, some for milk, and kept in deplorable conditions in an enclosure of deep mud with hay and other carefully controlled nutrients in troughs round the perimeter. Each one's condition is continually monitored by computer. The glazed hopelessness in the eyes of the calves and cows and bullocks - all in their separate prisons - was unmistakeable. There used to be a battery hen house, now rusting away and empty, but for economic, not humanitarian reasons. They grow cotton too; but they realised early on that they could not survive by agriculture alone, and there is also a furniture factory - now closed, and to be transferred to Jordan, where wages are lower than even the purely hypothetical ones on the kibbutz; a fish farm, now mainly for goldfish, many exported, especially to the UK; a garden centre; and a plastics factory, with huge American machines. Here, pellets of plastic are melted, and then air is blown through the mass to produce a vast expanding balloon towering up into the roof space. This "film" is then conducted onto a succession of rollers which fold it, print elaborate images, names, barcodes on at lightning speed, seal and cut it at intervals and - hey presto! a million plastic bags for milk and other foodstuffs flop into cardboard boxes...

Rafael has worked in this factory, as in just about every other area of the kibbutz. Devora has also done many different jobs, including teaching Hebrew on a crash-course for which this kibbutz is a centre: a very international group live in the houses set aside for it, including Japanese. When they first arrived, in the 1930s, Rafael and Devora were given a tent - British Army issue, a round "bell-tent". Then they built little wooden semi-detached bungalows, each family being allowed ten square metres of space (in which Joel rode his tricycle); next, breeze block houses were built, which soon suffered subsidence and had to be demolished. All the buildings now rest on columns sunk deep into the ground, with the actual floor above the ground, not resting on it. There is just a thin layer of soil over rock; Rafael is (typically) dubious about all the very tall and flourishing trees: their roots were meant to penetrate into the rock, but he believes they haven't; some don't stand quite straight, and he is confident they will come crashing down one day in a high wind. But all the houses have their little gardens, a bit amateurish perhaps, with various citrus trees, some bananas, and huge clumps of bird-of-paradise plants, hibiscus, poinsettia trees, and many others we had in Uganda, and still others that are familiar from our time in Portugal.

Watching a group of children running along past my room with their teacher on some outing from kindergarten, I was struck by the variety of races represented. Some had silvery blonde hair, others crisp African curls, and just about everything between. What does it mean to be a Jew? It certainly isn't a race. People are fat, and thin; tall, and short;there is NO racial type, no racial unity, such as we saw in Uganda, where you could clearly distinguish the Bantu and the Hamitic types. nor is religion an essential part of Jewish identity. Rafael and Devora, devoted to the Jewish cause, have no religion, and there is no synagogue on this kibbutz. I heard a lot of very unfavourable remarks about Rabbis and Rabbinical laws and customs. The Sabbath and some festivals like Hanuka are observed, much as we do Sundays and Christmas, just for the pleasure. So what IS it so many died for?

*

Joel, the oldest son, now well on in his fifties, arrived in a huge brand-new Land Rover - a stocky, well-preserved man who within minutes of his arrival was telling me that the kibbutz, the whole idea of a kibbutz, is WRONG, being communist: you have everything in common, the knives and forks, the work, the land, the women ... I was shocked, especially at the sexism in that last remark; but he said it again: Yes, the women too, just ask my parents! By now I knew that he had been working on the kibbutz, in charge of buildings, but had moved out when he married his first wife, with whom he had five children. Then she left him, and he divorced her, under rabbinical law, which meant she has no rights whatsoever, gets nothing from him, and he had custody of all the children - the youngest being then, I think, seven - though he let her keep the oldest...

Joel drove us over to his home near Haifa, where he lives with his partner Livnat, a slim, vivacious and very warm and demonstrative Moroccan - also an excellent cook and housekeeper, a loving stepmother and step-daughter-in-law. Their house is very big, with rooms for five children as well as themselves, though all the children have now grown up and moved out. The food was lavish, served on a massive glass-topped teak table from Thailand; under the glass was a fabulously carved jungle scene with trees and elephants; the backs and fronts of the eight chairs ditto. All the young people were there, some with their partners: Joel's son had gone to Italy to get married to a large and lovely young woman, a producer of TV commercials. He was still studying, and working part-time, in computers. (There are no grants or loans for students in Israel; they all have to have part-time jobs.) There's quite a trade in these weddings abroad, with agents who will set them up anywhere in the world and in any guise, though the most usual is the nearest, Cyprus. Within Israel there is no alternative to the rabbinical wedding, so the non-religious get married abroad - and the Israeli state recognises these marriages. The youngest daughter had just finished her military service; she had opted for the two-and-a-half year period as it meant she could be an officer, though most of the time she worked as a secretary to some high-ranking officer. Her real ambition was to be an actress, so we swapped notes on that. I was struck with the similarity in style between these large, healthy-looking, restless, noisy, confident young people, with their careers apparently mapped out for them, and some others we met at Burghausen in Germany earlier this year, and mentioned something of the kind to Devora: whereupon the young newly-wed man piped up. Actually, he had no idea what he wanted to do. - I thought you were into computers? - Yes, and working for Bill Gates' company. But I hate it! It seems all he really wants to do is to work with wood. He wants to make all the furniture for their home.

*

Sunday morning, my third morning on the kibbutz. Devora had a medical appointment; so Rafael and I breakfasted together in the refectory and then set out for the "Handtuch", the towel-shaped area where they first settled in 1934: now impossible to identify exactly, with the new roads and buildings and trees. But the Tower is still there, and a concrete replica of a bell tent, and one of the wooden houses – Rafael said every other nail was hammered in by him – which is being used as a sort of ramshackle museum, in which they store the odd primus stove, mouse trap, brush, tin plates, fruit press, the things they used in those early days, a bed with a mosquito net. They were infested with bugs and malaria was rife.

Now there are virtually no insects. I counted seven butterflies (and the weather was warm and sunny, with some thundery rain one day). Insects have been exterminated because of malaria. Every kibbutz and settlement had to appoint an insect-monitor – Rafael was one for a year – who had to give every pond and puddle, every water-way, a coating of oil; and in addition there were huge spraying programmes (with DDT, I think). Rafael seemed pleased when he saw a lizard, to think that sufficient insects had returned to support it.

We went into the watch tower, three floors, originally with a wall-mounted ladder, now a steep staircase. There was a lamp on top which could be rotated by means of a metal handle to illuminate the perimeter fence – more to scare off Arab infiltrators than actually to make them visible, as they would have been unseen if they had simply kept still. There were windows and shooting slits at various levels, and there was one occasion when things got very serious, and Devora actually fired a shot, hoping that she had missed... Later they found bales of straw dotted around; if they had not driven off the attackers, they would have set fire to the place. In the end it was the British army that dealt with them, I was told. The land had been bought with money from the Jewish Fund, to which Jews all over the world contributed; but the payment had gone to a few rich land-owners who lived in luxury in Paris and other places; their tenants got nothing, until, after some time, they were paid half the original price. But Rafael made no bones about it; they had driven out the Arabs and they had to fight to keep hold of the land. Had there been no Hitler, he said, there would be no Israel; and of course it was unjust that the Arabs should pay for the sins of the Nazis. But he could see no alternative.

I found myself wondering how this fitted in with the "mass of stones" I had been told was all they had found when they came; and that again wouldn't fit in with the information that the Arabs had been growing grapes, but the Jews had failed to and had turned to cotton instead. I suppose different bits of information apply to different bits of the land.

All that day there were low-flying fighter planes tearing across the sky. Rafael assured me they were training flights - climbing steeply and swooping down to land. But I feared for poor Lebanon. There was a break around 3pm but the flights started again around 6.

In the evening, Jehuda Zuntz and his wife Edith came with their son Itai and his wife. Like the Tabors, they are in their eighties, their youngest offspring forty. Jehuda and Edith, again like the Tabors, have lived on their kibbutz since their thirties. It is called Sde Elijahu, after one of the very few rabbis who supported the kibbutz movement. It is extremely hot, being well below sea level; he brought us a large bag of dates. Later we were joined by Naamit and her daughters, so we were quite a crowd. Itai and his wife only speak Hebrew, so for some of the time I was out of what was clearly a lively conversation. Then Jehuda and I spoke in German, with Edith, Devora and Rafael joining in. (Nobody really wants to use German in Israel, understandably.) Jehuda is the great researcher into the Zuntz family history, who - still working at technical drawing, on his kibbutz - has produced the monumental book which gives details of hundreds of our kinsfolk going right back to Zons and Frankfurt in 1488.

But I'm not in it, nor my brother and sister and mother. As with "*Who's Who*", only Fe's second wife and their children are included. Jehuda sympathises with my exasperation. Some time ago, he told me, a Professor Canitz from Tübingen University got in touch with him on what he felt were rather spurious grounds and asked to be allowed to visit him. Jehuda thought it was a bit odd but agreed. In the event Canitz gave Jehuda the only information he had been able to get about Günther, my father, asserting that he had been married just once, with an English woman, and had just the three children with her. Now Tübingen was the university which enabled my father in his old age to complete his colossal classical Greek language course, with every example of a grammatical point an authentic quotation from a classical Greek author, which he regarded as his greatest gift to the human race, opening the door to the glories of Greece by way of the language. I mentioned this to Jehuda, and he immediately linked it to the visit by Canitz; though why this Professor should have any interest in perpetuating the denial of our existence is beyond me. But if that was his purpose in visiting Jehuda, he succeeded. Of course, it is also possible that Canitz himself believed that my father had only been married once, and that his visit to Jehuda was simply due to a wish that Fe should not be left out of the family history.

On the Monday, Naamit picked me up from the refectory, fetched a key from an office and led me to the carpark, where there were about twenty identical white cars. We got into the one with a big red 6 painted on it and drove out onto the motorway, then turned onto the almost deserted road up Mount Carmel to the monastery of Elijahu-Elijah. She expounded the story depicted in a large relief in which Elijah challenged the worshippers of Baal to a competition. Both teams had a sheep (dead, I trust) lying on a pile of sticks right here on Mount Carmel for a burnt offering. The team whose sticks caught fire was to be the winner - the favoured of God. Well, Baal's side lost. So of course Elijah's team killed the followers of Baal, all two hundred of them. Nice story, isn't it, Naamit commented. Later she took me to a Druze village - a town, really - for a stroll along the street of souvenir shops and a glass of tea. The Druze are welcome in Israel. Unlike the other Arabs, they serve in the armed forces. I mentioned that I had seen Wallid Jumblatt's Druze village in Lebanon and we wondered why these people keep their religion such a dark secret - even from most of the members of the sect! Naamit, like me, is baffled by other people's religious beliefs. In fact I felt we have quite a lot in common, and hope to see more of her. When I said that she must be very satisfied with kibbutz life, since she was born and bred there and now her three daughters are growing up there too, she wrinkled her nose. What alternative is there? Her husband was coming home soon for a holiday, and it might be possible for the whole family to join him in Mexico next year. But he cannot find work in Israel outside the kibbutz since all the fish farms belong to kibbutzes - and they are over-manned.

Then we went to Haifa and we took a lift to the top of the University building which stands on top of a hill like a vast wafer. We watched the crimson ball of the sun sink into the sea beyond the circling strings of lights of this small, hilly town. Then home to Hazorea; a long chat with Rafael and Devora; a bread and cheese supper, and to bed for the last time in my guest room.

On the morning of my departure I had time to walk through the kibbutz, past the now empty swimming pool and the tennis courts and Naamit's house and out onto the hillside where there had been a forest fire some years ago. The forest was regenerating itself naturally: small, fluffy green pines and undergrowth. Perfect, cloudless weather, hot, a slight breeze, and looked down at the kibbutz, this happy valley, enclosed in its high fence. I didn't go far. A few

weeks ago a tourist had been killed in the forest nearby. A robbery?
No: hate.

Later, Rafael said: I want to explain this place to you. And why
we can't be pacifists. And why we need the atom bomb.

Back in 1934, he said, I was sick of the humiliations we Jews were
exposed to in Germany, wearing the yellow star, the Aryanisation
of the Zuntz coffee firm where I was working, being told to keep
out of sight when high-up Nazis came... Of course that was nothing compared to what came later, or indeed to the long history of
cruelty, not only in Germany, but in Spain under Ferdinand and
Isabella, and in Poland, and everywhere. And I asked myself: Why?
And I concluded that it was because we Jews had no country of our
own. So I converted to Judaism, though I had been brought up a
Christian, and I joined the Werkleute, the Jews who were preparing
themselves to live and work in Palestine, and in due course we came
here. But They want to "push us into the sea". Even after Oslo. And
They will do so if we aren't strong and if we don't have nuclear weapons. Because They have them. Iraq has germ warfare, Pakistan has
the Bomb. Iran nearly has. So we cannot do without. This I wanted
to explain to you. But the worst thing is this: that the Jews cannot
agree among themselves.

Then it was time to get into the taxi back to Tel Aviv. This time
my driver was an ebullient fat young Moroccan who spent a lot of
the time talking into one or other of his two mobile phones. In the
airport, uniformed young women asked me a string of questions.
Evidently I passed; and after the usual long long wait - again the
plane was an hour late - I was up in my Boeing 757 looking down at
the lights of Tel Aviv, thinking how crazy it was to think that this
sliver of a country should be prepared to commit nuclear suicide
in the name of self defence, thinking too how idyllic old age in the
kibbutz would be...if it all survives.

Chapter 13: Visiting Poland, May 2002

KRAKOW

We three - David, my cousin Dudu (Susanne Bessac, of Missoula, Montana) and I wanted to visit the places in Poland where Olga Hempel, known as Oma Drübbelchen - our grandmother - had lived. We flew to Krakow on Monday May 6, descending through the clouds to a city with countless high-rise blocks of flats strewn across the countryside round it. We travelled from the airport to the city by bus in a thunderstorm, and had the satisfaction of watching people in summery t-shirts running through the rain to catch up with us at the next bus stop. They all looked quite cheerful and healthy. Here let me say at the outset that throughout our ten days in Poland we saw no sign of the economic collapse, high unemployment, high crime rates, pick-pockets, and drunkenness we had been warned of by just about everyone we told we were going to Poland. On the contrary, we were all struck by the good looks, slender figures, tasteful clothes, friendly faces and ready smiles of the people we saw. They looked as if they were enjoying life, and whenever we found ourselves in difficulties because of our ignorance of the language, someone - usually a young woman - would appear from nowhere to help us out with sometimes excellent, sometimes rather hairy English.

The bus took us through the green countryside at first, with some villages consisting of large houses built to resemble a child's drawing of a house, based on a capital A. Soon we were in the outskirts of Krakow, with the usual anonymous blocks of flats you see everywhere on the Continent, and then in more historic looking suburbs, with attractive two or three storey terraced houses. Finally we were disgorged from the bus at the big railway station, and went in to buy tickets for the next leg of our tour, to Wroclaw, where we were going two days later. Krakow has a splendid station, with vast chandeliers and vistas down long Turkish style marble floored halls. Here we did see a few drunks, shabby elderly men, propped up against the pillars, shouting and singing incoherently. After a fairly long series of enquiries, we got our tickets and took a taxi ("You want to go Auschwitz?" asked the driver - we assured him we didn't) to the apartment hotel David had so cleverly booked by email, where we occupied the two attic rooms, very nicely (and recently) done up, with superb en suite bathrooms, and a view across trees, noisy with magpies, to the flats opposite, and straight into their windows.

We took a bus back to the station, and walked into the centre of Krakow, which is a huge market square or Rynek. Across one corner it has a red brick Marienkirche with two spires, one slightly taller than the other "because they were built by two brothers who each wanted his tower to be the tallest. In the end one brother shot the other and was declared the winner." A trumpeter starts playing a certain piece every evening, and breaks off suddenly at the exact note and the exact moment when a predecessor, hundreds of years ago, was silenced by an arrow through his throat. Perhaps it was the brother? A golden crown surrounds the topmost metal spike on the tower. We saw golden crowns everywhere in Krakow - golden crowns even surround each of the railings round a pavement café. Inside the church, the walls are most wonderfully painted in stripes of warm colours, brown, rose, sage green, and the arched ceiling is deep blue, studded with golden stars. Poland is certainly a religious country. There seemed to be non-stop services going on in this and the many other churches we saw, with hymns sung with loud, strained voices; numerous bevies of nuns moving about the streets; parents and children going in and out of the churches at all times of the day.

This Rynek has another tower (it was being repaired) belonging to the Town Hall, and a statue of the poet Adam Mickiewicz, under which two French horn players performed exceedingly well. The extensive market hall is given over to tourist trap shops, with every conceivable variation of amber artefact, and numerous figures of rabbi musicians with the black hats and the long black ringlets playing musical instruments.

The next day we joined crowds of tourists, many of them school parties, at the Wawel, which was the palace of the kings of Poland for hundreds of years, until uniting with Lithuania made a move to Warsaw seem called for. It has a cathedral, a former parade ground, numerous buildings, and an Italianate piazza with splendid royal apartments on four floors and elegant staircases. Here each little horde of well-behaved children was given a history lesson by earnest teachers.

After lunch, David and I left Dudu contentedly drawing in the Wawel, and wandered along the river Vistula / Wisla / Weichsel, where many people were enjoying the warm sunshine - an impressive Japanese Cultural Centre is on the opposite side - and then inland to the suburb called Kasimierz, the former Jewish quarter, with numerous wine bars and art shops now installed in the houses, and many closed synagogues. One is now a museum. This was the first synagogue I had ever been in, and the explanatory notes were helpful. There was a structure in the middle like a giant parrot's cage, from which the Torah was read. All round the walls there were reminders of the Jewish men (no women) who had worshipped here (Judaism is a very sexist religion) and though the whole area was not as claustrophobic as the ghetto in Trier, or as gaunt and desolate as the one we saw in Venice, it was impossible not to feel dismal, knowing what had happened here, so close to Auschwitz-Birkenau.

Wroclaw (Breslau)

The next day we took the train to Wroclaw (formerly Breslau) because Drübbelchen - Olga Hempel, nee Fajans - had studied here. (So had Dudu's paternal grandfather, Friedrich Leppmann.) Olga was one of the first women to study medicine, she had done the first, theoretical part of her medical studies in Freiburg in the Black Forest. In 1899 she came here for the practical part, and in her memoirs she remembers most of the doctors who were her mentors with great fondness and respect - especially the professor of surgery called Jan Mikulicz. In Wroclaw, Andrej Teisseyve - a friend of a friend of Dudu's - took us on a conducted tour. Again, as in Krakow, there is a huge and splendid Rynek, with an extraordinary Gothic town hall. He led us through an alleyway to the Leopold University, which was being cleaned up in readiness for the celebration of its 300th anniversary. Thence along the river Oder / Odra to Tumsky (Cathedral) Island, where nuns with a microphone were leading children along the road, singing a doleful sounding hymn. A service was in progress in the wide-open Cathedral, the priest leading prayers with a powerful loud-speaker. Then up the road - to David's delight - came a marching band; but when they reached the Cathedral, they hushed their noise and marched away again on tip-toe till they felt free to blast away again. Back across the river again, and a busy road, to what Andrej called "the medical university" - and here was a street named after Mikulicz, and the surgical department he had founded, an extensive golden coloured building, not destroyed in the War, unlike most of Wroclaw: in fact, the very building where Drübbelchen had studied! Nearby, on a wall, was a plaque showing Mikulicz being crowned with a wreath of bay leaves. Oma was not the only person who had admired him!

We stayed in a big, old-fashioned, luxurious hotel called the Monopol. After a good night's sleep and an ample breakfast, we wandered through the squares and streets and by the river. We wanted to see the old synagogue which was clearly marked on the street plan; but at first we couldn't. In the end we came upon it by accident - curiosity led us through an archway into an untidy yard where there were a few parked cars and some heaps of builders' materials. On the left a tall, shabby block of flats, with a sign: 1900-1901; on our right, a magnificent horse chestnut tree in full bloom; and ahead, behind a corrugated iron fence, an imposing, square-set temple building, with classical style pilasters and, just visible, a dome in the centre of a flat roof. Round the front, stone steps led up to a locked door. Through the tall windows we could see some plastic chairs, as if some kind of group activities, classes or group therapy perhaps, took place inside. But great cakes of plaster had fallen away from the brick walls; small sycamores were sprouting from cracks in the masonry. Decaying splendour! But was it necessary to build quite such an imposing building? Could what happened have been avoided if there had been less emphasis on the Jews' separate identity? Of course, for most of their history most of the Jews of the diaspora were anything but enviable. Whatever one thinks, the melancholy of the place was underscored when we read a notice - it was in Hebrew and German - saying it was from that yard that the Jews were transported to the extermination camps.

Then a man came out of the flats and drove one of the cars - a taxi - out through a narrow alley. We followed slowly. It led past an ultra-modern building, almost all glass, on the left, and a raw brick wall on the right, framing the tower of the old German military church, with a metal dome on top that resembled a helmet. It reminded one that all this area had been German with German names for rivers - Wechsel - and towns - Breslau, Danzig, etc. There was a student festival going on, "for humanity": huge loudspeakers on a platform roared out dreadful singing, culminating in a deafening rendition of "Blowing in the Wind". The merrymaking continued - slightly muted - most of the night. I looked out of our hotel window at 3.15 am to see a long line of taxis, their doors open, their drivers gathering in small groups round one or other, talking and laughing - bursts of side-splitting laughter. Young people, the girls (as Dudu observed) all looking like Barbie dolls, the boys slightly more baggy, were striding along, also talking and laughing, enjoying each others' company, having come from some party or other, unencumbered by any bags, and not, it seemed, at all drunk.

Here's David's poem:

SYNAGOGUE

I see it still, a drab Greek temple
With pitted grey pilasters
Statement of Jewish pride
That muscled in beside
The goyim city-masters.
For over fifty years this place –
So drab, so grey and gaunt –
Has heard no chants or prayers.
Only the ghosts of rabbis haunt
The office desks and chairs
That seem to give this tragic site
A trivial purpose now.
Perhaps the heaps of builders' stuff,
Their huts, their vans, their scaffolding
Portend a greater thing?
The tenements that shut it in
Have windows with no views.
Were those who lived here years ago
Beside this drab grey holy place
German or Polish Jews?
At all events, the yellow-starred
Assembled in this yard.
Who lives still who witnessed how
The army lorries bore them off
To Auschwitz-Birfkenau?
And now it's rows of fading ghosts
That shuffle silently,
The only sweet distraction here:
The flourishing menorah of
A candled chestnut tree.

TORUN (THORN)

Next we took the train to Torun. Railway workers were stripped down to their scanty y-fronts as they dug a drainage ditch along the track, the weather was so hot. We travelled for hours through a flat, green world, with here and there a solitary blue-clad peasant forlornly hoeing in the middle of the vast plain. We saw no cattle, little cultivation, plenty of streams and canals; no hedges, no fences, very few small villages, hardly any churches; no pylons, only tele-phone poles; virtually no roads. All the trains we saw were covered in graffiti. After Poznan (Posen), where we entered Pommerania (Pommern), we saw more trees; there were great balls of mistletoe in the poplars; hawthorn and horse chestnuts were in bloom. We came through some little woods with graceful silver birches and tall pines with reddish trunks, reminiscent of many German folk songs. Dudu opined that the land had been deforested to provide fuel for the brickworks. Certainly we saw few really old trees - and brick is the almost universal building material. The few houses we passed had white and purple lilacs in their gardens. There were a number of industrial sites in this area too, with modern box-shaped "units".

At Torun station, while Dudu and David queued up for the next day's train tickets, I went to an Information counter, hoping to find accommodation for the night (this was the only place David hadn't booked in advance) - but the only Information there was about trains. Soon, everyone in the queue was trying to divine my purposes. However, the young woman behind me understood me despite not knowing any English (she was intelligent AND kind) and led me to an inter-active computer in a dusty corner of the station. But here she too was flummoxed. However, another young woman who spoke excellent English took over, found several rooms availa-ble, decided which would be best for us, led us to the taxi and told the driver where to take us. This was just one of many incidents which made us feel like welcome guests, not bloody foreigners who hadn't even bothered to learn the language ....

Torun - Thorn - is where Olga was born. Her cousin, the painter Julie Wolf, added Thorn to her name because Wolf was so common; she signed her paintings Julie Wolfthorn. Unlike Wroclaw, Thorn was not devastated in the war, although it too had been declared a "fortress" by Hitler, who wanted these and other town-fortresses to be besieged by the advancing Soviet armies and to defend themselves fiercely, partly to pin down Soviet forces, and partly to become the pivots of the great fight back he envisaged if, as he hoped, the Western allies joined forces with Germany to destroy the Communists. Torun was ruled by the Teutonic Order (Deutscher Ritterorden) for 260 years, until the citizens revolted, destroying the knights' castle in 1454. After a war lasting 16 years the Treaty of Torun ousted the Ritterorden from the area. Thorn prospered because of the river-borne grain trade - in which Olga's father, having moved downstream to Gdansk, became extremely rich. Thorn, like Breslau, was a completely German city until the great population shift westward after the Second World War.

The River Wysla/Weichsel/Vistula is very wide and fast-flowing, excellent for carrying the rafts of timber loaded with grain, with little huts for the rafters' families, downstream. Now there are no boats of any kind on it, perhaps because it is shallow. It is separated from the town by a long brick wall, pierced by arched openings. A little millstream goes rushing down to it, the scars left by the mill wheel clearly visible on the old mill house. From the Town Hall tower we could see the grid-like layout of the town, all red brick, except the fine facades of the houses on the two squares. Well away from the old town, there is an arc of some 40 or 50 tower blocks. Our hotel was on one of the squares, with a great, elaborate brick Post Office and a busy church on one side, an open-air café, the town hall - and opposite: Dwor Artus - Arthur's Court. It is an Arts Centre, founded in the 19th century, when stories about King Arthur and the Knights of the Round Table were all the rage. (One is reminded of Kennedy and his "Camelot".) We enjoyed a concert there (Dvorak, Schubert and a local female composer, M. Cynk) in an ornate hall, something like Oxford Town Hall, but much brighter, with splendid chandeliers.

Early in the morning, I followed the smell of fresh bread and came to several bakeries where people were buying their breakfasts. One little boy was carrying a large bagful home to his family, kicking a football as he went. The streets were virtually car-free. Beyond a huge supermarket there was a traditional open-air market in full swing, selling fruit, vegetables, fish, meat - carpets - furniture - clothes - everything.

GDANSK (DANZIG)

The train to Gdansk went through more flat, green country - Pommern - with more small farms, lakes, rivers. Our apartment in the "Artist's House" hotel had two large rooms, TV, as all hotel rooms have these days, bath towels instead of sheets on the beds, a kitchen and a bathroom where hot water would thunder into the bath for a moment, then turn stone cold; finally one could coax a lukewarm trickle out. Outside, there were sudden fierce altercations between seagulls shrieking at each other as they chased each other off their perches on trees and rooftops round a school playground, disturbing the pigeons who were drinking from the puddles there and trying to persuade each other to be amorous. Looking the other way, you saw a great church tower made of brick - but where was the glowing red brick Olga enthuses about in her memoirs? Dudu said she (Drübbelchen) thought that amazing colour was due to the effect of sea spray on the brick; but now all the old bricks were quite blackened. They had been painstakingly picked out of the rubble produced by British and American air bombardments; perhaps the blackness was the effect of the fires in those awful weeks in 1945 when Danzig, too, was a "fortress". The whole of the old centre had been rebuilt in the 1950s, by the Communists, though it was a "bastion of capitalism", as a replica of what had been there before, shown on numerous etchings; so we were able to see the town Olga grew up in, just looking rather artificial, like a stage set for an opera, a bit too good to be true.

We had supper in a small riverside pub, and looked at the ships moored opposite by Granary Island, where brilliant red brick ruins reared out of the bright green foliage of the shrubs sprouting in the rubble. So that had not been refurbished. But there was a washing line among the ruins of the great granaries where, presumably, Great-Grandfather's stocks of grain waited to be loaded and transported through the Baltic to London and other parts of Western Europe. Further along on the hither side was the great black crane which the dockers had used in the past. As in Thorn, there was a wall all along the river front, with archways in to the fine old streets that ran inland. The chief of these, Ulica Dluga (Langgasse) is fabulously beautiful, with ornate, tall, colourful, Dutch-style terraced houses, topped by human or animal figures or a golden sun or star. It widens out into a square where there is a fountain with a fine figure of Neptune, with a seahorse which flicks its tail up obligingly to conceal Neptune's private parts. Here street vendors and shops were selling lovely and very inexpensive amber. One shopkeeper told us it was millions of years old, and can still be found in the sand by the sea. Unpolished, it looks dull and opaque. I asked him how you could tell if it was amber or plastic. He demonstrated, holding a burning match to a piece: it smelled of woodsmoke. Plastic would simply melt. But dare one try this out on the wares of the street vendors?

In the evening, an acquaintance of my friend Jean Kaye's, Piotr Ruckewicz, who had found this hotel for us, came and talked for while. He teaches English linguistics and his English is excellent. He remarked that there had been no unemployment under the Communists; now, it's 20%.... "The stronger always wins," he said, "which the Japanese should have remembered before they attacked Pearl Harbour". He thought America's treatment of Native Americans was comparable to Russia's Gulags. He is a deeply pessimistic man: It would be best, he said, if our galaxy would collide

With David in the early stages of dementia

with another, scattering our atoms through the universe. Then at last it would no longer be important whether we were Marxist or Catholic or Muslim or Jewish or American or African. We saw him again two days later. He is an atheist, though both his parents were devout Catholics. "My mother used the 'rhythm method' of contraception and had eight children - the last was stillborn. She never had a holiday." "They say God is love, and forgives everyone in the end, after purgatory, even Hitler, even Stalin - so why should we try to be good?"

Olga grew up in a house on Hundgasse (Ulica Organa) which runs parallel to Langgasse. It may have had one of the high porches or terraces with fine stone figures and wrought iron which are a feature of many of the houses. The business premises were on the ground floor, with store rooms containing samples of grain in a basement; the family, and all their relations, lived above.

Next day, Dudu wanted to draw at the riverside. David and I headed for the Lenin shipyards and the memorial to the famous Trade Union, Solidarnocz. We walked along a filthy little canal - overtaking and being overtaken by a family whose young son, in a smart suit, had obviously just had his First Communion - so had various girls we saw in snowy white dresses - the families looked very proud, the youngsters quite overwhelmed by their own importance. We went on, past some huge blocks of flats and a shopping centre, and thought we could see the monument, a brownish structure rearing out of some trees on a hill to our left; but crossing the railway on a big busy road bridge we saw the shipyards were all over on our right, clusters of drooping, inactive derricks extending across a huge area. Still I was intrigued by this green, wooded rise and we followed a path that led past a building covered with the Solidarnosc logo and some workers' flats and up into the trees. Drübbelchen had written about the town with its red brick churches "embraced by the green arms of the ramparts", where she, her father, his Scottish friend Stoddart and their dogs had gone for their daily

walks before breakfast "to the Russian Grave". The brownish structure turned out to be a fine example of modern art: two huge plastic
girders, slightly warped, erect, and an inscription commemorating
the Millennium. We left it, descended into a steep little valley – the
First Communion family was strolling along the lane there, while
the smart boy and his sister went rushing along the muddy path
above – where numerous brick buildings in the hillside were clearly
some sort of military bunkers. So these were the defensive ramparts
Oma had remembered! We climbed up the slope on the other side,
and followed a pleasant path along the ridge and came to another
monument, not quite as tall, made of stone, blank on the first three
sides we looked at, but with an inscription in Russian on the fourth!
And a mosaic of St George and the Dragon! It must be "The Russian
Grave" she had written about, in memory of Russian soldiers who
had died in successive battles for Danzig in 1734, 1807, 1813 and 1898.
We walked on, past more brick-built bunkers, along the ridge which
indeed curved slightly in an arc round the city on our left, a path
much used by dog walkers to this day – and I indulged in fantasies
of two sober-suited gentlemen and a lively little girl running hither
and thither with two dogs, in this place, 120 odd years ago.

Sopot (Zoppot)

Wanting to get the train to Sopot, we walked through lovely
Langgasse (Ulica Dluga) and the Golden Gate to the busy ring road
– and were lost. I went into a bread shop to ask for directions to the
station, and a young girl said, in English: "I will show you." Took me
out and was filled with doubt. "Eh – this way? Or this way?" Older
women came out and here was another of these conferences. Finally
one said, in no uncertain terms: "I will tell you good way. Always
along here. On left. See big clock tower…"

In fact the station was only a stone's throw away. We got our tickets from a friendly woman who explained with sign language where
platform three was and that the train left in four minutes.

It was a grubby little train, rattling through the suburbs, and stopping frequently. It took about 20 minutes to reach Sopot. This was presumably the line used by Olga and her sisters and brothers when, during the summer months, they lived in the family's summer house in Zoppot and needed to go into Danzig. And there were other prosperous families who had similar houses out there. One of them was called Schubert, owners of a popular bakery and tea shop in Danzig. And they had a son called Hans, about three years older than Olga.

"One day" (she writes in her memoirs) "I was lying on the beach at Zoppot, as I often did. I was a healthy, happy girl of 14. A young man of about 17 walked past. And I fell in love with him, then and there; and this love dominated my whole being for at least ten years." That was her "Schubert".

A big road leads from the station down to the front, where there is a long pier built since Olga's time. We walked through a park to the beach - off-white sand stretching as far as the eye could see in both directions. Garish little kiosks served beer and ice cream. There were dustbins at regular intervals on the soft sand. It was easier to walk at the water's edge, where jackdaws competed with seagulls for the few edible bits there among tiny shells and colourful stones.

Dudu settled down to paint some fishing boats, while I walked along the front and through the shrubs and roses at the top and across a cycling road into a small park, wondering if this was where, one September 25, (a special day for her for the rest of her life) after three years of doubt and hope, Olga had reason to believe that Schubert loved her as much as she loved him. There was a police car at the entrance, inscribed, in English: "SOLID SECURITY"; two policemen inside were fast asleep. This park was now a holiday camp, with little wooden houses under the tall pines.

We had lunch in a newish restaurant at the edge of the beach - absolutely phoney wooden beams and a blue plastic "sky". Dudu went back to her painting while David and I strolled back into

Zoppot. Later I walked along the beach on the other side of the pier; again, there was a park with trees and benches inland; I was looking for the "Koliebka grotto" in which, after ten years, Olga's hopes were finally dashed; but I saw nothing resembling a grotto.

WARSAW AND HOME

We travelled to Warsaw through slightly undulating country with shallow lakes, isolated farms, some afforestation and strip cultivation, a few solitary peasants crouching in huge fields, weeding presumably, or walking slowly with big scythes over their shoulders like Old Father Time. Again, no hedges or fences, but some long embankments - there were terrible floods in Poland in 1997. A smart Polish woman sharing our compartment started speaking in excellent American - most of her relatives now live in the USA and she often visits them. The Sales Director for a Finnish chocolate firm (Faver), she was very helpful and obligingly answered all our questions. She considers the Polish people fundamentally lawless. Why? Because under foreign domination for so long - most recently Russian - it was patriotic to break the law imposed by those foreigners. Now they can't stop.

We did not spend much time in Warsaw. Our hotel was near the University, and we spent a few hours in the evening and the following morning strolling through the nearby streets, all totally reconstructed after being pulverised by the Nazis as a punishment for the 1944 uprising. It did not seem as attractive as Gdansk; most of the buildings were dull and heavy, a bit like Whitehall, and the streets were noisy with hectic traffic. We had a drink on the terrace of an "English Pub" overlooking the Wysla/Weichsel/Vistula far below, but were driven in by a cold wind. There was a pervasive smell of drains, and indoors everywhere smelled of stale tobacco. There were lots of dogs being taken for walks or watching the passing scene from windows, their paws resting comfortably on the sill. In a little park we came across a group of boys probably truanting, drinking pop and throwing stones. They looked quite terrified when we came upon them; presumably school attendance officers here are more effective than in England.

Next day we flew home. A group of pallid Jewish men, with black hats and ringlets, were on the plane, like the little figures we had seen in Krakow, and I found myself wishing they were not like that. I had to remind myself that in all probability they had nothing to do with the barbarism in Sharon's Israel, any more than Germans one meets nowadays have anything to do with Auschwitz.

Chapter 14: Living with Dementia

We're going for our daily walk. Millions of daisies, like snowflakes across the fields, each one stirring in the wind, fulfilling its destiny, from seed to flower to seed to death. And the trees, now in full leaf again, each with its own special leaves, each leaf a perfect shape, its own special shade of green – and waves of sweet smell from the hawthorn blossom in the hedge. I try to say something about it all, about the twittering of the skylarks – but what's the point. Any words would drop into a void; no response; no echo.

Of course I do speak, – and he does light up when he sees the grey and silver clouds, the vapour trails of aeroplanes: "Just look at that! That's wonderful!" And it's all right, he is himself again, and I can carry on.

I am a carer now – that's all: a member of the "invisible army" much praised by politicians – "the octogenarian carers saving the state millions" in a newspaper headline. It means my days – and nights – are entirely devoted to keeping the routines going: guiding, coaxing him through the days. Helping him get up, washed, dressed. The reverse process at bedtime. Trying to keep him active, to stimulate his darkening mind, thinking of games, outings, TV programmes – *Dad's Army* again and again – each showing a revelation to him (but not to me ...); giving him simple jobs to do, like stirring the soup, or washing up, or putting things away, anything to make him feel useful, to ward off the despair that's hanging over us both – and swallowing my exasperation when I find he's put the crockery away in the freezer, or is trying to shave with a plastic teaspoon, – or, asked to lay the table, find he's put on his anorak and gloves. It would be comical if it wasn't so serious.

The tedium is oppressive. And no one and nothing is trying to "stimulate" *me* ...

But a break in the routine is much worse.

I emerge from the shower and find he has put his shirt and trousers on over his pyjamas. And for a moment it feels quite simple – he'll have to take them off again, take his pyjamas off, and get dressed properly. "I will NOT!" he bellows. "These are MY things. You CANNOT have them!" His eyes are glaring, his voice is deep – he is a different person, no longer the gentle good-humoured man I have known for 60 years. He goes on shouting, threatens me, finally does attack me, throws a chair at me. Is this a Jekyll and Hyde moment? Will he stay like this?

I discover a trick. I pretend to cry. It brings him back to himself. Suddenly mortified, he begs forgiveness. ... Then it just takes about thirty minutes to get him washed and dressed.

I understand his emotion, his desire to be in charge, to have his decisions validated – but I have to correct him, to explain that he's made a mistake, to make him see, to laugh at his absurdities. Sometimes he says, very quietly, "I don't know what to do. I'm stupid. I'm finished. Just waiting – waiting – for – for the end of the world."

When the children were small, I sometimes felt motherhood was a kind of slavery. This, now, this second childhood, is worse, without the compensating factors. Here, now, the certainty is that it will get worse, and worse.

For more than half a century, it was David's job to prepare the grapefruit for breakfast. In fact he often mentioned, with some pride, that he once had a job that involved preparing the breakfast grapefruit for the Lord Mayor of London. In his old age, he was still in charge of preparing grapefruit for breakfast. He would put a couple of half grapes and a slice of apple on top to make it look like a smiling face. It was mildly amusing the first time, but he did it every single time, and we gradually realized that it was a sign of the onset of dementia. He also had the slightly unnerving habit of talking to food just before he ate it. He would put a small potato on the end of his fork and say "I'm going to eat you. Is that all right?" And then he would put on a funny squeaky voice, pretending to be the little potato, and say "that's all right, I don't mind!" – upon which he would eat the potato. Again, it was mildly amusing the first time, but after hundreds of repetitions it became depressingly obvious that it was part of his mental decline.

I remember sitting in the garden with him during summer holidays. He would always get excited if an airplane went over and would point at it and tell everybody else to look at it because the vapour trail was so beautiful. He also used quite often to point at the statue of the prodigal son in the garden. One of the last things he remembered was how he got that statue. One day when he was taking some Magdalen College schoolboys on community service, they painted the house of an old lady who let them have some old sculptures that were lying around behind her garage. He himself received this statue of the prodigal son being embraced by his father on his return home. He could still recount that anecdote in some detail long after he had forgotten almost everything else, even his own name.

Our last trip abroad together was a holiday in Italy in March 2014. We travelled by train all the way from Oxford to Rome, with an overnight stop in Paris. In Rome we met up with Tom and Manami. We explored Rome, Naples, Sorrento, and took a hair-raising bus ride along the clifftop road from Sorrento to Amalfi. David enjoyed every moment, in his slightly vague and detached way. The day we went to Pompeii was especially memorable. The very last stop on our tour of the ruins was the Circus Maximus, the shell of which is remarkably well preserved. We sat there on the grass and experimented with calling in various directions to test the echo. Then we left, going through a small tunnel to reach the outside of the stadium.

David and I held hands and sang a little song as we left through a little tunnel.

David was very reluctant to give up driving. For a long time he insisted that he was OK to drive, and one day Tom went out with him, to make sure he really was safe. He was not safe at all, and nearly killed both of them by wandering across the central line into oncoming traffic - more than once. I finally made him return his license, and had to hide the car key to stop him trying to drive. But on one occasion he did manage to find the key and had even rolled a few yards along the driveway before we noticed and stopped him. Later he would pathetically attempt to unlock the car door with his house key.

I started to keep a dementia diary. Here are a few typical entries.

February 5, 2015

Today he fell - again - but flat on his *back* this time. He had been preparing our desserts, as he usually does, but in the kitchen, not the dining room, and using a breakfast grapefruit, not the fruit in the dining room - so he was confused. He was holding a bowl in each hand as he came into the dining room ... He was badly shaken but not, I think, hurt, and he recovered over lunch.

February 18, 2015

He disappeared during a trip to the museum. I couldn't find him; asked an attendant if he'd seen him. He called up his colleagues, and one of them said - "He's gone out. He said he couldn't find his wife, so he was going home". Would he find his way? I hurried to our usual bus stop. When I got home, there were several people standing by our front door - including him. A young neighbour had seen him struggling up the road with blood on his face - she had been having a driving lesson - and she and the instructor had helped him home, and called an ambulance, which came quickly. The paramedics ascertained that he had broken his left knee. He must have fallen at some point - perhaps when getting out of the bus - but I will never know, as he didn't remember. He will have to spend some time in hospital, and many weeks with his left leg in plaster.

March 16, 2015

What happened in the night? In the morning he was lying on the mattress which was *on the floor beside the bed*, wet and smelly, muttering "I'm finished. I'm finished." He couldn't explain what had happened, beyond saying it was "terrible". He recovered his spirits later and made a surprise suggestion: to get a bus into town and have lunch at the Nosebag. So we did, negotiating the steep staircase up to the restaurant carefully. As was his wont, he spoke to each forkful of the food: "I'm going to eat you. Is that all right?" Then in a squeaky voice: "Yes that's all right, go ahead" before putting it in his mouth. The young man who had served us was amused. He later followed us down the steep stairs - patiently, as each step had to be carefully negotiated - to give David his walking stick, and me my handbag, which we had forgotten ...

April 5, 2015

His mind has got worse. He asks me, again and again, to explain the appointments next week - i.e. Tuesday: Trauma Unit; Wednesday: Physiotherapy; Thursday: Diabetes eye check up. Finally satisfied, he puts down the diary or the letter with the appointment - only to pick it up again, and ask again ...Then there are the "knee exercises" which the physiotherapist said should be done three times a day. He seems to forget them every time and has to be shown them again - and again .... The trouble is, I get exasperated. Can't always control the impatience boiling up inside me.

He often fails to shave properly, or clean and fix his dentures - and is a bit incontinent. He's happiest when busy at some job like washing up, or mowing the lawn - but gets very tired, before he's finished.

April 22, 2015

The splint has been removed from his fractured knee, and I thought: Hurrah, at last he can have a proper bath. He did - but then he couldn't get out of the bath. Panicked. Of course he did get out in the end, but swore he would never enter it again… so it was back to "washing" with a flannel. I ordered grab rails to be fixed by the bath and also by the lavatories. Three days ago he emerged from the bathroom saying happily: "I've just had a lovely bath!" The next two days he had showers – seemed to have reverted to the pre-knee break pattern. But today he only shaved. I had to spend a long time, persuading him to have a shower, or at least a wash.

April 28, 2015

Break in the usual routine – he got up when I was still asleep. That's probably responsible for his total confusion this morning, He normally does the washing up, but today he stood by the sink, his mind a blank. "How do I wash up?" I had to show him the bowl – turn on the tap – at each stage he was amazed, as if he'd never come across these things before.

Later he was his usual self again – but he discovered that his trousers were wet …

May 26, 2015

Today David is spending most of the day at the Limes Club for people with dementia for the first time. Hurray! If this is successful, Tuesdays will be freedom days for me!

June 1, 2015

I think his brain has shrunk further. I asked him to fetch the waste paper baskets from the bathroom and bedroom. Three times he went up – and came back empty handed. Said he didn't know where the bathroom was. Or the bedroom. Or what a waste paper basket was. Finally I managed to make it clear to him and watched him go upstairs and "find" the bathroom. Later I found he had removed the towels from the bathroom, folded them neatly, and put them in the bedroom …

June 26, 2015

I woke up about two a.m. and found David was wearing my blouse over his pyjama jacket, and my trousers. His pyjama trousers were sopping wet and a large puddle lay by the bedroom door.

I must get some practical advice about *incontinence*...that is the worst thing I have to deal with, being disgusting - and infuriating.

September 13, 2015

Doing physiotherapy exercises with him can be quite exasperating. When I get irritated, because he gets these simple things wrong again and again, he sometimes gets angry, shouts ...

Yet he still seems quite normal, chatting, laughing, blowing his trombone, obliging, co-operative, trying (unsuccessfully) to lay the table correctly, to put things back where they belong ...

September 18, 2015

We set out for a walk about 6.30. At first he was walking really well, longish strides, quite rapid. But after about an hour he started lurching to one side, walking very fast, almost running - I could hardly keep up. I asked him to slow down - he said, irritably, "I'm tired". Then in the park he caught his foot on a broken branch and fell full length. Tried to get up. I tried to help him, but he was too heavy for me. He kept saying "I'm done for. I'm finished." Fortunately a young man (with three dogs) came along and helped him up quite easily.

October 18, 2015

He has a bad cold - cough, catarrh, and there's pus in the corners of his eyes. Persuaded him to come down for breakfast, and later to have a bath. He panicked, thinking he couldn't get out of it. But he did, got dressed, had lunch. But he seems to be physically weak, and his understanding is minimal - he doesn't really know where he is.

October 20, 2015

The doctor prescribed amoxicillin for his chest infection, and kind and patient people from the "Bladder and Bowel" have visited and arranged for a huge supply of padded disposable pants to be supplied. But he seems to have lost muscular control completely - struggles to get up from his chair, and defecated helplessly in the bathroom ... horrified, disgusted, in despair. He thinks he must die soon.

His poem *The Vanishing Trick* has won First Prize in the Alzheimer Society's poetry competition. His poetry is his main interest. He spends a lot of time rereading his poems and likes nothing better than reading them aloud to people.

November 1, 2015

He seems much better now - cheerful, and going for daily walks again, but gets extremely tired and starts tilting to the left.

December 2, 2015

At the Gerontology Clinic, the memory test score was *down* from 18 to 11...in a test with questions such as "what is today's date?" and "what is this?" (showing a pencil). There was not much cheer from Dr. Sharon Christie.

January 1, 2016

New Year's Day! And it started so well! He slept peacefully, didn't toss and turn, didn't push his duvet on the floor - and went on being peaceful, not wanting to get up - and when at last he did - he was dry!

June 17, 2016

It's the Wednesday routine, so we're in town, at the market, and suddenly I realise that he's not with me anymore. I look round. I go back to the market stall we were at before, I ask people who have seen us here every Wednesday if they've seen him; I hurry to our usual Wednesday destinations, I ask familiar buskers, the *Big Issue* seller, if they've seen him - everyone shares my concern. "We'll keep him here if he turns up."

I go back to the baker, and ask him to call the police. In no time there are police men and women everywhere. A police car moves slowly up the pedestrianised road. It occurs to me that he might have gone to our usual bus stop, and I suggest this to a young policeman. But before he can answer there's a call on his intercom. "I've got his wife here," he says; and to me: "He's been found." He leads me to a police car and I'm driven half way home to find him sitting in another police car. He had walked a great distance. We are driven home together.

"Why did you go away from me?"

"I didn't know where you were."

"I was just in front of you."

"I can't remember."

Then there are forms to be filled in, a photo to be attached – in case it happens again. The police are very friendly, good humoured, apologise for the formalities. I tell them how impressed I am with the speed and efficiency with which they found him.

"Do you often get asked to find people?"

"About once a month on average for older people. More often for children."

Now I try to make sure we are together all the time. If I get absorbed in some activity, I interrupt from time to time to check up on him. To see what stupid thing he's doing now – getting into bed fully clothed, or trying to drink some sunflower oil. Then the struggle begins to persuade him, to find something else for him to do. I give up what I was trying to do. And get out the Junior Scrabble. Or the Snakes and Ladders.

There were several other occasions when he went on walkabouts. One was when he was at the day-care centre in Polstead Road and managed to slip out while the care workers were concentrating on helping other members to use the toilet. I think he pushed the bar on one of those doors that only open from the inside, and off he went. The police found him a couple of hours later, near the canal next to Port Meadow.

February 20, 2017

Yesterday we went to Rosemary Pountney's "Commemoration" at St Anne's College where I taught for a time. It has grown enormously since then, and the entrance is now on Woodstock Road – so it was a long walk from Frideswide Square. David dozed during the hour long panegyrics about Rosemary. Then we set off back to Frideswide Square, very slowly. On Hythe Bridge he suddenly fell down, full length, so suddenly that I tripped over him and also fell. In no time solicitous people had gathered round us and someone phoned for an ambulance. David was in great pain and wouldn't let anyone move him, sat leaning against the railing, his legs stretched out across the pavement. The ambulance came after about a quarter of an hour and the two paramedics, after some discussion, managed to get him – shouting and cursing – onto a stretcher and into the ambulance. At the John Radcliffe Hospital we did not have long to wait, and with great difficulty, using a special sheet of plastic, about six nurses and paramedics got him – shouting and cursing again – onto a bed. All this awful shouting continued whenever the nurses attended to him: I was ashamed of him. They got some Paracetamol into him, and partly undressed him, and he was wheeled to the X-ray department, where they found that his right hip bone was cracked. Today – no waiting! – they will make a small cut in his hip and pin the bone with some metal studs. The doctor said they do this very often, hips being fragile – they had done three that morning! But he will have to stay in bed in the hospital for some time. I spent a lot of time there with him and got to know the nurses and their routines – also a physiotherapist who encouraged David to take a few steps along the corridor – which he found extremely difficult.

March 11, 2017

David has been transferred to the Fulbrook "City Hospital" in the grounds of the Churchill Hospital. I have been visiting him every day – brought little treats like grapes or biscuits, which he shared with some of the other men – all, like him, convalescing after operations.

April 13, 2017

He is to come home tomorrow. A hospital (adjustable) bed has been delivered and placed in the back room – and a hoist – to help him get upright and out of bed. We created the space by donating the round table to Emmaus, a charity that recycles old furniture. Two carers are to tend to him four times a day.

(These carers had to put up with a lot of bad temper from David as they cleaned him, moved him, tried to get him onto the hoist, tried to feed him… he would furiously resist and swear at them using shocking language. There were about half a dozen carers, and they were all women, except for one African lad, and two of the women were Romanian. They put up with his tantrums with incredible patience, and sometimes would even succeed in calming him down. Then a seraphic smile would come to his face and he would say "thank you very much" and even, on rare occasions, apologize. More than once I found him lying on the floor beside the bed and had to phone for a paramedic to come and help me get him back into bed. On another occasion he assaulted one of the carers - a tough woman who used to be in the army - trying to pull her hair and sending an earring flying into space. She said it was a cherished present from her son. I and several others spent hours searching for it, but it never did turn up.)

May 16, 2017

David has difficulty breathing and has been taken to the A&E at the hospital.

May 19, 2017

At about 4 am he stopped breathing.

*

He saw it coming, and wrote this prescient poem, which won the 2015 Alzheimer's Society Poetry Prize:

THE VANISHING TRICK

Don't take me for permanent,
Don't think I'm a monument
accreting grey lichen.
Don't think I'm a totem
with creosoted root.
Don't think I'm a stayer.
I'm more of a Friday afternoon,
a smile on a moped

at knocking-off time,
I'm the last day of September,
I'm the instinct that ranges
swallows on phone wires,
I'm the mellow sunset
for every muster,
an evasive mister,
an easy-going fellow
fleeing over stubble-fields
in my own evening light
to the western ferries.
When I greet you these days,
my faithful, my on-going friends,
my eyes are saying good-bye.
When you take me for the man
I was yesterday,
you're mistaken:
I'm half that man,
and running out fast.
You've little idea
how much of me's gone
with the autumn flights
to other lands.
My thoughts are already abroad
in foreign railway compartments:
already they wear the rags
of foreign words.
I'm the ring-stain
where the glass was,
a cat-smile, no more
above the garden wall,
a fading shape in an archway,
a raised arm on a distant quayside...

Chapter 15: Revisiting Germany

October 2018. I was 85 years old, and a widow, free of responsibilities. I decided to travel. In October, I spent three weeks in Germany, moving from place to place, visiting old friends and relations. First I wanted to see the convent of St Lioba, in Günterstal, near Freiburg. I was born there, just before Hitler came into power, and the crazy antisemitism made life difficult and dangerous to half jews like my family. But the nuns there were kind and helpful, until we were able to get out of the country as refugees. As you know, my earliest memory is of lying on a bed in a shadowy room with a nun - who was prepared to look after me while my mother was away. So I saw the convent - a beautiful building, a golden yellow colour, Italianate in style, with a large cultivated area in front, and the burial places of past nuns behind. One elderly nun was attending to the flowers round the graves and smiled. Considering the upheavals the country has been through - defeat, division into Communist East and Capitalist West, and then reunification - it is astonishing how many things have endured unchanged - like St Lioba.

I was keen to see **Emil Hahn**, who had been a member of Hitler's army, and hadn't questioned the order he grew up in. We got to know him when he became a Prisoner of War in one of the PoW camps near Oxford - his job was to drive other prisoners to the farms where they worked, and pick them up at the end of the day to return to the camp. In between he came to our house in Oxford - my mother had responded to an appeal to befriend PoWs - and visited us. My mother talked with him and made him aware of the evils of fascism and what Germany - the "land of poets and thinkers" *ought* to be proud of. He admired her and became very fond of her and all of us. We kept in touch after he was repatriated, and I visited him with his grand-daughter Joanna in the care home in Freiburg where he now lived, widowed, very old and slightly confused, but still maintaining that my mother was *eine wunderbare Frau*. I happened to have the address where my grandmother lived about 1920 after she had left her husband in Berlin - he had joined the National Socialists and was generally insufferable. I asked Emil to take me see to see the house and he recognised it: as painters and decorators he and his father had refurbished that house, especially the attic, where she and her children (including the girl who was to be my mother) lived for years.

Ute Scherb had got in touch with me when she was researching the early women students in Freiburg, one of whom was my grand-mother, Olga Hempel, and I was able to tell her about that revolu-tionary progressive woman. Ute is a sociologist. I contacted her and told her I was coming, so we met in Freiburg. Among other things, she took me to see the square now dedicated to the old syna-gogue which had been there since the 1700s, till it was burnt down quite early on in the Third Reich by the Hitler Youth. The Jews were deported to Gurs, in "Free France", en route to Auschwitz. The ground plan of the synagogue has been marked by a low wall or kerb - it is filled with water - it is a paddling pool. I felt this was a humane memorial to the Jews and others who were denied life by the Nazis.

I felt I ought to see a concentration camp. It was with **Alfred Blazek** that I visited Dachau concentration camp, not far from Munich. Along the road on which we drove there was a series of sculptures showing human figures walking, staggering along close behind each other - representing a *Todesmarsch* - a death march. When the end of the war was imminent, the prisoners were simply let out without any provisions or support, and did indeed die on the road.

Dachau was not actually a concentration camp, but a work camp, an *Arbeitslager.* The prisoners left the camp every morning to work in weapons factories. We saw the *Paradeplatz,* the huge square where the prisoners had to stand for roll call, often for hours, whatever the weather, when they returned from the factories, till they could go into the barracks. There was one open wash room, and beyond it the stacked wooden cots in which they were to sleep - most would have to climb over the lower cots - there were no ladders - till they could collapse in an empty one.

After the war, Nazis and SS men were imprisoned in the camp. Later it was used for refugees and homeless people. In 1964, it was opened as a *Gedenkstätte* - a memorial - with the motto: *Nie Wieder!* Never Again! Everyone I was in touch with would echo that *nie wieder,* so did most of the numerous political parties. No doubt Angela Merkel's opening Germany to refugees from Syria was partly inspired by remorse for all the refugees - like my family - that left the country to escape extermination. But one person I spoke with on a train journey blamed Angela Merkel for the upsurge of extreme right-wing populism - because she had opened the floodgates to so many refugees without proper provision for them. This, she argued, had given rise to xenophobic and racist emotions.

The *Burg* at Burghausen has a long history as a defensive castle - it is on an escarpment above the river Salzach - which is salty, and marks the frontier with Austria. Over the years more and more courtyards with gateways and turrets were added, to the point where it is now "the longest castle in the world". The **Wirners** have owned a flat in one of the towers for a long time, and we have stayed there more than once. I was happy to stay in that circular room with its eye-level view of the tower of the church in the valley below. **Elisabeth** has lived in Bavaria all her life - another example of the continuity which surprised me. She took me to visit her very old

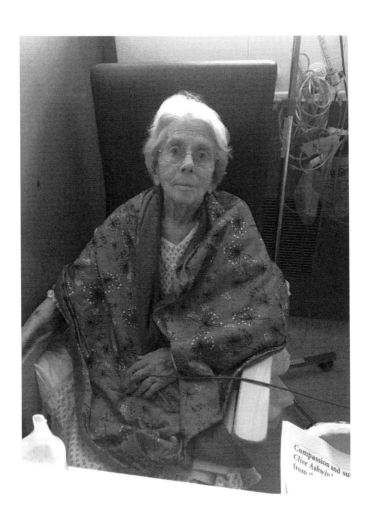

In the John Radcliffe Hospital, Oxford, in April 2022

mother who still lives in the farmhouse where Elisabeth grew up, an idyllic, peaceful place, and she described how she would walk to the village school through the fields and later travel by train to the Gymnasium, the secondary school - we saw this little train that still links villages and farmsteads, trundling through fields and woods once an hour - often completely empty. A little stream runs through the meadow in front of the house to a lake. Now the old places are enjoyed by the grandchildren. That little train is an example of practical commonsense which is apparent in many ways in Germany. All big buildings have an underground carpark, with a space allocated to each occupant - many involve an ingenious device to accommodate cars in two layers. At the Municipal Cemetery in Munich, a team of gardeners were at work replanting graves - one could pay to have one's grave cared for in this way, but Elisabeth prefers to care for the Wirner family grave herself. Yes, we are both widows now. Helmut and David met, I think, in a Youth Hostel in Paris and were friends all their lives.

My next destination was Leipzig. Now I was in the former GDR - the communist Eastern part of Germany - and I heard frequent references to it: comparisons often introduced by "*Zu DDR Zeiten*" (back in the GDR times) or "*vor der Wende*" (before the change), some saying it wasn't all bad, that there were some good things in those 41 years in the Soviet Bloc. My Leipzig friends, **Hartmut** and **Gundula Friedrich**, had lived in it all their lives- till 1990. Hartmut maintained that Communism was as bad as National Socialism as far as personal freedom was concerned. If one didn't conform to the diktats of the party, one risked being "sent to Siberia". His father Peter had been David's pen-friend since they were both at school, trying to learn each other's language, and they and their families continued to be friends.

They live in a large house, with its own underground car park which opened automatically as we approached, and quite a big garden at the back. There was plenty of open space indoors, which was all wood. Every movement, every plate put down on a table, echoed and re-echoed. There were targeted lights, big potted plants, a corner with sofas and a coffee table: all spotlessly clean and tidy. This is where they had brought up their three children - only one, Tilman, was in residence. But we met Lovisa next day, in Meissen, and it was touching to see how pleased the three of them were to see each other. Lovisa, who is nearing the end of her Business Studies course at nearby Dresden, had come by Stadtbahn (the light railway). She is a lovely young woman, finding something amusing in every situation. The river Elbe was a mere trickle in the middle of mud flats - there has been no rain for months, and the heat was unbearable.

Further east in Saxony is the ancestral farm at Zschoppach. Another example of traditions maintained through thick and thin, this farm has belonged to the Hempel family since 1860 - passed down from father to son. When we first visited, in 1972, it was part of an "LPG" (Landwirtschaftliche Produktionsgenossenschaft) - a collective farm. In 1995, after the *Wende*, it was private again. Reinhardt Hempel had a herd of cows and was supplying milk to Müller & Co. But now, in 2018, he was 82 years old, and none of his sons wanted to farm. He had given up the cows, planted apple trees on their meadow, and kept just two cows with three calves - as a hobby. The farm buildings, some dating back to the 18th century, set on four sides of a big yard, are big and impressive. But trees and bushes have grown up in the yard, there are huge pieces of farm machinery lying idle, and in the great barns some firewood has been stacked up, with logs and branches and rubbish thrown in. One side of the yard is a long half-timber two-storey building with a number of rooms, bathrooms and bedrooms - presumably accommodation for farm labourers in the past, but now useless, a dumping ground for unwanted things. Just one corner of the quadrangle, nearest the farm gate, has been modernised - here Reinhardt and Martina have two bedrooms, a kitchen and a bathroom. What will become of the farm? Can it be sold? Perhaps not. A number of people have left the village of Zschoppach, leaving abandoned farms, empty houses. The village is being depopulated.

*

About the time when Louis Hempel took on the farm - 1840 - one Christian Friedrich Weber founded a textile company, CF Weber, in another part of Saxony, called Spitzkunnersdorf. The business is still called CF Weber, but it has been passed down the generations by the female line; Weber (weaver) - so appropriate for a textile firm - is not the current family name, but Friedrich: yes, it's another branch of the Leipzig Friedrich family. The present director, Klaus Friedrich, is Hartmut's uncle. Klaus and his wife Martina live in a big house overlooking the bleak, slightly hilly landscape - with the big shiny factory in the foreground. Why is it here? There are hardly any other buildings, certainly no industry, far and wide.

Martina explains that local farmers grew flax and used its fibres to weave linen to augment their income. Many of the older houses in the area have walls reinforced with an arched second wall, to withstand the rocking movement of the loom. CF Weber bought up the pieces of linen and marketed them. Now hundreds of huge mechanical looms in the factory are thumping away to produce textiles; Klaus and his son travel far and wide, visiting trade fairs to sell their textiles and study the market. Like the farm at Zschoppach, CF Weber was taken over by the State in the Communist era, and they were ordered to accommodate several families in their house; but the company continued to be managed by the Friedrichs - another example of continuity through thick and thin.

In the evening we discussed politics. Germany is a federal republic, with 16 Länder like Bavaria and Saxony represented in the Bundestag. There are 19 political parties, but to get a seat in the Bundestag the party must gain at least 5% of the votes. At present just six parties qualify. Elections are held at different times in the separate Länder and in the *Landesparlamente* the smaller parties have

seats. While I was there Bavaria voted - and the *Grosse Koalition*
of Christian Democrats and Christian Socialists (CDU and CSU),
which has been in power for a long time, suffered a loss of support,
while the Greens did well. A new party, *Alternative für Deutschland*
(Alternative for Germany), qualified for seats. This is an extreme
right wing nationalistic party. The *AfD* wants a strong German
Army and *armed* frontiers to keep out refugees. It is similar to Nigel
Farage's UKIP - xenophobic, opposed to the European Union, and
it wants foreign troops and arms, including nuclear ones, removed
from Germany. The Green Party (*die Grüne*) is totally opposed to
all nuclear weapons - but not for nationalistic reasons, like the AfD.
Their overriding concern is for the environment, and they have
widespread support - far more than the Greens in Britain.

Not far from Spitzkunnersdorf is the pleasant town of Herrenhut,
centre of the worldwide Moravian Church. Moravia - Mähren in
German - is the Eastern part of the Czech Republic. Here, followers of Jan Hus and the Reformation were persecuted, and fled to the
West, where Count Zinsendorf gave them protection and space. In
1722 they founded the town with a large, airy central meeting place.
The Church sends missionaries to countries all over the world to
preach Christianity. They have a strong pacifist tradition and will
choose prison over conscription at time of war.

*

German railways - the *Bundesbahn* - seemed to me to be exemplary,
very efficient, compared with the British privatised system. At major
stations, smaller local trains - the Stadtbahn - serve nearby towns.
I had bought my ticket for the journey from Dresden to Hanover
days before at a travel agency, for a certain train, with times stated
for departure and arrival. And it all happened exactly as foretold.
At Hanover, **Peter Kühn** met me and drove me to Münster and
Warendorf, and a warm welcome from **Karin Schimmelpfennig**.
Next day we saw an excellent Julie Wolfthorn exhibition.

Julie was a cousin and friend of my grandmother's, an artist and feminist and activist - and of Jewish descent. Once the Nazis were in power she could no longer practice her profession and suffered all the restrictions and humiliations that the State meted out to Jews. In 1942 she and her sister were deported to Theresienstadt concentration camp where she died, aged 79. Karin wanted to bring her back into the light of day. She and Heike Carstensen researched her life and collected her works and organized exhibitions like this one at Ahrenshoop. It used the words she wrote to a friend when she was about to move to Theresienstadt - *Vergessen Sie uns nicht* - Do Not Forget Us - as the title for the exhibition. I had recently published an article about Julie ('Don't forget us!': Julie Wolfthorn, artist [1864-1944]' in *Women's History*, Spring 2017 volume two issue 7, 32-35).

My next destination was Neuss, which is near Karin's home in Krefeld, so we travelled together - and l got a very different impression of the Bundesbahn. We hadn't been travelling long before the train stopped, in the middle of nowhere, and stood still. Another train whizzed past. The indicator told us we would be five minutes late. Moved on a bit, then stopped again. Passengers started theorising: we were near the Hambach forest - there have been many demonstrations against its threatened destruction in order to mine lignite - perhaps the protesters were on the line, to stop the train. Or - a power failure. Or - a suicide. We were never told. We moved on a bit, stopping and starting. A notice came up saying this train would not be going to Krefeld - why not? - there was no explanation. So Karin got off when we crawled into a station and waited for the next train, hoping that would go all the way. When I finally got into Neuss my friends the **Goddes** had been waiting for over an hour - they had not been given any explanation either - but they mocked my admiration for the *Bundesbahn* - today's confusion is just typical, they said, it's hopelessly inefficient.... They live in a pleasant flat with a balcony and views of other similar blocks of flats. There are trees around, and a lovely park nearby. They are an affectionate couple, good humoured, intelligent, concerned for each other's health and wellbeing - and their sons and grandchildren live nearby. Edmund was a schoolteacher, and it shows: he likes to explain things in carefully formed sentences.

For my return journey I had to travel to Brussels to join the Eurostar there. I didn't realise that there are lots of stations in Brussels and only one serves Eurostar. I was the last person in the queue when I finally got there, and found to my horror that my passport was not with my ticket. It must have been stolen. It took some time to explain this at immigration, so I missed that train and had to wait two hours for the next. Then at last I was travelling across part of the North European plain, under the Channel, into London - and then by bus home to Oxford.

Three years later, after an excruciating bureaucratic ordeal, I was finally granted German citizenship and issued with a German passport.

Once I was a refugee and had no nationality. Now I have two. And until the next time I lose one, I have two passports as well. I have been British – but never English! – for eighty years. And now the country that wanted me dead before I was even born has finally accepted me. Perhaps it is time for me to stop feeling like a refugee.

Chapter 16: It's My Turn Now

… my turn to be white-haired, my face as wrinkled as a walnut. My turn to have a mind like a murky pond with bits of thought - of memory - of worry - odd quotations - floating around. Dependant on dentures and hearing aids - which vanish and have to be searched for …

… my turn to be addled and confused, like old Miss King - not knowing the date, or the day, leaving my bag on the bus, forgetting why I'm here in this room, and having to go back to where I was before - trying to trick the person I'm with into mentioning their name, which I've forgotten - wishing people wouldn't mumble so - missing the point when everyone else is laughing - wondering who that leathery, wrinkled, walnut-like person staring at me is, till I realise I'm looking in a mirror - being in the right place, at the right time, but on the wrong day - trying to identify the tune, or the poem, I've got on my brain -. It's just your memory, dear, that's all, it doesn't matter, it's quite natural, quite normal - .

… sitting up suddenly in bed in the middle of the night, remembering something I should have done, but didn't, cudgelling my head with my fists with remorse…

… my turn to keep forgetting what I'm supposed to be doing, why I've come here - better go back, perhaps then I'll remember - to have scraps of memory floating up out of nowhere to be puzzled over - quotations to be identified on Google … to write things down quickly before I forget and then later find the note and wonder what it means -

Maud, the senile old lady in Emma Henley's 2014 novel *Elizabeth is Missing*, exasperated her daughter, but if my daughter is exasperated, she doesn't show it. Yes, that brown baby, that wild teenager, has turned into a stout and warm hearted and efficient middle-aged woman. She is like a Home Help, or a Carer, for me, in charge of me, takes me shopping and to medical appointments, and devises special treats for me, just telling me there will be a magical mystery tour, for which I must be ready on a certain day at a certain time, and has me guessing where we're going till finally we arrive at the arboretum, or the botanical gardens. She phones me to make sure I'm OK and to ask about the black cats, Jack and Molly, which she got for me as kittens and are now quite big and beautiful and occupy our minds and time.

Once, only once, never again, never,
The idle curve my hand traces in air,
The first flush on the cloud, lost in the morning's height,
Meeting of the eyes and tremble of delight,
Before the heart is aware
Gone! to return, never again, never!

Futurity flows toward me, all things come
Smooth-flowing, and ere this pulse beat they are bound
In fixity that no repenting power can free;
They are with Egypt and with Nineveh,
Cold as a grave in the ground;
And still, undated, all things toward me come.

Why is all strange? Why do I not grow used?
The ripple upon the stream that nothing stays,
The bough above, in glory of warm light waving slow,
Trouble me, enchant me, as with the stream I flow
Lost into the endless days
Why is all strange? Why do I not grow used?

Eternity! Where heard I that still word?
Like one that, moving through a foreign street,
Has felt upon him bent from far some earnest look,
Yet sees not whence, and feigns that he mistook,
I marvel at my own heart-beat.
Eternity! how learnt I that far word?

I am haunted by those words. Who wrote them? My son, consulting the all-knowing internet, tells me that I am recalling Laurence Binyon's amazing poem, *I Have Heard Voices Under the Early Stars*. But they describe me, as I am now: I am being carried along on the stream, backwards, looking back at the endless days, at the ever more distant, darker past, but often surprised to remember, to experience past events again, vividly… eighty years have passed, but how clearly I recall being called a "dirty little German rat!" by Eunice Coghill.

Another vivid memory: In 1945, Anne Martin and I spent a holiday with her paternal grandmother, who lived in a home for clergymen's widows in the country. It was a warm, wet summer and we roamed around in the damp meadows, reciting *The Lost Heifer*, a poem we had learned at school –

When the black herds of the rain were grazing,
In the gap of the pure cold wind
And the watery hazes of the hazel
Brought her into my mind,
I thought of the last honey by the water
That no hive can find.
Brightness was drenching through the branches
When she wandered again,
Turning sliver out of dark grasses
Where the skylark had lain,
And her voice coming softly over the meadow
Was the mist becoming rain.

What did it mean, lovely as it was, and so relevant to where we were? We resolved to write to the poet, Austin Clarke, and ask him to explain. We had no idea that it was in fact an elaborate nationalist metaphor about the plight of Ireland in 1936.

*

Over the years, I have returned to Germany many times. I have touched the *Stolpersteine* - memorial stones in the pavements that mark the addresses of those who were not so lucky. I have visited a concentration camp - at Dachau - which the totally reformed Germans have established as an educational and tourist centre, with groups of school children being shown the huge *Paradeplatz* (parade ground) where the prisoners were obliged to stand to be counted, often for hours, whatever the weather, after their day's toil in munitions factories, before they could return to their dormitories, to use the open washroom, before clambering up the storeys of wooden bunks to collapse - and rest and sleep, perhaps to die - of hunger and exhaustion...

Surely being an Enemy Alien was much much much better than being a victim of the holocaust.

But it felt very bad.

I was ashamed of myself. I was ashamed of my name, of my German parents, I didn't want people to know that I spoke German. There must be something wrong with me - like a bad smell - which made me so unpopular, so friendless - after Anne I had no close friend. I struggled to fit in, to perfect my English, to imitate the popular girls at school.

I was jealous of Gillian Shepherd. I was even jealous of her name, so pleasing, so English, so like her... She was the captain of the Hockey team, always reasonable, relaxed, she could exclude someone from the team before a match in such an amiable, reasonable way that no offence was taken. I was not excluded. I was Right Wing, I could run fast, I could dribble the length of the field and shoot a goal.

"Jolly good shot, Garbi", said Gillian - who had shot plenty of goals herself without any histrionics.

Gillian wasn't particularly tall. She had curly fair hair, freckles, a short nose, rather broad shoulders; she carried her hockey stick casually, as one might hold the lead for a dog. She was an epitome of Englishness: fair minded, cool, successful. Not brilliant academically, but she passed all the tests and exams. She was on good terms with everybody from the headmistress to the groundsman. Not eloquent. The famous English understatement came naturally to her. How we refugees admired it! But couldn't emulate it.

Oh to be like that! To have an English name, an English passport - to belong here, to be cool, relaxed, confident, secure, simply and naturally patriotic - whereas patriotism was such a dreadful quagmire for us.

Yes, I was jealous of Gillian Shepherd. And still am, really.

I struggled to conceal my identity, not to reveal my knowledge of the German language, became aware of the different word order in the two languages - (*I have yesterday by bus to town gone*). I changed my very German name - Gabi Zuntz - to a bland English one - Irene Henry - as soon as I was able to. And for years I succeeded - worked hard, did well (*too* well, typical Jew...). But I was walking on thin ice, and despair overwhelmed me again and again. The rep theatres I joined when I thought I could be an actress all failed, were bankrupted, as theatres were converted into cinemas. The stories and plays and poems I wrote gleaned nothing but rejection slips. I wrote this poem about it:

> The taste of failure is a bitter one
> Puckers the skin in the mouth,
> Constricts the throat.
>
> A paper wall, or less, a word

Divides Failure from Success:
So slight an alteration,

From "Sorry, No" to "Yes,"
To put an end to loneliness in the shadows
The forced smile, the need
To congratulate others.

The children of Success smile in the sunlight.
Theirs is the manna of friendship
The honey of fame,

While Failure scrabbles about in her possessions.
Don't try to console her: however carefully chosen
Your words will contain Pity: a verdict.

But Time, the old Gipsy man, kept the ice solid; I never fell through. Time did have someone in store for me; someone I could admire without envying him; who actually approved of my German origin. I recall the library, in Foster Court, at University College London, and there was David, and we found that we both loved Nietzsche's poems - so different from his doctrine! - and so found each other.

Heiterkeit, güldene, komm!
   Serenity, golden one, come!
Du des Todes
   Thou, death's
Heimlichster, süßester Vorgenuß!
   Most secret, sweetest foretaste!
Lief ich zu schnell meines Weges?
   Did I run my way too fast?
Jetzt erst, wo der Fuß müde ward

Only now, when my foot grows weary,
Holt dein Blick mich noch ein
    Does your glance catch up with me,
Holt dein Glück mich noch ein.
    Does your bliss catch up with me.
Rings nur Welle und Spiel.
    Around me only wave and play.
Was je schwer war
    Whatever was ever hard
Sank in blaue Vergessenheit...
    Sank into blue oblivion.

We marvelled at the music, the image, the emotion of such verse, the beauty of the German words. Not many people know that the promoter of the *Wille zur Macht* (The Will to Power) could experience such feelings – and express them in such poignant verse ....

The next vivid memory is of a shadowy room on the Adriatic island of Krk – which we had chosen because of its absurd name – where we spent a steamy week. What a thoroughly *English* person he was! Civil, modest, kind, generous ... and what excellent poems he wrote in the years we were together! Quirky, original, touching, sincere – with precise words selected from his huge vocabulary – modest, sceptical observations.

When he was getting old, and needed a hearing aid, he wrote this poem:

HEARING AID

My plastic humming-bird hovers
behind my ear
and daylong
lips

the tiny transparent French horn
of the ear-mould
blowing snatches of tune
from the phonic world.
I ought to bless
the NHS
for keeping me in sound
like this
but as I place the aid
beside my bed,
I see a cockle
scoured and dead
to which the waves
have bid their last farewells,
- and think of all my
unheard decibels.

His warm and sympathetic heart was often stirred to anger - but the famous English *understatement* made his protest poems more powerful than any rhetoric. This is one he wrote about a blind Iraqi student who stayed with us for some time:

A LITTLE COLLATERAL DAMAGE

The team who designed it knew nothing of Muhammed Adnan.
Nor did the armourers who eased it into place.
The pilots who carried it hundreds of miles
hadn't heard of him either. But when the missile struck
the family farm on the edge of Baghdad
it was Muhammad Adnan, all of eight years old
and his brother and sister, whose faces were torn
into patterns of blood, and whose cries rang out
in the desolation, never to reach the pilots

who fired it, the armourers who fixed it,
the designers who made it. Nor would the bosses
of the big corporations who sold it, hear
in their sleep the slightest incision
of a hurt child's voice.

He wrote hundreds more, and they swim in and out of my consciousness as I look back on the good years we had together - in Britain, Portugal, Uganda, Japan, Germany...running Oxford CND - family holidays in Wales, Scotland, Devon ... organising our micro-school, Oxford Residential English ... and for long periods my Refugee Complex was a sleeping dog in the cellar.

But if I did not receive an expected invitation, when neighbours walked past me chatting with each other and ignoring me, it rose up again. I dreamed of confronting them - "Tell me what it is about me that you don't like" - but never did, as I knew in my heart that they would have shaken their heads and asked me what on earth I was talking about. Not even David's unquestioning love and approval helped. But I kept it secret. I didn't tell him or anyone that I was so deeply ashamed of myself.

*

The next big thing, presumably, will be death.
When I was young, I was terrified of death.

"It is simply this, and no more:
That I dread to feel
the air stop short at my nostrils -"

- I wrote, finding more and more heart-stopping images for the absolute loss of existence, swallowed up or cancelled by Time, that terrifying, incomprehensible force. I was too sceptical to take the resurrection and the life everlasting seriously, and was - still am - baffled that so many people do, somehow, subscribe to it. But I like toying with the idea - expressed in so many hymns and poems - of being reunited with those who have "gone before". Sitting on a cloud with David, dangling our legs over the edge ... would be nice.

Buddhists seem to think that when my body dies, my self, my ego, will continue to exist - perhaps in a newly hatched bird, or a seedling tree, only I won't be aware that this is actually *me*, so what's the point?

In some sense, people who are present in my memory, my consciousness, do still have a kind of existence; and I suppose I will be remembered for a time.

But whether remembered or not, everyone, everything that *has been* will always *be* - there, in the past. As Time carries me backwards in Time, looking at the past, the lengthening past, and discerning people, events, places, reading diaries, I feel reassured.

What will it be like? Sometimes, feeling tired, I lie down, and think - "Perhaps this is it? Perhaps I'm dying?" But so far, obviously, I'm not.

Memories arise unbidden in my mind.

Nyakasura. A little boy, so blond his hair was almost white, with big blue eyes, and a solemn, deep voice. "Musses Gull," he would say, "Can we have the car?" I would get out Tom's toy jeep and he and Tom would take turns sitting in it and hold long, baffling conversations. They were together most days. But early one morning his mother, Kay, came and told me Neal had died. It took me a long time to grasp what she was saying. She told me he had had acute stomach ache and when she took him to the doctor he diagnosed a ruptured appendix. He was rushed to the hospital - the last Kay saw of him he was sitting up on the trolley waving to her - but he looked like a little old man in his pain as they wheeled him into the operating theatre. He died under the anaesthetic.

We were all dumbfounded with the shock of his death. Tom was the one who suffered most. When I told him, he was flushed and broke away from me. He was silent and very hot - for weeks he had a temperature. I tried to talk to him about Neal, but he remained silent - just once he shouted "Stop talking about -" but he couldn't say the name.

I asked him recently if he remembers Neal. Sadly, he does not.

*

I wake up in the middle of the night - bright moonlight - it's a full moon, visible through a gap in the curtains. What an amazing number of things have coincided to produce this - the position of the moon, the gap in the curtains, the position of my head! It won't last long - the moon will move on from that precise position ... I close my eyes, and think how my mother, Mu, would have reacted. She would have gone out into the garden, worshipping the moon, - singing

THE END

Guter Mond du gehst so stille
An den Abendwolken vorbei ...

Der Mond ist aufgegangen
Die goldnen Sternlein prangen
Am Himmel hell und klar
Der Wald steht schwarz und schweiget ...

Dear moon, you move so quietly
Past the evening cloud

The moon has risen
The golden stars are shiny in the sky
Bright and clear
The woods stand black and silent...